Working men's bodies

MANCHESTER
1824

Manchester University Press

Working men's bodies

Work camps in Britain, 1880–1940

JOHN FIELD

Manchester University Press
Manchester and New York
distributed in the United States exclusively by Palgrave Macmillan

Published by Manchester University Press
Oxford Road, Manchester M13 9NR, UK
and Room 400, 175 Fifth Avenue, New York, NY 10010, USA
www.manchesteruniversitypress.co.uk

Distributed in the United States exclusively by
Palgrave Macmillan, 175 Fifth Avenue, New York,
NY 10010, USA

Distributed in Canada exclusively by
UBC Press, University of British Columbia, 2029 West Mall,
Vancouver, BC, Canada V6T 1Z2

British Library Cataloguing-in-Publication Data
A catalogue record for this book is available from the British Library

Library of Congress Cataloging-in-Publication Data applied for

ISBN 978 0 7190 8768 4 *hardback*

First published 2013

Typeset in Minion by
Koinonia, Manchester
Printed in Great Britain by
TJ International Ltd, Padstow

For Annie

Contents

Abbreviations

AD	Arbeitsdienst
BJN	*British Journal of Nursing*
BLPES	British Library of Political and Economic Science
BMA	British Medical Association
BMJ	*British Medical Journal*
BUF	British Union of Fascists
BWTA	British Women's Temperance Association
CCC	Civilian Conservation Corps
CCWTE	Central Committee for Women's Training and Employment
CPGB	Communist Party of Great Britain
CSC	Community Service Council
CUA	Cambridge University Archives
CUB	Central (Unemployed) Body for London
CUSS	Christian Union for Social Service
DM	*Daily Mirror*
DW	*Daily Worker*
ELCS	English Land Colonization Society
FAD	Freiwilliger Arbeitsdienst
GF	Grith Fyrd
GH	*Glasgow Herald*
GPO	General Post Office
GTC	Government Training Centre
HHC	Hull History Centre
HMSO	Her/His Majesty's Stationery Office
HTC	Home Training Centre
IC	Instructional Centre
ILP	Independent Labour Party
ITB	Industrial Transference Board
IVS	International Voluntary Service
JC	*Jewish Chronicle*
LCC	London County Council
LEA	Local Education Authority

LGB	Local Government Board
MP	Member of Parliament
NA	National Archives
NAS	National Archives of Scotland
NCSS	National Council for Social Service
NSB	North Sea and Baltic
NSDAP	Nationalsozialistische Deutsche Arbeiterpartei
NSEE	National Society for the Employment of Epileptics
NUWM	National Unemployed Workers' Movement
OSC	Oversea Settlement Committee
OSD	Oversea Settlement Department
OWC	Order of Woodcraft Chivalry
PAC	Public Assistance Committee
PRONI	Public Records Office of Northern Ireland
RAD	Reichsarbeitsdienst
RCPL	Royal Commission on the Poor Laws
RCUI	Royal Commission on Unemployment Insurance
SLCA	Scottish Labour Colony Association
SOSBW	Society for the Overseas Settlement of British Women
TIC	Transfer Instructional Centre
TUC	Trades Union Congress
UAB	Unemployment Assistance Board
UCUC	Universities Council for Unemployed Camps
USSR	Union of Soviet Socialist Republics
WTC	Women's Training Colony
YMCA	Young Men's Christian Association

Acknowledgements

Despite its intrinsic interest, as well as its wider significance, I stumbled across this topic almost by accident. While greatly admiring Gareth Stedman Jones' monumental study of *Outcast London* when it first appeared, only much later did I pay any attention to his occasional references to labour colonies.[1] What triggered my interest was a reminiscence by Len Edmondson, a trade union militant and Independent Labour Party member who had been active in the National Unemployed Worker's Movement during the 1930s. Edmondson briefly mentioned that one of his brothers had been sent to a work camp at Kielder, while he himself spent time in a camp at Brandon.[2] At the time, I was teaching a course on interwar Britain, and drew on both Edmondson's memoirs and a chapter from another contemporary account, Wal Hannington's *Problems of the Distressed Areas*. Subsequently, one of my students decided to tackle the Ministry of Labour's camps for his diploma dissertation; Dave Colledge was determined and systematic in tracing men who had worked in the camps, and published his findings in a study that has too long been out of print.[3] I disagree with his interpretation of the period, which seems to me heavily reliant on the Marxist views and language of Wal Hannington (of whom more later on), but I have drawn on the oral and written testimony that Dave gathered, some of which is available in his book.

I have benefited enormously from the help of friends, colleagues and archivists. Several people helped me by passing on source material. They include Reevel Alderson, of BBC Scotland; Allen Bordoley, whose uncle Shalom trained at the David Eder Farm; Dr Georgina Brewis, of the Institute of Education; Dr Cathy Burke, University of Cambridge; Wilma Burns, Stirling Central Library; Dr Mark Freeman, University of Glasgow; Professor Martha Friedenthal-Haase, Friedrich-Schiller-Universität Jena; Dr William Lancaster, University of Northumbria; Professor Keith Laybourn, University of Huddersfield; Gerry Moore, Weeting History Group; Dr Ian Roberts, Bellingham Heritage Trust; Dr Kevin Ryan, National University of Ireland, Galway; Ann Shrive of Brigstock Historical Society; Brian Walker of the Forestry Commission; David Wilson, of Kettering; and the members of the Just William Society. Malcolm McGregor arranged permission to use a photograph owned by Liddesdale Heritage Association, Philipp Rodriguez arranged permission to use photographs from the Archive of Service Civil International.

Others helped in equally valuable ways. I received financial support for travel to archives from the Carnegie Trust for the Universities of Scotland. The University of Stirling granted me research leave, meaning that my colleagues in the School of Education covered my teaching and administrative duties while I was enjoying myself elsewhere; they continue to provide congenial and stimulating company. Neil Thompson of the Scarborough Scouts arranged for me to visit the impeccably maintained huts of Langdale End Instructional Centre. Last but never least, frequently curious about what I was up to, and always willing to share her ideas and expertise, Julie Allan was an invariably cheery companion when we set out to explore some of this island's most beautiful areas in search of old labour colony or work camp sites, staying calm even when we were set upon by midges in Strachur and geese in North Yorkshire. I am most grateful to them all, and cheerfully claim all flaws as my very own.

Notes

1 Gareth Stedman Jones, *Outcast London: A study in the relationship between classes in Victorian society*, Penguin, London, 1970.
2 In K. Armstrong and H. Benyon (eds), *Hello, are you Working? Memories of the thirties in the North East of England*, Strong Words, Durham, 1977, 66.
3 D. Colledge, *Labour Camps: The British experience*, Sheffield Popular Publishing, Sheffield, 1989.

Introduction

Work does you good. A whole mountain of social and psychological research confirms the importance of our job to our identity (who we think we are), how we feel about our lives (our well-being), and our sense of community (our social capital). Generally, we get paid for work, which in turn lets us do other things as a result, though interestingly researchers have found that many of the benefits of working also apply to voluntary work.[1] And it shapes how we see others, particularly those who do not work, especially if we see the workless as parasites who are failing to shoulder their duty to the community. Marie Jahoda, a pioneer in the social science of well-being, identified five factors that she believed were fundamental to how we feel about ourselves: time structure, social contact, collective effort or purpose, social identity or status, and regular activity. All of these, Jahoda argued, were provided for most people by their jobs, but were often absent from the lives of people who were unemployed.[2] More recent research has underlined Jahoda's argument, showing that unemployment strips people of their social networks, and reduces their sense of value and worth, in tangible and measurable ways.[3]

Of course, much of this may now be changing in our fast moving world. While Karl Marx famously defined work as the core of what distinguishes humanity from other species, the environmental thinker André Gorz argued that work's central place in socialist thinking was an ideological burden, a hangover from the industrial past.[4] As Gorz noted, more and more people found themselves in precarious work, or moving ever more rapidly between jobs, so that ideas of an identity rooted in one's job were increasingly tenuous. The steady feminisation of paid work, as well as the ever more porous borders between work and retirement, are also reshaping the terms of debate. Whether or not work will continue to hold its central place in our culture and lives for much longer is therefore a matter for debate. But it is hard to ignore its continuing importance, symbolically and culturally as well as financially and practically, to our lives.

Krishan Kumar traces the modern primacy of work to the early industrial period.[5] In pre-industrial Britain, he argues, ordinary people earned their living from labour, to be sure, but did not depend solely on their ability to sell their labour to others. Employment only became the sole precarious base of one's living during the nineteenth century. Hence, Kumar argues, the importance of the New Poor Law after 1834 was less as an attempt to underpin a victorious and ruthless capitalism than the last attempt of the old order to distinguish between the 'deserving' and the 'undeserving', with its imposition of the workhouse test on the 'able-bodied' male poor.[6] In many ways, early British work camps – the labour colonies of the 1880s and early 1890s – were both a reaction against the New Poor Law and an acknowledgement that the workhouse system had failed. By this time, Britain was a fully-fledged industrial and urban society, and most of the male population were employed by others, while most of the adult female population were working without a wage in the family home. Britain's industrial cities, and the rhythms of the trade cycle, stretched the New Poor Law to breaking point and beyond. It is fitting that the two decades which witnessed the first labour colonies also produced a new term – 'unemployment'.[7] By the time that the language of unemployment was in common use, and hesitant steps were being taken to understand and reduce it, the German sociologist Max Weber was writing his first essays on the Protestant ethic and the spirit of capitalism. Among other concerns, Weber noted that the religious sense of a calling to work was fading away, and being replaced by a Franklinesque rationale for hard work and thrift as strategies for producing an independent citizenry.[8] Work, in short, was a duty to God as well as to one's fellow men; not only was it an obligation to others to work if one could, but it was also necessary to ensure that others could fully share in its benefits. For over fifty years, then, it seemed perfectly reasonable to pack at least some of one's fellow citizens off into the countryside, where they would live and work, at least for as long as it took for labour to heal their ills.

Work camps may seem strange to us, but before 1939 they were a normal part of the landscape. In one of her *Just William* stories, published in May 1940, Richmal Crompton described how William and his gang were driven to seek revenge on a 'band of toughs' from a nearby 'unemployed camp'. The Outlaws come out on top in the end, thanks to the intervention of a short man who turns out to be the former British lightweight boxing champion.[9] In William's seemingly timeless Home Counties commuter village, Crompton thought it quite unremarkable that someone should open an unemployed camp. Before the Second World War, work camps were scattered across Britain, though not many were close enough to the suburbs to spark off ill-will and anxiety among the middle class. In general, work camps – whether for the unemployed, for epileptics, for alcoholics, for former prostitutes, or for utopian visionaries in search of a better world – were placed in remote country communities, far away from the rest of the world.

This book examines the story of those camps, the men and women who created them, as well as those who inhabited them. It starts in the mid-nineteenth century, just after the Chartist and Owenite communities had come to an end, and when the debate over the failures of the 'new poor law' was under way. By the 1880s, the idea had emerged of the labour colony – an organised settlement, where people (usually men) worked the land, often in order to prove their willingness to take work or to improve their ability to perform it, and sometimes as a preparation for a life on the soil as a peasant farmer. At the outset, most of these ventures were voluntary initiatives, associated with the churches or with reform movements. Increasingly though, local government became involved, initially through poor law boards dominated by radical politicians who believed that progressive policies on unemployment could easily be reconciled with land reform, and subsequently by agencies interested in labour colonies as a treatment for conditions as various as learning disability and tuberculosis. After the Great War, there were work camps for veterans and work camps for peace-builders, as well as work camps for nationalists of various kinds. By 1939, government was playing a far more central and strategic role, directly through its national system of work camps for unemployed men, and indirectly through a range of partnerships with voluntary organisations.

Why have we heard so little about these ventures? The main reason is simple: work camps have had a pretty bad press. Ever since British soldiers walked into Bergen-Belsen on 15 April 1945, and sent home photographs and films of what they found there, people have tended to see Nazi Germany's labour camps, concentration camps and extermination camps as a more or less equally oppressive and murderous. Of course, this gross oversimplification is easily understandable, but it jumbles together a gamut of different types of institution, from those designed to eradicate undesirables to those that were intended to build healthy National Socialist manhood. The images of Auschwitz also tend to overwhelm earlier work camp systems, including the plethora of voluntary work camp systems that sprang up in response to unemployment in the final years of the Weimar Republic. In the United States, it is perhaps easier to escape from this flattened view of the work camp: faced with record unemployment levels, along with a series of environmental disasters, President Barack Obama turned straight to the Roosevelt era and its Civilian Conservation Corps for inspiration.[10] In Europe, however, it is all too easy to dismiss all work camp systems as variants on a Nazi theme.[11]

If the language of the work camp is likely to provoke immediate and negative reactions, the language of the labour colony probably sounds archaic. In our post-colonial culture, it is easy to forget that the word can mean a land settlement (deriving from the Latin *colonus*, a farmer or husbandman). Radical Owenite cooperators happily adopted the Roman habit of calling their communities 'colony', as did housing reformers when building groups of homes for skilled workers in Victorian cities.[12] As well as the borrowed splendours of ancient (civic) Rome, the term offered radicals an opportunity of lampooning the inequalities of modern Britain. As early as 1827, the Owenite, Quaker and scientist William Allen published a pamphlet called *Colonies at Home*, proposing villages of small farmers as an alternative to emigration.[13]

The dream of re-establishing the peasantry – or, in England, a yeomanry – presents an exceptionally clear version of the idea that people are improved by living and working on the land. Most of the work camp systems featured in this book were less ambitious, and were mainly intended to develop men's bodies, and only secondarily their minds, with little thought at all of their contribution to a more equal and community-minded way of living. Our bodies are at the centre of who we think we are. Each of us, of course, has more than one body. There is the material flesh, weighed and examined as it is, not least by ourselves: we prod our midriffs, stroke our hair, ponder our reflections, and exclaim in surprise at the stranger staring back in our photographs. There is the equally material but unseen muscle that is the brain, whose workings constitute, store and process what we think we know. Then there is the imagined body, the one that we would like to have, the self-portrait against which we judge the alien in the mirror. There is also the body we imagine we will have in the future. For most of us, this will simply be an older body, though it is more likely that many of us will at least entertain the hope that one day, soon, we will look a bit more trim and muscular, lithe and attractive. To achieve this, a lot of us invest serious money in products, services and behaviour that are supposed to help reshape our body.

Why does the body matter so much? Partly, it is because we all see the body as a way of making judgements about one another – and therefore intuitively know that others are making similar judgements about us. In our reflexive and consumerist world, as Susie Orbach says, 'Looking after oneself' has become 'a moral value', a 'worthy personal project'.[14] In 2011, a survey found that four out of every five British men wanted to be more muscular. All but a handful said they had heard demeaning comments about men's bodies, built around unrealistic dreams of a lean and muscular ideal, but many were frightened to go to a gym, while one in eight had considered taking steroids.[15] Little wonder, then, that sociologists are studying 'body work' with renewed interest. While much of their research concerns the effort people put into their own body and its appearance, some people have been looking more closely at the relationship between the body and work.

Men's bodies have entertained and fascinated people for countless generations. Of course, they come in different shapes and sizes, and in the twentieth century one particular category came to the fore: the bodies of the male working class. In the early years of the century, and especially after the catastrophic military set-backs of the Boer Wars, the sport-playing middle and upper classes of Britain gazed with concern on the puny bodies of industrial Britain, fearful that these unhealthy slum-dwellers might hinder what they called 'national efficiency'.[16] By the 1920s, an ideal workman's body was starting to take shape: brawny, muscular, upright workers became symbolic figures, whether representing the international proletariat in Communist iconography or the healthy Aryan people in Nazi propaganda. By the 1970s, the working man's body had emerged as a gay archetype, epitomised by the hard-hatted Construction Worker in the popular disco band, the Village People. At the end of the century, the gym-joining middle and upper classes gazed anxiously at the flabby, obese, waddling bodies of people poorer than they.

For academics, this is a relatively new interest. Sociologists mostly followed Marx and Weber in seeing work and employment as something that happened increasingly in large organisations, run on impersonal lines, and taking it for granted that male working bodies were, physically at any rate, fit. Male working-class muscularity can partly be understood, according to Pierre Bourdieu, as an instrumental investment in the body that in part seeks to compensate for the lack of other resources, such as social connections and educational credentials, which demand at most an 'essentially hygienic' approach to sport and exercise.[17] Thanks to feminist debates over women's bodies and their contested meanings, these widely held assumptions are now being questioned and explored. Carol Wolkowitz writes of three broad approaches to the sociology of embodiment: the everyday work we do to keep ourselves going, or 'reproductive work', such as washing and feeding; the activities we engage in to make ourselves culturally acceptable, from dieting and dressing smartly to body building and piercing; and job-related body work, undertaken by ourselves or others to maintain our viability as workers.[18] While these are not hard-and-fast distinctions, the third type of body work is what chiefly interests me here, and especially the development of institutions that are deliberately designed to work on other people's bodies. Work camps are, of course, a great example.

For a historian, the work camp movement is also unusual – though not unique – in the amount of information that survives about the experiences of some of our most marginalised fellow citizens. Alcoholic women, epileptics, vagrants and the unemployed do not stand at the centre of our thoughts, and they do not fill too many shelves in our official archives. Most of the records relating to labour colonies, instructional centres and other work camps were compiled by their administrators or by official observers of some kind. J. D. Clarke, a clerical worker, was unusual in recording his impressions of a three-week stay in Lingfield Labour Colony in 1899. Writing afterwards to thank the Charity Organisation Society, who had funded his stay, the Londoner reassured his sponsors that he had not been on holiday:

The heat is intence & we are out in it all day, hoeing, haying (finished), fruit & pea picking – we rise at 6, I wouldn't mind if it were 4, for I am an easy early riser. Breakfast at 7 out till 12 back at 1 & work till 5.30 … We are allowed 6d a week to pay for washing collars &c, get thread, cotton, stamps, notepaper &c.

Desperate to return to office work, Clarke stressed that he was not complaining, simply expressing gratitude for its support.[19] His letter provides the first account by an inmate of this new type of institution – new for Britain, at any rate – dedicated to making men stronger and more employable by living together and working on the land. It is part of a much wider and diverse collection of material that allows us to explore attitudes to different types of bodies – mostly male, often unemployed, sometimes addicted or sick – and to their treatment. This is a largely neglected story, and one which has considerable wider significance for our understanding of social policy, masculinity and the many meanings of work in the development of modern Britain.

Notes

1 For example, M. Musick and J. Wilson, 'Volunteering and Depression: The role of psychological and social resources in different age groups', *Social Science and Medicine*, 56, 2, 2009, 259–69.

2 M. Jahoda, *Employment and Unemployment: A social-psychological analysis*, Cambridge University Press, Cambridge, 1982.

3 C. Wanberg, 'Individual Experiences of Unemployment', *Annual Review of Psychology*, 63, 2012, 369–96.

4 A. Gorz, *Farewell to the Working Class: An essay on post-industrial socialism*, Pluto Press, London, 1982.

5 K. Kumar, 'From Work to Employment and Unemployment: the English experience', in R. Pahl, *On Work: Historical, comparative and theoretical approaches*, Blackwell, Oxford, 1988, 146–8.

6 Ibid., 151.

7 Kumar notes that 'unemployment' in its modern usage first appeared in the Oxford English Dictionary in the late 1880s: 'From Work', 164.

8 M. Weber, *The Protestant Ethic and the Spirit of Capitalism*, Routledge, 1992, 14–16.

9 R. Crompton, *William and the Evacuees*, George Newnes, London, 1940, 160–88.

10 http://articles.cnn.com/2011–02–16/politics/obama.conservation_1_ land-and-water-conservation-action-plan-president-barack-obama? (accessed on 11 October 2011).

11 For an extreme example, see http://libcom.org/library/concentration-camps-in-england-1929–39 (accessed on 29 August 2012).
12 R. Rodger, *Housing the People: The colonies of Edinburgh: A history of the Edinburgh Co-operative Building Company*, Edinburgh City Council, 1999.
13 W. H. G. Armytage, *Heavens Below: Utopian experiments in England, 1560–1960*, Routledge & Kegan Paul, London, 1961, 88.
14 S. Orbach, *Bodies*, Profile, London, 4.
15 Central YMCA, 'Body confidence – not just a women's issue', www.ymca.co.uk/bodyconfidence/campaign/men (accessed on 29 February 2012).
16 G. R. Searle, *The Quest for National Efficiency: A study in British politics and political thought, 1899–1914*, Ashfield, London, 1990, 34–53.
17 P. Bourdieu, 'Sport and social class', in C Mukerji and M Schudson (eds), *Popular Culture: contemporary perspectives in cultural studies*, University of California Press, Berkeley, 1991, 369.
18 C. Wolkowicz, 'The organizational contours of "body work"', in E. Jeanes, D. Knights and P. Martin (eds), *Handbook of Gender, Work & Organization*, Wiley, Chichester, 2011, 178–9.
19 J. D. Clarke to COS 30/7/99, London Metropolitan Archives, A/FWA/C/D254/1.

1

Colonising the land

In 1850, Britain was reaching the peak of her international power. Hyde Park rang to the hammers and cries of two thousand labourers, erecting the vast Crystal Palace. Most Britons were duly impressed by the Great Exhibition's eclectic celebration of Britain's ingenuity, prosperity and power, but not Thomas Carlyle. Faced with such vanity, pomp and pride, the veteran satirist modestly proposed that 'the Pauper Populations of these Realms' be conscripted into 'Industrial Regiments', recruited to fight not the French, but 'the Bogs and Wildernesses at home and abroad, and to chain the Devils of the Pit which are walking too openly among us'.[1] In the complacent Britain of 1851, the idea of a regiment of paupers was a satirist's fantasy. By the 1880s, it had assumed a more realistic shape, in the form of the labour colony.

The idea of the labour colony drew on earlier traditions of thinking about the poor. By the 1880s, workhouses were coming under increasing strain; as well as the able-bodied poor, their inmates included pauper children, the elderly, the insane and the sick. Conservatives such as Carlyle often thought that a dose of rural life would prove healthy economically as well as socially, drawing the poor away from the malign influences of city life, and reminding the landowning class of its obligations. Land settlement schemes took deeper roots among radical and working-class movements. Chartists, Utopian socialists and Owenites all invented schemes for bringing the urban poor into rural communes, where they would live off the land. Robert Owen himself, pioneer cooperator and theorist of the cooperative movement, developed remarkably detailed proposals between 1817 and 1840 for home colonies, on which some 2,500 men, women and children would support themselves.[2] Later, John Stuart Mill so admired the Chartist Land

Plan, which settled urban working-class families on five planned rural estates of well over 1,000 acres, that he considered it as a lasting solution to Ireland's persistent land problems.[3]

Visions settling the urban poor on the land captured the imagination of radicals and rural conservatives alike throughout the nineteenth century. Radicals took a particularly active interest in land reform, and debates over the rights and wrongs of landlordism reached a peak in the 1870s and 1880s.[4] Given increasing public criticism of the Poor Laws, and growing recognition of its inability to deal with unemployment, it is not surprising that these two concerns came together. In his account of public responses to unemployment, underemployment and poverty in Victorian London, Gareth Stedman Jones has explored the unstable balance between belief in civic progress and moral anxiety over urban degeneration that by the 1880s characterised middle-class attitudes towards the poor. Emerging socialist groups occasionally found an audience among the unemployed, organising demonstrations that often spilt over into violent outbursts.[5] Fears of class war were further inflamed by union activity among unskilled and casual workers and, above all, the London dockers' strike of 1889.

For many late Victorian Britons, urban conflicts and aspirations were one side of a coin. Land reform, of one kind or another, was the other. In imperial Britain, long-term changes in food supply were producing a contraction in the amount of land under cultivation. Some large landowners turned portions of their estates over to game, causing further resentment and hostility over land ownership patterns, while some land reverted to scrub and moor. From the early 1880s, radicals, socialists and rural traditionalists alike were promoting debate about land reform, and were particularly interested in land settlement, seeing it variously as a means of promoting manly independence and national stability and undermining the power of aristocratic 'feudalism' in the countryside while helping resolve the problems of urban life, unemployment included.[6]

During the early 1880s, public attitudes towards the poor started to shift. Stedman Jones highlighted a number of different elements to this process, including recognition of the Poor Law's failures, changing middle-class attitudes towards charity, the impact of Charles Booth's enormous survey of London's poor, and the spread of social imperialist ideas linking British unemployment with colonial settlement.[7] There were also more proximate causes, including a sharp rise in the numbers of the poor when the severe winter of 1885–86 put a stop to much outdoor work, at a time when depression had already led to job loss. The economists Alfred Marshall and John Hobson had started to write and speak about unemployment, a term that had barely entered the language before the 1880s, as a product of the way the labour market is organised.[8]

The main mechanism for relieving poverty, the Poor Law, was demonstrably ineffective at dealing with cyclical unemployment in the industrial cities, and was under massive strain in cities like London, where the importance of casual labour meant that huge numbers of men and women hovered between work and despair. Nor was the Poor Law any better at handling the other social and health problems, from madness to old age, that were passed on to it. By January 1908, while the Royal Commission on the Poor Laws was chewing over the competing propositions of Fabian socialism and liberal idealism, almost a million people in England and Wales – around one person in forty – were receiving some form of poor relief.

One reason for advocating labour colonies, then, was as an alternative to the existing poor law institutions. Advocates could point to earlier experiments, like the workhouse farm opened by Sheffield Board of Guardians in 1848. Isaac Ironside, a radical Guardian who briefly lived on the Owenite New Harmony community in his youth, vigorously defended the 'New England' farm, declaring that it allowed the able-bodied poor not only to provide productive labour but also to become 'better citizens'.[9] Once economic conditions improved, the farm declined, and the Sheffield experiment came to an end. Nevertheless, workhouse farms continued to provide a focus for debate. Fifty years later, one poor law guardian presented a paper on workhouse farms at a conference on land reform, citing such examples as the workhouse farm at Wyke, near Winchester, on which able-bodied male paupers grew some of their own food, with the infirm men caring for the workhouse pigs, and the 100–acre Craiglockhart farm, which employed pauper 'imbeciles' from Edinburgh poorhouse.[10]

The Liverpool Unitarian Herbert Mills, founder of the Starnthwaite colony in 1892, argued in 1886 that unemployment resulted from mechanisation, which then reduced demand for goods, creating a vicious cycle that could not be tackled by existing poor law institutions. For Mills, the workhouse encouraged anything but

work: on the contrary, he was impressed by the uselessness of such
tasks as oakum-picking and stone-breaking, the disdain with which
officials treated the poor, and in general 'the extraordinary amount
of yawning that goes on'.[11] What was required, he concuded, was
an 'English experiment' in cooperative land settlement.[12] He spelt
out more detailed proposals in a speech to a Mansion House conference in 1887, claiming moreover the support of the eminent economist Alfred Marshall.[13]

Far better known than Mills, the East Ender George Lansbury
was also a Christian Socialist and critic of the workhouse. A radical
Liberal who moved steadily towards socialism, Lansbury was also
an active campaigner for poor law reform, though as a railwayman's
son Lansbury had not spent his childhood in poverty, and unlike
Will Crooks and Keir Hardie he had not spent time in a workhouse
until he became a candidate for the Poplar Board of Guardians.
'Abandon hope all ye who enter here' was his judgement on the
Poplar workhouse, when he visited as a newly elected Guardian of
the Poor.[14] Lansbury continued to serve on Poplar Board of Guardians until 1929. His base lay in London, as part of a generation of
Labour leaders whose constituencies were associated with populist
radicalism and – occasionally – the threat of public disorder.[15] For
these politically minded men, poor law boards were a point of entry
into local government.

Lansbury was active on a number of fronts, including the drink
trade, child labour, advertising, gambling (on the Stock Exchange as
much as in the street), and clerical hypocrisy. Perhaps his chief hate
– along with freemasonry – was 'the sinfulness, the crime against
society, which the mere fact of landlordism entails'.[16] The land was
created by God for all humanity, and Lansbury thought that there
was no foundation for private ownership other than past violence
and oppression.

> The progressive workman is asking himself with a very bitter insis-
> tence how it is that he and his should be cooped up, in the great cities
> (yes, and in the tiny villages too), in little bits of houses with scarcely
> room to breathe, whilst all around him are hundreds of thousands of
> acres of land practically unused, and great parks, with walls and rail-
> ings surrounding them, used only for the pleasure and convenience of
> just a handful of people.[17]

Poor law reform, then, provided an opportunity to pursue practical
land reform at the same time.

Initially, Lansbury proposed punitive labour colonies for 'the treatment of the habitual casual and repression of the loafer'.[18] In 1895 he persuaded the Poplar Guardians to develop plans for a labour colony in Essex which would take both men and women for a one-year period. Alarmed at the cost, the Local Government Board (LGB) rejected the plan, offering instead to allow Poplar to extend its workhouse.[19] By the late 1890s, however, he appears to have shifted gear, moving away from an authoritarian perspective on the 'under-class', and developing a view of labour colonies as a school for citizenship on the land. Labour colonies, Lansbury wrote, would help so-called 'unemployables' to become 'self-respecting citizens' only if they led to land settlement.[20] He developed this theme in a speech to the Christian Social Union at Oxford University, proposing that there should be several different types of labour colony – including one for vagrants, one for able-bodied workhouse inmates, and one for ordinary unemployed – all leading to land settlement in 'co-operative communities'.[21] He also drafted a thirteen-page Bill for Land Colonisation in the United Kingdom, with detailed plans for extensive 'State Colony Farming Operations'.[22] In a House of Commons dominated by vested interests, the Bill had no chance of success, but that was precisely its point.

Lansbury was appealing to a deep-rooted tradition in land agitation. British radicals had long dreamed of communally held or inexpensive land as way of releasing them from the grim conditions of urban, industrial life. Massively damaged by the collapse of the Chartist Land Plan in 1851 (a collapse partly engineered by Chartism's enemies in Parliament), the British land reform movement did not revive until the 1870s, when a number of organisations emerged with the aims of reforming land-owning patterns and supporting the extension of smallholdings. By the 1880s, a number of campaigners, including several active in the Liberal Party, were speaking warmly once more of the Chartist settlements.[23] The movement was given added process by the writings of Henry George, an American economist whose ideas of a single tax on land values attracted many in Britain who wanted to see large landholdings broken up.

The idea of land settlement had old roots in British labour and radical movements. It fed from hostility towards the landed gentry, and especially those aristocrats who had inherited large estates. This can be seen in the work of the English Home Colonisation Society, created in 1893 by John Brown Paton and Harold Moore to promote land settlement through publications and advice, as well as by supporting such institutions as cooperative smallholdings and rural credit banks, with labour colonies to train would-be agriculturalists from the towns.[24] Paton and Moore, along with Herbert Mills, were enthusiastic advocates of a return to the land, and one of the Society's earliest publications was a report on labour colonies and farm settlements.[25] As well as civic and economic goals, it also couched its arguments in national terms. Reverend J. L. Brooks, director of Lingfield Labour Colony, described the Society's basic aim as 'making agricultural Englishmen independent in their own country', by reviving 'the yeoman class', once so 'hardy, full-blooded and resourceful'.[26]

National motifs also appear in Charles Dawson's arguments for labour colonies. Dawson, an Irish home ruler, blamed the Reformation rather than urbanisation or industrialisation for the evils of modern poverty. Problems created initially by abolition of the monasteries were only reinforced when the English poor law was 'forced' on Ireland in 1838.[27] Citing the ideas of 'Prince Krapotkin' and Charles Booth, Dawson proposed to combine land settlement for the people with forced labour for the lazy: 'Let the land of England and Ireland be opened up to the labour of the people. Let labour stations be established to indicate employment to the "want works". Let the "won't works" be sent to forced labour farms to make them work, and, at the same time, to develop the National resources and to increase the National wealth.'[28] Dreams of a thriving countryside continued after the turn of the century. In 1912, the Radical Liberal MP Percy Alden – a Congregationalist who believed that 'land monopoly' was the most 'serious obstacle to any solution of the unemployed problem' – was complaining about Norman feudalism, and contrasting it with Saxon peasant independence.[29] Ten years later, Alden was blaming modern unemployment for the 'break-up of the manorial system and the decay of communal cultivation'.[30]

It was not just Irish nationalists and Christian Socialists who dreamed of a return to the land. The cultural critic John Ruskin and the economist Alfred Marshall were both said to be supporters of the Home Colonisation Society and its plans for settling colonies of unemployed men and women on the land.[31] A number of Fabians expressed interest in land settlement and afforestation, partly as a form of counter-cyclical stimulation and partly as a step towards 'the better distribution of labor', counter-balancing the drift towards the towns.[32] According to its constitution, the Fabian Society aimed at 'the re-organization of Society by the emancipation of Land and Industrial Capital from individual and class ownership, and the vesting of them in the community for the general benefit'.[33] Not all Labour figures took this view. Will Thorne, secretary of the Gas Workers and General Labourers' Union, thought that a large part of the unemployed 'would not possibly go back to the land at any price'.[34]

Healthy bodies and a strong nation

Mary Fels, who supported the labour colony movement as much as her husband Joseph, believed that Britain's rural population had been dumped in the industrial cities 'to wither and decay', depriving the country of 'an element of national strength' that elsewhere arose from a vigorous peasantry.[35] Such critics blamed urbanisation and industrialism for the physical condition of Britain's poor. For those with a social conscience, such as Mary Fels, this was the natural consequence of 'the general disregard for life and health accorded to the wage-earning population'. Fels recalled the way in which the Boer War had 'disclosed to England many ugly conditions within her', including 'a proletariat rapidly deteriorating in fitness as well as in the means of subsistence'.[36] Similar ideas were pervasive; socialists had campaigned for school meals and school medical inspections well before the public panic over working-class physical weakness during the Boer War.[37]

The Reverend John Brown Paton expressed similar views in more archaic language. He harked back to the days when 'England was … held and cultivated by a splendid type of men, who owned their own land and tilled it with their own hands; men who were made strong in body by healthy labour, and who had the virile temper and the freedom of spirit which grow naturally from such independence and industry'. Now, through urbanisation and industrialisation, 'the whole of this order of men has been exterminated'.[38] Others held less radical versions of the same sentiments. National and imperial considerations weighed heavy with more conservative minds. Dr Donald MacLeod, convener of the Church of Scotland's home mission committee, told the Kirk's 1891 assembly that persistent beggars should 'be packed off to a labour colony'.[39] Richard

Lodge, professor of history at Edinburgh, favoured labour colonies as a way of preventing such degeneration, for after 'a few generations of slum life, our city population needs to renew its strength by contact with mother earth'. Lodge believed that 'in the extension of small holdings and properties lies the salvation of our race'.[40]

Such concerns over working men's bodies long pre-dated the Boer War. Walter Hazell's first venture into charity formation was through Samuel Barnett's Children's Fresh Air Mission, which from 1884 provided a seaside holiday to several thousand poor London children every year.[41] In 1888, Reginald Brabazon, Earl of Meath and a noted philanthropist brought together a collection of materials on physical education and technical training, arguing that state intervention was justified by the fact that, while the physical abilities of the upper classes were improving, the health of the urban lower classes was degenerating.[42] Meath, who was scouting commissioner for Ireland and a founder of the Empire Day movement, drew inspiration from German models of gymnastics as well as of the labour colony.[43]

Meath was one of many who admired and drew inspiration from labour colonies abroad. The first German *Arbeiterkolonie* (workers' colonies) opened in Wilhelmsdorf, attracting a horde of admiring visitors from Britain and elsewhere. By 1900, the idea of the labour colony was everywhere. As well as Germany and Britain, reformers drafted labour colony schemes in the United States, Australia, Holland, Belgium and Scandinavia. The Congregationalist Dr John Brown Paton recalled that it was through Meath's writing that he first became aware of the German colonies, though it was Miss Julie Sutter's book that gave 'great impetus' to the movement in Britain.[44] Sutter herself also showed interest in training the body, describing the clientele of the German *Arbeiterkolonien* as 'sinking men'.[45] Her proposal for national training colonies for young women and men addressed the body human and the body politic: 'Fitness would be the aim and citizenship the reward.'[46] Paton enumerated the advantages of labour colony work: first, it 'is interesting, full of variety, and health-giving', particularly in so far as it involves 'intensive and hand industry'; second, it 'contains high possibilities of social life', through cultivation of leisure in the evening, while avoiding the 'massing together of large numbers in a barrack-life'.[47]

Concern over the working-class male body was shared across a wide spectrum of opinion. The Fabian socialists Sydney and

Beatrice Webb contrasted 'strong, disciplined and trained men' with the 'half-starved and physically incompetent weaklings' who were first to fall out of work, so that training rather than idleness would produce 'obvious improvement in physical efficiency' while also having 'a bracing effect on character'.[48] William Harbutt Dawson went further, arguing that to punish vagrants by sending them to detention colonies 'is not enough'; rather, 'these evaders of all social obligations would learn, or at least would be taught, both how to work and the duty of industry'.[49] Some resorted to medical metaphors. One journalist, reporting sympathetically on the Christian socialist colony at Starnthwaite, described unemployment as 'the visible result of a series of diseases'.[50] Drage saw colonies as useful in removing 'the contaminating influence of a section of the permanent surplus'.[51]

Following the Boer War, the government established a committee to investigate 'the deterioration of certain classes of the population'.[52] Everyone knew what was meant by 'certain classes'. Provoked by widespread anxiety over the high proportion of army recruits who had to be rejected on physical grounds, and following on from Meath's Royal Commission on Physical Training in Scotland, the committee found no real evidence that Britons were deteriorating, calling for government to undertake a regular 'anthropometric survey', and warning against exaggeration of 'the evil'. Taking environmental factors – poor housing, diet – as the main causes of poor physique, it also proposed a number of interventions to prevent 'such physical degeneration as is no doubt present in considerable classes of the community'.[53] And while it was 'much impressed' by the Salvation Army colony at Hadleigh, and praised smallholdings and the garden city movement, the committee concluded that the state should treat labour colonies as a 'last resort' for those who 'are incapable of independent existence up to the standard of decency which it imposes'.[54]

This brings us to the more punitive approach. In 1906, an inquiry into vagrancy had called for the establishment of industrial labour colonies where habitual vagrants could be sent, along with a smaller number of severe penal labour colonies, where those who proved uncooperative might be sent for between six months and three years.[55] The Webbs, in a report published after the Royal Commission on the Poor Laws, argued for benefits to be conditional on 'such training – physical and mental, general and technological – as may be found appropriate'.[56] The Webbs restated the Minority Report's proposal for two or three 'Reformatory Detention Colonies', where men who had been sentenced for offences under the Vagrancy Act, or for failing to maintain their families, would be 'subjected to the best influences that can be discovered with a view to effecting a reformation of character', including 'compulsory segregation'.[57]

The Webbs shared this authoritarian streak with others. Thomas Smith, superintendent of the Mayland land settlement colony, also favoured penal colonies 'for the incorrigibly lazy'.[58] Hubert Hammond, superintendent at Fambridge Labour Colony, also favoured the penal colony for bad cases.[59] But socialists seemed particularly keen. In London, the Battersea and Wandsworth Trades and Labour Council issued a manifesto in the poor law elections which included a proposal for placing habitual vagrants in labour colonies.[60]

Ideas of compulsion often rested on a belief that the poor and unemployed could be more or less firmly classified. The Reverend Wilson Carlile, founder of the Church Army, identified six groups, from those who had asked for support but were yet to be classified, to 'beggars, habitual vagrants … [and] feeble-bodied and drunken folk', who would be made to go to 'land colonies or adult reformatories' until they were fit to work or emigrate.[61] Bolton Smart, experienced charity worker and by then the superintendent of Hollesley Bay, recommended three types of labour colony: first, the training colony, designed for men able and willing to settle on the land; second, a testing colony, for those 'suffering from defect of character or physique', who might be rescued through open air life and regular feeding'; and the detention colony, aimed at those who 'have made up their minds never to work again'.[62] William Harbutt Dawson, a Yorkshireman by birth who had been educated at Berlin University and was a great admirer of things German, saw labour colonies as one way to 'stamp out' what he called 'the social parasite of every kind'.[63] As well as persistent vagrants, Dawson wanted 'forced labour' for 'several other classes of notorious delinquents', including deserting husbands, idle paupers, and 'Unmarried women of inferior mental and moral capacity, dependent on the rates, who have had more than one illegitimate child'.[64]

International models

German and other continental European models attracted considerable attention. In February 1895, the Reverend John Brown Paton wrote to Charles Loch, secretary of the Charity Organisation Society (COS), inviting him to join his campaign to recreate the yeomanry of old. Paton, a Congregationalist and advocate of Christian service, directed his argument to Loch's own rather authoritarian views on the poor, singing the praises of the 'wonderful results' of the German labour colony movement in eradicating 'the curse of loafing trampers' and restoring the unemployed 'to an honest and self-reliant livelihood'.[65] This startling achievement, Paton wrote, was the brainchild of Pastor von Bodelschwingh, of Bielefeld, whose work Paton greatly admired. Loch was not impressed, but many others were.

Friedrich von Bodelschwingh, son of a senior Prussian civil servant, had been a playmate of the future Kaiser Friedrich III. After studying agriculture, he became an estate manager, before returning to university to study theology. After a time working with the German Lutheran community in Paris, he took a position managing a care home for epileptics in the city of Bielefeld. While in Bielefeld, Bodelschwingh was associated with the foundation of a number of *Arbeiterkolonien*. Starting with one colony at Wilhelmsdorf, by the end of the 1880s there were twenty-one *Arbeiterkolonien* with almost 2,500 places.[66] Bodelschwingh's movement was soon well known in the English-speaking world. A brief description appeared in 1886 in the *Daily News*, in a letter from a reader who gave his address as the Reform Club.[67] His ideas were presented to the West Midland Poor Law conference in the following year.[68]

Meanwhile the Foreign Office issued a brief report on the German colonies, compiled by its consular representative in Stuttgart.[69] Daniel Stevenson, secretary of the Glasgow Social Union, visited two German colonies, warmly recalling his meeting with 'the good pastor'.[70] Back in Scotland, the lawyer who edited the *Poor Law Magazine* thought the idea of replicating this German model 'a most excellent one, both as regards its suitability for the health and morals of the colonists, and as regards its ultimate benefits to the community at large'.[71] Stevenson's own thoughts were embraced by the *Belfast Newsletter*, whose editor thought that the German model showed Ireland how to 'provide employment, check disaffection, afford comfortable holdings to farmers, and keep our countrymen at home'.[72]

Bodelschwingh's Lutheran background no doubt appealed to Congregationalists like Paton. Paton claimed that the Christian Union for Social Service (CUSS) had been 'formed to adapt the methods of Pastor von Bodelschwingh to the conditions of English life'.[73] English social reformers being no better at speaking German then than they are now, Paton had absorbed Bodelschwingh's ideas at second hand, through Meath's articles and a book called *A Colony of Mercy*, written by Miss Julie Sutter.[74]

Sutter was unqualified in her enthusiasm for von Bodelschwingh's ideas. She wrote one book as an open letter to John Burns, President of the LGB and stringent opponent of the labour colony movement. While Burns had recently visited labour colonies in France and Belgium, he had not visited Germany, so Sutter politely recommended that his next trip might extend to the *Arbeiterkolonien*. Interestingly enough, Sutter now regretted translating the latter term as 'labour colonies', preferring now to substitute the more grammatically accurate 'working men's colonies' for the 'unhappy appellation' of her earlier study.[75] She then presented a detailed scheme, involving a national network of 'training colonies' for the young, girls as well as boys; and a parallel system of training colonies for the 'surplus labour' found in each city. This, she argued, would supplant both the poor law system, which failed to prevent unemployment at source, and the rigid mindset of the voluntaristic COS, which she criticised as lacking authority and concentrating excessively on the individual rather than the cause of poverty.[76]

For Paton, Bodelschwingh's *Arbeiterkolonien* represented the blueprint for a new social order that would render the Poor Law marginal. Loch thought this folly, noting grumpily that 'Miss Julie Sutter has not a critical mind.'[77] A highly competent organiser and prolific writer, Loch became secretary of the COS in 1875; his outlook on the poor, including the unemployed, was shaped by a firm grounding in classical economics and individualistic philosophy.[78] Emphasising the discipline of markets, combined with family responsibility and the strictest enquiry into each individual's application for charitable support, Loch denounced the 'injury and inutility of this pseudo-employment', and had no intention of being influenced by Paton.[79] For Loch, the failings of the Poor Law were to be resolved by strict discrimination between deserving and undeserving, based on information gathered systematically through casework and personal acquaintance, and not by make-work initiatives inspired by half-baked ideas of a return to the land.

Nevertheless, the movement continued to gather momentum. In 1888, the House of Lords received a report from its Select Committee on the Poor Laws, which had heard a number of witnesses – including Herbert Mills – extolling the merits of labour colonies, all citing models from continental Europe.[80] Further, very detailed information was provided when the Board of Trade, whose Labour Department was undertaking an investigation into unemployment, asked Professor James Mavor to compile a special report on labour colonies.[81] Mavor had moved to Toronto University by the time of the inquiry, but he had previously lived in Glasgow; as a member of the Glasgow Social Union, he knew Daniel Stevenson, who was an enthusiastic admirer of von Bodelschwingh's *Arbeiterkolonien*, and he joined a group who visited Germany with Stevenson, concluding on their return that 'the system is capable of adaption to the conditions of our own country'.[82]

Mavor's study covered labour colony systems in Denmark, France, Holland, Switzerland and Germany; and he was particularly impressed by the German *Arbeiterkolonien*, which had their origins in the industrial depression triggered by the Franco-Prussian War.[83] In his view, the labour colony offered a solution to several costly problems, for if the poor were given the opportunity of working,

> then the vagrancy law may be put stringently in force, the unemployed rogue put in prison, and the idle 'chivvied' into the colony with the alternative of being shut up in the jail.[84]

So far as genuinely unemployed workmen were concerned, Mavor thought that the labour colony had value only 'to a modified extent', and would mainly be of benefit in hardening up physically weaker workers.[85] Mavor's report was widely read at the time, and visits to European labour colonies became popular with policy makers, particularly after the Boer War.[86] By the time Herbert Samuel became President of the LGB in 1914, he had examined labour colonies in Belgium, France and Germany.[87]

Sociologists and the poor

While nonconformity and the land reform movement played important roles in the early labour colony movement, it also attracted
interest from social scientists. The Webbs' interest has already been
mentioned, but Beatrice had been introduced to empirical social
research through her cousin Charles Booth, who employed her as an
investigator for his monumental study of poverty and the London
labour market. Booth retained a conventional moralistic view of
poverty, but also aimed to provide clear and rigorous evidence as
a basis of classifying the poor. In particular, he provided a ratio-
nalist basis for distinguishing between what he thought of as the
residuum of unemployables, who invariably dodged honest work at
every opportunity, and the respectable working class, who sought
to provide for themselves, but sometimes fell on hard times. Booth
saw the first group, which he called Class A, as beyond rescue; they
ought to be broken up and dispersed by coercion so as to reduce the
threat they posed to society at large. But in between the respectable
workers and the unemployable residuum lay a class on the margins
of employability. In his schema, Booth defined the key group as the
members of Class B, the very poor living on casual earnings, and
Class C, the unskilled labourers whose labour market position was
precarious because of competition from Class B. Booth's proposal
was designed to improve the position of both by removing unemployed men from Class B to labour colonies, where they would
learn the responsibilities and duties of honest labour.[88]

John Brown has estimated that had Booth's plan been adopted,
around 345,000 of London's poor would have found themselves in
a labour colony.[89] Yet Booth's thinking provided a clear empirical
basis for thinking of the labour colony as a rational intervention in
tackling at least one source of poverty.

By studying London, with its huge market for casual labour,
Booth had selected a city of huge symbolic significance.[90] He was
not the first social scientist to endorse labour colonies as a solution
to the problems of sweating and casual labour, for the economist
Alfred Marshall had in 1884 proposed shifting low-paid Londoners
to 'a colony in some place well beyond the range of London
smoke'.[91] More important in the longer term, William Beveridge,
the future architect of the welfare state and then a youthful civil
servant at the Board of Trade, shared much of Booth's thinking.

Beveridge saw unemployment as partly what we would call structural in nature, but he also accepted that there was a small number
of 'unemployables', though he argued that their defects were often
the result of the casual labour market, and they might be remedied.
Unlike Booth, he thought that the border between the 'can't works'
and 'won't works' was an open and changing one, and dismissed
attempts to distinguish clearly between the two.[92] But he did not
break with all of Booth's thinking, and in particular he did not,
as Mary Langan suggests,[93] reject the idea of the labour colony.
Beveridge had closely studied the labour colonies of 1905–6, and
his evidence to the Royal Commission on the Poor Laws shows that
he saw a distinct role for the labour colony, provided that it had a
clear educational focus.[94] For Beveridge, the colony could serve as a
'technical school', training for 'some specific well-assured demand',
such as emigration; or as 'a hospital' for the reintegration of 'men
broken down through privation or vice'. Finally, he also saw a role
for penal colonies, to discipline the few who were 'incurably defective or idle'.[95] So labour colonies continued to occupy a place in his
thought, alongside other institutions designed to remove obstruc-
tions to the free flow of labour.

The sceptics

Loch, of course, was scathing. He publicly denounced plans for
labour colonies in *The Times*.[96] He dismissed the German colonies as 'only a method of treating vagrancy. I don't think that they
succeed in putting men back into the labour market. I don't think
this experiment necessary.'[97] He devoted a third of an acid review
of Geoffrey Drage's book on the unemployed to condemning labour
colonies. His main objection was that the opportunity of entering a
labour colony was a form of charity, as 'is not earned: it is given',
and this was precisely 'what we ought to avoid'.[98] Loch's objections,
whether understood as arising from principle or ideology, were
deep-rooted. Others, though, voiced more practical objections.

A number of critics questioned the financial viability of the
project. The radical economist John A. Hobson thought it absolutely
impossible for a labour colony to become fully self-supporting if its
main role was to rescue the unemployed. 'The very name Training
Colony is sufficient to indicate that it cannot be self-supporting',
Hobson asserted, adding for good measure that: 'No educational

work can be self-supporting.' Returns on investment in labour colonies could be seen 'in certain unmeasurable forms of public good, the improvement of the industrial character of certain workers, the public guarantee of a decent livelihood without degradation, a certain direct relief of the low-skilled labour market'. The question was then whether these public goods were worthwhile, and if so whether the returns were on a scale to merit public intervention. Hobson thought this possible, concluding that labour colonies were the 'largest and most serviceable of the palliatives' which the state might use to tackle the effects of unemployment, while being of little value in addressing its underlying causes.[99]

Others returned to long-held beliefs about the innate idleness of the poor. H. B. Lees Smith thought that the labour colony, attracting as it did 'the poorest class of workmen', did not offer a real test of willingness to find work in the market for labour.[100] General Booth, said the editor of a Preston newspaper, was assuming that all could be made to work: 'That is just what will not happen, let him plant his city suburbs and farm colonies as he may.'[101] The House of Lords was equally unimpressed, grilling witnesses such as Herbert Mills who advocated colony settlements. Such schemes, their lordships concluded, were fraught with risk, though it was 'hardly necessary' to set out in terms 'the serious objections to extensive schemes of this kind'. They then went on to spell out one objection, which was their lordships' fear that public interventions such as these 'would lead to a wide-spread belief that it is the business of the Government to provide work at suitable wages for all who apply to it for employment'.[102] The existing powers of the Poor Law, they pronounced, were quite sufficient.

Similarly hostile to state intervention, if from a very different standpoint, was John Burns. Burns had a politically chequered career. He trained and worked as an engineering worker, joining the Social Democratic Federation in 1881, getting himself arrested during the unemployment demonstrations, and becoming a leading socialist speaker in London. Rising to fame as a leader of the 1889 dockers' strike, he was then elected independent Labour MP for Battersea, before switching to the Liberal Party during the Boer War. In 1893, while still a socialist, he denounced labour colonies as a 'will o' the wisp' that would attract either bad workmen, who could not be disciplined and therefore would not improve, or good workmen, who did not need them. Instead, Burns favoured shorter working hours and municipal winter relief works as solutions to unemployment.[103] He held on to this position through his later changes. Later on in his career, as President of the LGB, Burns was to rule out most local applications to form municipal labour colonies.

While many socialists saw labour colonies as a means of combining land reform with labour market interventions, some shared Burns' misgivings. R. H. Tawney, an economic historian and adult educator, thought that relief works in general, labour colonies included, effected 'little permanent good'. Much unemployment in London was caused, he thought, by an over-supply of casual and general labour, and the solution therefore lay in a national system of labour exchanges to promote mobility, combined with higher educational standards to reduce the supply of unskilled workers.[104] A rather more esoteric response from the left appeared from the Guild Socialists at *The New Age*, who asked with a flourish: 'Is it by now superfluous for us to remark that all these labour colonies, all these labour exchanges, all this State organisation, informed and permeated by clever Fabianism, are all designedly rendered subservient to the maintenance of the wage system?'[105]

Policy formations

Despite the chorus of hostile voices, a number of thinkers took the idea of the labour colony seriously. While many thought the better route lay through voluntary provision, some influential voices argued for state intervention. Reflecting on the experiences of the Scottish Labour Colony Association, for example, the *Manchester Times* reflected that such schemes 'can only work on so small a scale that it seems but a drop in the ocean of poverty', urging government and the larger municipalities to take advantage of low land prices and establish a national system. Policy interest probably reached its peak during the Royal Commission on the Poor Laws, which paid considerable attention to the question of labour colonies, and made a number of recommendations on their future contribution. Brief periods in a temporary colony of the type envisaged under the Unemployed Workmen Act, it thought, were 'almost if not entirely useless', as their main role was to provide relief.[106] For those who required retraining rather than temporary relief, it advocated 'industrial or agricultural institutions or labour colonies' where 'the capacity of the individual could be properly tried and his physique improved'.[107] For the 'derelicts of industrial life', who were fundamentally workshy, it recommended a sentence in a 'detention colony', administered by the Home Office rather than the public assistance authorities.[108] In short, the Commission saw a role for labour colonies, but not in relieving unemployment, and certainly not as a means of relieving crowded urban labour markets through land settlement.

If it saw a specialist role for labour colonies in Britain, the Commission took a rather different view of the labour colony's potential in Ireland. The Commission emphasised the differences between the Irish and British labour markets; while Britain was predominantly urban and industrial, most Irish people depended on the land. There was also a dense network of charitable support, both through the Roman Catholic church and through the family. The Commission saw no role for training colonies, as there was limited demand for retrained labour, but it did commend proposals for 'modified Labour Colonies' to take vagrants, habitual drunkards, and the won't works. Most should be voluntary institutions, which were

> both curative and restorative in treatment. The discipline should be strict. The open air life will conduce to the rehabilitation of those subject to its influence; there should be attached to each institution sufficient land to employ a number of persons.

In addition, it proposed a small number of state-run 'detention colonies', for utterly hopeless cases.[109]

When it came to the role of the labour colony, the Minority Report from the Royal Commission shared much with the majority. In a book based on their involvement in the Royal Commission, the Webbs argued that the experience of local labour exchanges since 1909 had already confirmed that many of the unemployed lacked skills, which might be remedied through a network of 'small Training Establishments', run in conjunction with the exchanges, some residential in the country, some in day centres in the towns. In contrast to the existing colonies, they should be 'run exclusively as places of training', offering physical exercise and basic adult education alongside skills training; entrance should be voluntary.[110] Percy Alden, a social worker, land reformer and socialist activist who had studied the continental systems at first hand, similarly proposed a 'series of graded colonies dealing with various classes from the unemployable to the better class of unemployed', with the former being detained, while the latter learned to become smallholders.[111] Governmental responsibility for the training colonies, he believed, should lie with a single minister, whose department would also include labour exchanges, unemployment insurance and emigration.[112] Though a Liberal (and subsequently an MP), Alden was also a Fabian, and took a keen interest in unemployment. Like the Webbs, though, Alden thought the labour colony a serious proposal only if there was a clear distinction between their educational and their punitive roles.

Some historians tend to portray the labour colony and the labour exchange as mutually exclusive, the one looking forward to the modern regulated labour market of social democratic Europe, the other looking back to the workhouse and the Poor Law. Yet for all of the supposed opposition between the two ideas and sets of institutions, many at the time believed that both offered complementary rather than competing approaches to unemployment. In their text on social work, William Foss and Julian West thought the labour exchange sufficient to help good workmen and men in casual industries to find a new job, but would do little for 'unemployables' whose 'strength and will have been broken by illness or privation'. For this group, 'the best treatment is found in labour colonies, where they will receive physical training and will be brought to a state of fitness'.[113] If some contemporaries took a conservative view of the labour colony and rejected the labour exchange, then, others saw both institutions as working together, contributing to a modernist view of the benefits of instruction and information as ways of overcoming poverty and unemployment.

Notes

1 T. Carlyle, 'The Present Time', in *Latter-Day Pamphlets*, Phillips, Sampson & Co., Boston, 1855, 55.

2 R. Owen, *A Development of the Principles and Plans on which to Establish Self-supporting Home Colonies*, Home Colonization Society, London, 1841, 37–40.

3 M. Chase, '"Wholesome Object Lessons": The Chartist Land Plan in retrospect', *English Historical Review*, 118, 2003, 59.

4 J. Saville, 'Henry George and the British Labour Movement', *Science and Society*, 24, 4, 1960, 321–33.

5 G. Stedman Jones, *Outcast London: A study in the relationship between classes in Victorian society*, Penguin, London, 1970.

6 P. Readman, *Land and Nation in England: Patriotism, national identity and the politics of land, 188–1914*, Boydell Press, Woodbridge, 1978.

7 Stedman Jones, *Outcast London*, 297–314.

8 M. Langan, 'Reorganising the Labour Market: Unemployment, the state and the labour movement, 1880–1914', in M. Langan and B. Schwarz (eds), *Crises in the British State*, Hutchinson, 1985, 107.

9 W. H. G. Armytage, *Heavens Below: Utopian experiments in England, 1560–1960*, Routledge & Kegan Paul, London, 1961, 246–50.

10 W. Hazlitt Roberts, 'Employment of Pauper Labour upon the Land', in J. A. Hobson (ed.), *Co-operative Labour Upon the Land*, Swan Sonnenschein & Co., London, 1895, 93–7.

11 H. V. Mills, *Poverty and the state, or work for the unemployed: an inquiry into the causes and extent of enforced idleness*, Kegan Paul & Tench, London, 1886, 22.

12 Mills, *Poverty and the state*, 172–80.

13 H. Mills, *Home Colonization: Details of first colony*, Mansion House Conference, 1887.

14 Quoted in J. Shepherd, *George Lansbury: At the heart of old Labour*, Oxford University Press, Oxford, 2004, 51.

15 Shepherd, *George Lansbury*, 2004, 53.

16 George Lansbury, *Your Part in Poverty*, The Herald, London, 1917, 117.

17 Ibid., 118–19.

18 Quoted in Shepherd, *George Lansbury*, 61.

19 J. Harris, *Unemployment and Politics: A study in English social policy, 1886–1914*, Clarendon, Oxford, 1972, 139–40.

20 *Clarion*, 16 December 1905.

21 George Lansbury, Speech to Christian Social Union, Oxford, May 1907, British Library of Political and Economic Science (BLPES), Lansbury Papers 2.

22 Colonization in the United Kingdom – A Bill 1905, BLPES, Lansbury Papers 2.

23 M. Chase, '"Wholesome Object Lessons"', 74–6.

24 *Birmingham Daily Post*, 29 December 1893.

25 J. C. Kenworthy, 'The Work of the English Land Colonisation Society', in Hobson (ed.), *Co-operative Labour Upon the Land*, 117–18.

26 *Leeds Mercury*, 12 May 1900.

27 C. Dawson, 'Suggested Substitutes for the Present Poor Law System', *Journal of the Statistical and Social Inquiry Society of Ireland*, xi, 1906, 428.

28 Ibid., 438.

29 P. Alden, *Democratic England*, Macmillan, New York, 1912, 118, 239.

30 P. Alden, 'Unemployment', in Alden and others, *Labour and Industry: A series of lectures*, Manchester University Press/Longmans, Green &

Co., London, 1920, 27.
31 *Pall Mall Gazette*, 1 April 1892.
32 A. P. Grenfell, *Afforestation and Unemployment*, Fabian Society, London, 1912.
33 Fabian Society, *Twenty-ninth Annual Report*, Fabian Society, London, 1912, 23.
34 Cited in G. H. Duckworth, 'The Work of the Select Committee of the House of Commons on Distress from Want of Employment', *Economic Journal*, 6, 21, 1896, 151.
35 M. Fels, *Joseph Fels: His life-work*, Huebsch, New York, 1916, 31–2.
36 Ibid., 26–8.
37 P. Thane, 'The working class and state "welfare" in Britain, 1880–1914', *Historical Journal*, 27, 4, 1984, 895–6; G. R. Searle, *The Quest for National Efficiency: a study in British politics and political thought, 1899–1914*, Ashfield, London, 1990, 60–2.
38 J. B. Paton, *How to Restore our Yeoman-Peasantry*, James Clarke & Co., London, 1907, 8–9.
39 *Glasgow Herald*, 28 May 1891.
40 Cited in W. Foss and J. West, *The Social Worker and Modern Charity*, Adam and Charles Black, London, 1914, 81–2.
41 R. C. Hazell, *Walter Hazell, 1843–1919*, Hazell, Watson & Viney, London, 1919, 21.
42 Earl of Meath, 'Health and Physique of our City Populations', in Earl of Meath (ed.), *Prosperity or Pauperism? Physical, industrial and technical training*, Longmans, Green & Co., London, 1888.
43 I. Zweiniger-Bargielowska, *Managing the Body: Beauty, health and fitness in Britain, 1880–1939*, Oxford University Press, Oxford, 2010, 3.
44 *Minutes of Evidence taken by the Departmental Committee on Vagrancy*, HMSO, London, 1906, 182.
45 J. Sutter, *Britain's Hope*, James Clarke & Co., London, 1907, 3.
46 Ibid., 19.
47 Ibid., 82–3.
48 S. and B. Webb, *The Prevention of Destitution*, Longmans, Green & Co., London, 1911, 146.
49 Dawson, *Vagrancy Problem*, 1910, 73.
50 *Manchester Times*, 18 January 1895.
51 G. Drage, *The Unemployed*, Macmillan, London, 1894, 213.
52 *Report of the Committee on Physical Deterioration*, Vol. 1, HMSO, London, 1904, v.
53 *Committee on Physical Deterioration*, 13.
54 *Committee on Physical Deterioration*, 17, 35–7, 85.
55 *Departmental Committee on Vagrancy*, 122.
56 S. and B. Webb, *Prevention of Destitution*, 141.

57 Ibid., 151.
58 *Royal Commission on the Poor Laws (RCPL)*, Appendix, Vol. VIII, *Minutes of Evidence*, HMSO, London, 1910, 133.
59 Ibid., 158.
60 *Reynolds Newspaper*, 11 November 1894
61 E. Rowan, *Wilson Carlile*, 324–6.
62 B. Smart, 'The Problem of Unemployment', *Journal of the Royal Society of Arts*, 5 February 1909, 219.
63 W. H. Dawson, *The Vagrancy Problem*, P. S. King & Son, London, 1910, 4.
64 Ibid., 76.
65 Rev. Dr J. B. Paton, Congregational Institute, Nottingham, 27 Feb 1895 [letter to unnamed correspondent], London Metropolitan Archives (LMA), A/FWA/C/D254/1.
66 A. G. Warner, 'Some Experiments on Behalf of the Unemployed', *Quarterly Journal of Economics*, 5, 1, 1890, 6–7; H.-W. Schmuhl, *Friedrich von Bodelschwingh*, Rowohlt, Reinbeck, 2005.
67 *Daily News*, 17 December 1886.
68 *Birmingham Daily Post*, 19 May 1887.
69 *Bristol Mercury and Daily Post*, 4 January 1888.
70 *Glasgow Herald*, 27 May 1891.
71 *Poor Law Magazine*, 3, 1893, 426.
72 *Belfast Newsletter*, 22 October 1892.
73 J. B. Paton, 'Labour for the Unemployed upon the Land', in Hobson (ed.), *Co-operative Labour Upon the Land*, 85–6.
74 J. Sutter, *A Colony of Mercy; or, Social Christianity at Work*, Hodder & Stoughton, London, 1893.
75 Sutter, *Britain's Hope*, 3–4.
76 Ibid., 29–31.
77 Handwritten note, 1895, on CUSS appeal signed by J Carlisle and others, LMA A/FWA/C/D254/1.
78 M. K. Smith (2002) 'Casework and the Charity Organization Society', *The Encyclopedia of Informal Education*, at www.infed.org/ (accessed on 6 August 2010).
79 *Economic Journal*, 4, 16, 1894, 698–701.
80 *Report from the Select Committee of the House of Lords on Poor Law Relief*, HMSO, London, 1888, 247, 303, 405–6.
81 Board of Trade Labour Department, *Report on Agencies and Methods for Dealing with the Unemployed*, HMSO, 1893, 268–339.
82 *Birmingham Daily Post*, 13 November 1893.
83 J. Mavor, 'Labor Colonies and the Unemployed', *Journal of Political Economy*, 2, 1, 1893, 30.
84 Ibid., 26.
85 Ibid., 52–3.

86 *Parliamentary Debates*, 26 February 1903, 4 March 1903, *Parliamentary Debates*, 6 June 1905, C. Dawson, 'Suggested Substitutes', 437.
87 *Parliamentary Debates*, 31 March 1914.
88 J. Brown (1968), 'Charles Booth and Labour Colonies, 1889–1905', *Economic History Review*, 21, 2, 351.
89 Ibid., 353.
90 Stedman Jones, *Outcast London*.
91 A. Marshall, *Where to House the London Poor*, Metcalfe & Son, Cambridge, 1885 (repr. from the *Contemporary Review*, 1884).
92 W. Beveridge, *Unemployment: A problem of industry*, 2nd edition, Longmans, London, 1910, 12, 134–6.
93 M. Langan, 'Reorganising the Labour Market',110.
94 Beveridge (1910), *Unemployment*, 233.
95 *RCPL*, Appendix, Vol. VIII, *Minutes of Evidence*, HMSO, London, 1910, 15.
96 *The Times*, 1 November 1893.
97 Handwritten note, 1895, on CUSS appeal signed by J Carlisle and various others, LMA A/FWA/C/D254/1.
98 C. S. Loch, '*The Unemployed* by Geoffrey Drage', *Economic Journal*, 4, 16, 1894, 700–1.
99 J. A. Hobson, *The Problem of the Unemployed: An enquiry and economic policy*, Methuen, London, 1904, 143.
100 H. B. Lees Smith, 'The London Unemployed Fund, 1904–5', *Economic Journal*, 16, 61, 1906, 158.
101 *Preston Guardian*, 17 January 1891.
102 *Committee of the Lords on Poor Relief*, iii, vi.
103 *Leeds Mercury*, 22 September 1893.
104 R. H. Tawney, 'The Report of the Central Unemployed Body for London', *Economic Journal*, 18, 72, 1908, 646–7.
105 *The New Age*, 30 May 1912.
106 *Report RCPL*, 385.
107 Ibid., 426.
108 *Report RCPL Laws*, 429, 431.
109 *RCPL Report on Ireland*, HMSO, London, 59.
110 S. and B. Webb, *Prevention of Destitution*, 142–5.
111 P. Alden, *Democratic England*, 117; P. Alden, *The Unemployed: A national question*, P. S. King & Son, London, 1905, 17–31.
112 Alden, *Democratic England*, 1912, 120.
113 Foss and West, *Social Worker*, 74–5.

2

'We work amongst the lowest stratum of life'
The early labour colonies

Victorian movements for radical social and urban improvement often drew on a heady ferment of land reform and communitarianism. These ideas, often blended with Christian notions of service, inspired practical experiments in community living for several generations, from early labour colonies to the garden city movement.[1] In the case of the labour colony movement, two institutions were particularly influential: voluntary Christian social service and local government both generated practical support for labour colony movements. Frequently citing the example of the German evangelical theologian von Bodelschwingh, nonconformist Christians tended to view labour colonies as a practical way of helping the poor while furthering their mission. Local government initially paid for local paupers to spend time in a labour colony, then played an increasingly significant role in founding colonies once working-class political groups started to win control over poor law boards and local councils. By 1914, the labour colony had become a normal feature in the landscape of Britain's increasingly jumbled system of poor relief.

Faith and charity

In 1891, two colonies opened as by-products of missionary activity. Funded through the proceeds of Booth's Darkest England campaign, the Salvation Army's Land and Industrial Colony at Hadleigh stretched over 1,500 acres of land, with a further 1,400 acres of mudflats in the Thames estuary. This vast estate, five miles east of Southend, was a massive step in Booth's planned ladder of institutions that would turn the male 'denizens of Darkest England' into 'self-helping and self-sustaining communities, each a kind of co-operative society or patriarchal family', either on a labour colony overseas or a land settlement at home.[2] Newdigate, much smaller than Hadfield, and associated with Wilson Carlisle's Church Army, was more clearly Anglican in outlook. Its main purpose was to let Church Army social workers test and train potential emigrants, so that each would set across the oceans ready to 'plough and do enough rough carpentry to knock together his own shanty'.[3]

Organised non-conformist groups also set up their own colonies. The Congregationalist, businessman and Liberal politician Walter Hazell opened a private colony in 1891 at Langley, north Essex, before moving to a larger farm, near Chesham.[4] The Christian Union for Social Service (CUSS), supported mainly by Congregationalists, opened a colony at Lingfield, in Surrey, in 1896.[5] The Scottish Labour Colony at Midlocharwood in Dumfries opened its doors in 1897, after three years of fund-raising.[6] Driven by the Kirk, with its responsibilities for poor relief, the Scottish Labour Colony Association (SLCA) was formed by a group of Glasgow merchants and professionals after Daniel Macaulay Stevenson – leading Liberal, wealthy coal merchant and cousin of Robert Louis Stevenson – visited three German *Arbeiterkolonien* on behalf of the Glasgow Presbytery.[7] SLCA's main aim, Stevenson said, was 'to say to able bodied men who begged that if it was really work they wanted, they could have it'.[8]

Recruitment was easiest for the larger organisations, with their overlapping networks of missionary and relief activities. A survey of 253 Hadleigh colonists in 1893 showed that all but 86 had passed through an 'elevator', as the Army called its local centres in London.[9] The Salvationists' Prison Gate Brigade, which specialised in helping discharged prisoners, also passed men to Hadleigh.[10] After the first years, the poor law authorities for Hackney and Woolwich, as well as some private individuals supported by their families or by charities, also paid for men to spend time at Hadleigh.[11] The Self-Help Emigration Society (which Hazell had helped found) selected and financed suitable candidates for Langley.[12] The SLCA recruited through Glasgow COS, with the first group coming from their Kyle Street shelter.[13] CUSS used its own supporters' private contacts and connections with local boards of guardians to recruit men for Lingfield. By the end of the century, sixteen boards of guardians were sending men to Lingfield, and while most were London-based they also included Nottingham and Eastbourne.[14] In fact, the Reverend

J. L. Brooks, CUSS director of labour colonies, thought a northern pauper likely to be 'a better man than the London pauper'.[15]

Most early inmates came from the poor and unemployed. Around a third at Hadleigh were general labourers, and a tenth farm labourers, although there were also building workers, engineers, and a few shop assistants and clerks. They were relatively young: two-thirds were under 35, and only three among 253 colonists were over 55.[16] Newdigate inmates were also young, with an average age of 26; while most were single, roughly a quarter were married, and Brooks noted that a number were ex-prisoners or former soldiers.[17] Through its contacts, CUSS took a number of 'private cases', among them 'several civil servants', mostly inebriates, though one family sent a 'Christian Jew' suffering from religious persecution (he did not explain what he meant by 'Christian Jew', nor specify who was responsible for persecuting him), and another sent a man accused of 'indecency'.[18]

Once recruited, the men entered what was effectively a closed institution, with its own regime and routines. At Hadleigh, new entrants underwent medical inspection, were allocated a bed, and then undertook light work. After four weeks, the Army's officers classified them into four groups; men in the first class received four shillings weekly as well as board and lodging and were given semi-skilled jobs such as carpentry or paining, those in the fourth, comprising men judged capable only of the most limited labouring, received one shilling.[19] Hadleigh issued its own tokens, with the value reflecting the supervisors' view of each man's daily efforts; it was for each man to decide whether to spend the tokens on food or change them for cash.[20]

Classification and regimentation also characterised Hadleigh's living arrangements. Each dormitory, housed in brightly painted wooden buildings, was fitted with beds for thirty-two sleepers, with leather-covered mattresses and ex-army blankets; a Salvation Army supervisor slept in a small cabin at the end. By the time Henry Rider Haggard visited, in February 1905, the accommodation was graded: new entrants and poor performers slept on mattresses stuffed with seaweed, with twenty to a room, while higher grade men had better quality bedding, and slept ten to a room.[21] A fourth building served as a kitchen and canteen. And to clean the working, regimented bodies, the colony included a bathhouse, and a row of earth closets.[22]

Such complex and classified arrangements were not possible at smaller colonies. At Midlocharwood, a large whitewashed farmhouse provided space for administration, kitchens, a meeting room and a library, as well as accommodation for the superintendent and some of the men. Although its founders had planned for 200 men, the colony was small, with only sixteen inmates by the end of its first year.[23] The men slept in a dormitory, of questionable warmth and dryness.[24] In 1905, the Association drew up plans to replace the dormitory. The architect's sketch shows two pleasant single-storey buildings, each holding 29 beds, divided into three by screens, and linked by an enclosed porchway to a block with 4 WCs, 2 bathrooms and a washhouse.[25]

Religion featured in all of the early labour colony regimes. On Sundays, said Hadleigh's superintendent, 'we pray and praise all day'.[26] The Army's services, open to the local community, were held in a corrugated iron 'citadel'.[27] Attendance was voluntary, and according to Rider Haggard, transport was provided for those who wished to attend a local church instead.[28] At Lingfield, work was sandwiched between morning and evening prayers and interrupted by mealtimes. All were expected to attend prayers, including the small number of Roman Catholics (who were also encouraged to attend mass),[29] as well as Sunday services. Each colony also imposed its own system of discipline. At Hadleigh, as Booth put it, the colonists were to learn 'the elementary lesson of obedience[30] Alcohol was banned, with new entrants promising to abstain while resident in the colony, and to avoid any premises where alcohol was sold.[31] Breaches of rules, such as negligence in work, were punished with fines; more serious or repeated offences could lead to a reduction in classification, or even expulsion. With the nearest pub less than a mile away, temptation was close at hand, and 73 of the first 991 colonists were dismissed for drunkenness.[32] By contrast, the Midlocharwood men – four miles from a pub – were removed from what the SLCA called 'temptation of the sort which might interfere with necessary discipline'.[33]

Lingfield's arrangements followed a more communitarian approach. Imitating Bodelschwingh's *Arbeiterkolonie* at Bielefeld, CUSS appointed a house-father to supervise the trainees, with his wife serving as house-mother, supported by voluntary social workers known as 'brothers'. In 1907, William Henry Hunt, a former journalist who became house-father in 1902, described his

employers' internal regime to the Royal Commission on the Poor
Laws as based mainly on 'personal influence and moral persuasion'.
The brothers comprised 'fifteen to twenty young, earnest Christian
men, with enthusiasm for humanity, who are in training for institutional service'. Colonists and brothers wore the same clothing, so
that 'at work or at play it is almost impossible to distinguish the one
from the other, except as regards industry and bearing'. The sixty
colonists were divided into small squads, with a brother responsible
for each. Hunt concluded that the colonists 'soon get to understand
that there is a spirit of kindliness towards them, and there are very
few who do not respond to it.[34] Each colonist could earn 3d. a
week, as a tobacco allowance, 'if they are just decent', and 6d. a
week if they got a good recommendation from the farm bailiff or
the Brothers.[35] Those who worked well could move from a dormitory into a cubicle, where they slept on their own.[36] Hunt also fined
the men for misbehaviour, though he presented this as exceptional.

Sport and leisure also played a role. Cricket was played in the
summer and football in the winter, along with swimming, quoits
and other games, both indoor and outdoor. Brooks, Paton and
Hunt were 'muscular Christians' as well as educationalists. Brooks
saw rational leisure pursuits – sports above all – as a way of 'getting
at the social instincts of men, and humanising and inspiring them
with social conditions and educational purposes'. He thought it 'a
sort of law' that 'the boy or man who cannot or will not play will
never make anything'.[37] If such enthusiasm for sport was untypical,
most of the labour colonies made limited provision for games and
offered some basic adult education. As well as a twice weekly night
school for men who could not read or write, Lingfield taught light
carpentry and boot repairing. At Midlocharwood, sympathisers
donated clothing, magazines and illustrated newspapers. There was
also a recreation room with a piano, bagatelle board, draughts and
newspapers, while some men spent their spare time angling for eels,
roach, trout and herring.[38]

Yet work was always the main focus. Each day, apart from
Sunday, followed a regular routine centred on manual labour. At
Hadleigh, the colonists woke to the ringing of a bell, and breakfasted at 8.00 a.m., followed by prayers. They then went to work at
a quarter to nine, and worked until 8 p.m., with one hour for lunch
and a shorter break for tea. Dick Browne, who visited in 1896,
reported that some 800 acres were being farmed, most as pasture;

as well as cattle and sheep, the men learned to care for horses, pigs and poultry.[39] While many colonists worked on the farm and market garden, others were occupied in small-scale industries, including brickfields and a saw-mill. Women worked mainly in the laundry, kitchens and clothing workshops. The routine at Midlocharwood was comparable: the men rose at 6 a.m., with prayers at 6.30, followed by breakfast; a whistle blew at 7.00 to summon the men to work until 12 noon, and again from 1 p.m. until 6.00, with supper at 6.15, more prayers at 8.45, and lights out at 10 p.m.[40] As well as working on the farm and moorland, the men cooked their own meals and cleaned the buildings.

Brooks described Lingfield as a training colony, rather than a 'mere labour colony'.[41] This distinction was a fine one: Lingfield had a market garden, cattle and horses, and employed an experienced farmer to oversee the work, and like the other colonies it aimed at reclaiming and improving its inmates, by preparing them for a life on the land. But, as part of its wider role within the CUSS, Lingfield also served as a centre for social work training. Paid 5 shillings weekly, the brothers, according to Hunt, had sacrificed better-paid jobs to answer their calling, expressing the voluntaristic spirit of the colony.[42] The training itself lasted for three years and was, of course, largely practical, often requiring considerable Christian forbearance as well as sporting prowess. There was also an academic element, and the brothers attended classes in first aid, agriculture, bible study and social science (the set text in 1907 was *The Social Mission of the Churches*).[43]

All the early colonies faced money problems. As some of the critics had predicted, costs were high and the returns low. Initial investments were heavy, yet the land was usually too poor to render easy profits. The Midlocharwood colony, for instance, comprised 150 acres or arable land, 40 acres of reclaimed moss, and 300 acres of unclaimed moss, some of which was below the high-tide level, as well as the farm buildings themselves.[44] Funds were chronically short, and in 1900 the SLCA committee considered closure in the face of its 'serious financial condition'; an emergency appeal raised enough to purchase the estate for £6,500.[45] Ongoing subscriptions recruitment remained weak, and in 1903 the SCLA applied for certification as an inebriate reformatory, hoping to attract public funds.[46] Still Midlocharwood struggled, attracting around thirty men a year up to 1911, far fewer than hoped.[47] Hazell gave up altogether; while he received a weekly payment of 10 shillings 'from the friends of a few of the men', the burden of finding the rest from his own pocket was, his son recalled, 'necessarily heavy', and the colony closed in 1900.[48]

Money problems also dogged Hadleigh, which had become a showcase for the labour colony movement. Apart from the novelty of its sheer size, Booth was an able publicist, and visitors poured in, followed shortly afterwards by gossip and then scandal. Within a year, Booth was being challenged to show how funds had been spent, while south Essex traders complained of unfair competition, and farmers complained that the colony's generous wages were causing unrest among their workforce.[49] Booth convened an inquiry, chaired by the Earl of Onslow, who concluded that there was little in the criticisms.[50] The Salvation Army responded by closing ranks, refusing information to investigators from the Royal Commission on the Poor Laws.[51] Eventually, the Commission sent a delegation to Hadleigh, who returned impressed with the energy and discipline of the men, but sceptical about aspects of the management.[52] Yet the financial implications were clear: the costs of running a labour colony stretched even the largest charities to the limit, and accordingly, the labour colony movement turned increasingly to the state.

The poor law colonies

Before 1904, proposals for municipal colonies came to naught. Canon Samuel Augustus Barnett proposed in 1888, supported by Hazell, that the Local Government Board (LGB) should support poor law guardians in training 'able-bodied men in country pursuits'. Barnett, then vicar of St Jude's, urged the Whitechapel Guardians (of which he was a member) to purchase a plot of disused farmland within 100 miles of London, but was defeated by sixteen votes to eight.[53] A handful of authorities pursued the idea, and the Whitechapel Guardians established an Agricultural Homes Training Committee in 1893, but most gave up on finding that their powers for dealing with unemployment were 'utterly inadequate'.[54] Barnett turned his attention elsewhere, but the prospect of combining the relief of poverty with land settlement continued to attract attention.

Popular opinion in late nineteenth-century Britain was often suspicious of plans for state welfare. Members of friendly societies, who helped working people save and administered benefits such as sick pay and pensions, were often scathing about the 'undeserving', and aspired themselves to full employment and a 'living wage' rather than state benefits.[55] By the 1880s, socialist and working-class organisations were starting to expand their influence in local government, giving a platform to some enthusiastic advocates of the labour colony and land reform. Keir Hardie, the socialist MP, was one of several who noted that poor law authorities had powers to buy and work the land, proposing farm colonies as a way of combining social enterprise with land reform.[56] In the public mind, though, the leading Labour advocate of labour colonies was George Lansbury, for whom the labour colony reconciled the 'work test order without the pauper stigma', by mobilising the unemployed to build socialism with a communitarian face, on socialised land.[57]

First elected a guardian in 1893, Lansbury was a Christian socialist who believed that

it is only by basing our life and conduct on the teachings of Christ – to forgive all things, hope all things, endure all things by faith and love for each other – that we can make a clean and wholesome place of our country.[58]

This, he believed, meant substituting cooperation for competition, brotherhood for selfishness. He was particularly interested in the education of pauper children and the treatment of the aged poor, but also pressed the Poplar guardians to improve conditions in their workhouse for the able-bodied poor, while agitating nationally for modernisation of poor law administration.[59] By 1904, when Lansbury became chair of the Poplar board's farm committee, he had served continuously for eleven years. Along with his fellow guardian Will Crooks, he talked the Poplar board into establishing a training farm in Essex in 1895, a proposal promptly rejected by the LGB.

Meanwhile, with the return of mass unemployment in winter 1902–3, and worsening unemployment in the following year, Barnett had returned to the fray. Lansbury and Crooks, as well as reform-minded Liberals like Herbert Samuel, MP for Cleveland, joined the debate.[60] The Lord Mayor of London's Mansion House Fund was already financing men at Hadleigh during the winters of 1902–3 and 1903–4, at 10s. 6d. for each man, plus an allowance to their families averaging 14s. 6d. each.[61] On New Year's Day 1904, anticipating a bitter winter, the Lord Mayor of London appealed on behalf of the Mansion House Unemployment Committee, expressing 'a growing consensus of feeling that any help given ought to be afforded in the form of work'. The Committee agreed to send men to colonies at Hadleigh and Osea Island, using the 'work-test and the distance from London' as ways of deterring idlers and professional beggars.[62] Hadleigh was relatively well established; Osea Island, a newer venture, took in Londoners to help level land, lay roads, and build sea-walls and houses for a new teetotal holiday resort. They also had to agree to abstain while on the island, as its owner, Frederick Charrington, son of a large brewing family, was a temperance campaigner. Three of the first group of twenty-five men, unable to keep the bargain, decamped to the mainland, where one 'created a disturbance in the quiet village of Maldon'. Those who remained slept in bunks in large wooden sheds, warmed by stoves.[63]

For those who saw labour colonies as a solution to unemployment, such experiences – evaluated by William Beveridge, then at Toynbee Hall[64] – fuelled the case for municipal intervention. In October 1904, Walter Long, Conservative MP for Dublin and President of the LGB, convened a conference of London guardians to discuss the crisis.[65] The conference appointed what effectively became a central committee for the London Fund, setting up a number of sub-committees, including one – chaired by Lansbury – on working colonies.[66] Buoyed by this role, and with support from the London unemployed fund, Lansbury and his fellow Poplar Guardians opened the first municipal colony in 1904, on 100 acres of land at Laindon, in Essex, offered rent-free by the Philadelphian millionaire philanthropist and land reformer Joseph Fels. Long, as President of the LGB, approved the proposal.[67]

Fels, a disciple of Henry George, had been impressed by the work of Paton and Booth in Britain, as well as by labour colonies in his native country, and admired Lansbury's drive and vision.[68] According to Mary Fels, hardly a day passed for the 'next four months' during which Lansbury and her husband did not meet; they remained friends and collaborators for over a decade.[69] The new Laindon Colony opened in March 1904, with the men living initially in two corrugated iron buildings. As elsewhere, they followed a strict daily regime, rising at 6.45 a.m. in the winter months, going for breakfast between 7.00 and 7.30, then working from 7.30 until 4.30 p.m. with an hour for lunch. After work, the men ate their supper at 5.00 and went to bed at 8.00. Saturday afternoon and

Sunday were times of rest.[70] New men faced a probationary period of three months, working and living in the colony while their families were supported in London. If they passed this stage, they settled in cottages with their families, going on to learn more specialist skills.[71] The Boards of Guardians supplied clothing, and continued to pay relief to the men's families.[72] With the nearest pub three miles away, leisure options were limited, but by November 1904 there were plans for papers, games and books.[73] Fels donated a piano, that great symbol of working-class respectability.[74] Most early recruits were in their 40s and 50s: the colony's admissions book for July and August 1904 shows that 32 were between 50 and 54, while only 20 were under the age of 30 (one – Thomas Bankins – was 16), and none were over 60.[75]

Lansbury and his fellow socialist Guardians, as well as Fels, treated the colony as a showcase, issuing an illustrated brochure, and inviting journalists and others to visit.[76] Crooks, by now MP for Woolwich, put forward a scheme for three distinct types of labour colony: for the 'habitual able-bodied pauper', who needed 'his muscles hardened'; for 'habitual tramps', who were already physically fit, and needed to be kept separate from other groups; and voluntary colonies, where unemployed men would be trained in market gardening and farming.[77] Crooks had been sent to a workhouse as a boy, an experience that haunted him, and made him unusual in a labour movement dominated by skilled men. For Crooks, workhouse reform was personal.

Crooks proudly told one government inquiry of the 'remarkable' work of Laindon in taking 'idlers or loafers' and turning them into 'real useful men', while the workhouse tended to make them 'useless'.[78] Following their success at Laindon, Fels and Lansbury started planning their second colony. Hollesley Bay Colonial College in Essex had trained the sons of gentlemen in the skills needed for managing estates in the Empire, but by 1904 it had fallen on hard times, and was for sale. Fels wrote to the London Unemployed Fund offering to buy the estate and lend it rent free for three years; Lansbury moved acceptance, seconded by a socialist colleague from Woolwich. According to Mary Fels, the committee approved the decision before it realised what it had done, and the colony opened a few months later, with Bolton Smart as its superintendent.[79]

Hollesley Bay was an impressive sight. The neo-Gothic main building, with its offices and halls, survives today as part of Hollesley

Bay Prison; together with twenty-three cottages on the estate, it provided accommodation for about 350 men; most were in open dormitories of 50 men, while the cottages were usually reserved for men and families who were being prepared for emigration. There were hot and cold showers, with each man being required to bathe at least once a week.[80] It included a model dairy, farm buildings and workshops, all surrounded by about 1,300 acres of land, almost half of which was set to arable farming.

Under the Unemployed Workmen Act, responsibility for managing Hollesley Bay passed in 1906 to the Central (Unemployed) Body (CUB) for London. Local distress committees selected the men, who initially were married Londoners of good character, preferably with an interest in moving to the land. The men were employed for a month at a time, going home for two days to look for work and see their families, then returning to the Colony for the next month. As well as board and lodging, each had a weekly allowance of 6d.; wives were given 10s. weekly, minus one third of their earnings, with an additional sum of between 2s. and 1s. for each child under 14, up to a maximum of 17s. 6d.[81] The Colony supplied boots and leggings on loan, as well as a change of underwear for those men who had none. It offered a wide variety of work, including slaughtering, bakery work, drainage, basket-weaving, brick-making and work on the land and in a small market garden; it continued to breed the former college's prize-winning Suffolk Punch draught horses. The earth closet lavatories (converted from the open latrines used by the colonial trainees), provided manure, along with run-off from the urinals, for the land.

Leisure inside the colony was varied. There were regular classes on aspects of farm and garden maintenance, as well as an adult school on Sundays for those who wanted to improve their literacy. Alcohol was banned, though there was nothing to stop the men from visiting the two local public houses, three quarters of a mile away, as long as they were back by bed time. The local curate held a weekly service on Sundays for Anglicans, a priest from Bury St Edmunds ministered to the Roman Catholics, and Bolton Smart held a non-denominational service for nonconformists. There was a games room, with quoits, bagatelle and billiards, as well as a football pitch. Some men swam in the river, but this was judged dangerous, and by 1911 there was a swimming pool.[82] As well as football and cricket, there was an annual sports day and ploughing match every Easter. The men elected a committee to organise other leisure activities, including weekly concerts and debates; it also ran a tobacco shop, burial club and a small library, as well as a life insurance scheme subsidised by tobacco sales.[83]

While Hollesley Bay was distinctive in size and political ambition, several new municipal colonies opened under Long's legislation. The Act allowed local authorities to coordinate their relief work through a Central Body, or establish a local Distress Committee, giving these bodies powers to help unemployed workers with small cash hand-outs or temporary work, and establish local labour exchanges. It also opened the door for local bodies to support would-be emigrants. Finally, it defined the unemployed as, in Balfour's words, a 'limited class' of 'genuine workmen, usually in employment', who were 'honestly desirous of obtaining work but temporarily unable to do so from exceptional causes over which the applicant has no control'.[84] In London, the CUB established short-term colonies at Burnham-on-Crouch, Fambridge, the Garden City in Hertford-shire and Osea Island, and took over Woodbridge Farm Colony, in Suffolk, which had accommodation for 350 men (though only 52 were in residence when it was taken over on 12 December 1905). It also employed men under colony conditions at two Kent convales-cent homes.[85] It explored the idea of a farm colony for unemployed women, examining a 60–acre site at Swanley, which was suitable for fruit-growing and bee-keeping, but nothing came of it.[86] Mean-while, trade unions successfully lobbied the government to ensure that men who received relief under the Act would not be disenfran-chised like paupers, losing their right to vote.[87] In Blackpool, the annual conference of the Miners' Federation of Great Britain, long a supporter of land reform, unanimously agreed to encourage the government to use the Act to establish labour colonies.[88]

Both sides in the Royal Commission on the Poor Laws criticised the Act, which faded largely from memory after the introduction of unemployment insurance in 1911. Nevertheless, it had considerable symbolic importance, signalling a clear recognition that the state had responsibilities for easing the plight of the unemployed.[89] More practically, it provided a clear framework for local bodies to create labour colonies, particularly in London, provided they could get past the LGB. In March 1905, Long moved to the Admiralty, and his place at the LGB was taken by Gerald Balfour, who in turn was replaced by John Burns when the Liberals took power in December.

Burns disliked the Act in general, and its provisions for public works and labour colonies in particular, and as President of the LGB he repeatedly blocked proposals from local distress committees.[90] The radical orator of the 1889 dockers' strike had never been a supporter of labour colonies, and he detested Lansbury. In 1893, Burns had denounced all such 'nostrums' for unemployment, describing labour colonies as little more than 'the revival in another form of the hated casual ward'.[91] A skilled engineer by background, Burns was keenly aware of the gulf that separated trade unionists, who insured themselves against unemployment, from the poor, who looked for help elsewhere. The men he saw on a visit to the West Ham colony at Ockenden were 'Tired Tims, Weary Willies', he confided, even where 'skilled did not belong to trade unions'.[92] On becoming President of the LGB, Burns visited the 'doubtful experiment' at Hollesley Bay, walking from the nearest railway station at Woodbridge.[93] He promptly clamped down on Fels's and Lansbury's land settlement plans, blocking the building of small-holdings on the estate, and placing a sixteen-week limit on the time that London men could stay at the colony.

The labour colony movement was furious. Bitterly disappointed, Lansbury scaled down his involvement in Hollesley Bay, protesting publicly and frequently over what he saw as Burn's betrayal of a socialist project, while Keir Hardie took advantage of the Easter 1907 adjournment debate to challenge Burns's conduct.[94] Ramsay MacDonald attacked Burns for blocking land settlement at Hollesley Bay, and preventing local authorities from using labour colonies for 'educational purposes' such as farm training.[95] A decade on, Mary Fels still felt strongly about 'the harm done to the cause of progress by this one man'.[96] Lansbury bore his grudge for decades.[97] He mentioned Hollesley Bay in Parliament for the last time in a 1938 debate on the Unemployment Assistance Board, by which time it was a Borstal (Lansbury thought that the young offenders might usefully be used to reclaim the Wash, along with their own character and physique).[98] In his autobiography, Lansbury described the colonies at Laindon and Hollesley Bay as 'amongst the best pieces of constructive work that stand to the credit of any initiative'.[99]

Burns, though, was not alone in his dismissal of the municipal colonies. One Conservative MP set Burns up by asking a question about Hollesley Bay men who had been given public funds to go home and vote in municipal elections; it turned out that they had indeed been given the train fares, though the money came from private charitable donations.[100] James Davy, an inspector for the LGB, conducted an inquiry into alleged extravagance by the Poplar Guardians which fuelled a colourful press campaign over Laindon, with journalists delighting in tales of beer-swilling, coffee-glugging, cake-scoffing paupers, fed by hard-working, honest ratepayers.[101] However shrill and distorted the criticisms, the inquiry did little to improve the labour colony's reputation, and while the LGB was powerless to direct the CUB, it did instruct Poplar Guardians to send all able-bodied paupers to Laindon in place of an outdoor work test.[102] All this was grist to Burns's busy mill, giving him a ready-made reply to every parliamentary question from Lansbury and his allies.[103] He also blocked a number of new proposals, including one (involving Fels) for a women's colony in Kent. On behalf of the Women's Labour League, Margaret Bondfield wrote to the Prime Minister supporting the proposed 'country colony where women should be taught lighter work on the land', and complaining of Burns's obstructionism.[104]

Nevertheless, local authorities continued to push new schemes. Manchester Distress Committee opened a farm colony on Chat Moss, and the Labour MP J. R. Clynes intervened in Parliament on its behalf when he thought Burns was undermining it.[105] The Bradford Guild of Help, representing the city's leading charitable bodies, opened a short-lived land colony with the hope of settling the city's unemployed on smallholdings.[106] In the winter of 1906–7, Leeds Distress Committee created a small forest colony in Washburn Valley, supported by a grant from the LGB. Initially, a group of thirty were offered places, though ten apparently refused.[107] According to the chairman of the Distress Committee, the men were given bacon for breakfast, took a light lunch to eat at work, and received a 'substantial meal … of meat and potatoes' at the end of the working day.[108] Most substantially, in 1908 the Fulham Guardians acquired the old workhouse at Belmont to run as a labour colony.[109] According to Burns, 1,327 men were in Belmont by December 1910, of whom 422 were able-bodied, working on farm work, corn grinding, wood bundling, tailoring and other occupations, supervised by 56 male officers.[110] The jumbling together of different classes of inmate irritated Burns, who wanted to separate 'the goats from the sheep'.[111]

Burns held no sway in Scotland, where both of the largest cities tried to found municipal labour colonies. Edinburgh Distress Committee founded a small colony in 1907 at Murieston, fifteen miles west of the city beside the Caledonian Railway's line to Glasgow. The Committee converted a group of farm outhouses into accommodation for 60 men, treating the soil with 'Edinburgh city manure', and converting Murieston House into the manager's residence.[112] The men were set to work improving the 202 acres of clay land, which was to be prepared for rent or sale as a group of smallholdings. The accommodation was only fully occupied in the summer months, and even then the men went home at weekends, purportedly to find work, while in the winter months the men commuted in daily by train. In the same year, the LGB for Scotland approved proposals for a colony at Palacerigg, near Cumbernauld, where Glasgow Distress Committee acquired 591 acres and built temporary huts with the intention of housing 90 men.[113] In the year 1907–8, an average of 70 men lived in the colony, with over four hundred more travelling in each day by train.[114] As well as reclaiming bog land, the men worked at digging and processing peat for fuel and cattle litter, as well as raising crops and caring for livestock, and planting trees to protect the soil.

By 1908 both Murieston and Palacerigg were underfunded and on the verge of closure.[115] Richard Lodge, Professor of History at the University of Edinburgh and a social imperialist who thought land settlement 'the salvation of our race', concluded that Murieston, though an instructive 'experiment', had 'never been a labour colony in anything but name'.[116] Murieston was quietly run down, but Palacerigg was Glasgow Distress Committee's main source of relief work, with 800 being sent from the city in 1908 alone, mostly on a day basis.[117] The Distress Committee and LGB both aimed to run it 'strictly as a Labour Colony',[118] and on average, 80 men lived in the colony through 1908–9; there were still 40 in residence at the time of the 1911 census, along with four members of staff.[119] By 1912, it was claimed that over 80 were in residence at any one time, and the transport of day workers had ceased. Seventy men, on average, lived in the colony in 1914. By this time, men were spending an average of eight weeks at the colony.[120]

By the time of the Royal Commission, the municipal labour colony movement had lost momentum. While a number of colonies had been established, such as Laindon and Hollesley Bay, the overall results were disappointing, and demoralising. Looking back in 1909, Beveridge concluded that their main value was to show the scale of the problem.[121] Unemployment levels remained stubbornly high, and in creating the Royal Commission on the Poor Laws, the government was effectively accepting that private charity as well as public policy had proved unable to deal with unemployment.[122] Witnesses lined up to denounce labour colonies. William Beveridge, who in 1904 had claimed that the CUB colony experiment had 'to a very large extent realised the hopes of its designers', still praised those colonies which focused on training, naming Hollesley Bay in particular, but otherwise thought that their positive effect was largely short term, and that they tended to institutionalise the trainees.[123]

Even sympathetic policy thinkers like the Fabians increasingly thought of labour colonies in a new, rather punitive light. In an essay published in 1889, Annie Besant laid out a national scheme of County Farms, run by trained and experienced agriculturalists, to which 'will be drafted from the unemployed in the towns, the agricultural laborers who have wandered townwards in search of work, and many of the unskilled laborers'.[124] Sydney Webb, by contrast, already thought that their main role lay in stamping out vagrancy and idleness.[125] In 1890, Webb reassured readers that they need not 'fear that the Democracy will deal tenderly' with 'chronic cases of sturdy vagrancy, idle mendacity and incorrigible laziness' – these would go straight into a labour colony, carrying out useful work under strict supervision.[126] While the Fabians did not, as one historian suggests, turn away from the labour colony movement, their interest increasingly lay in proposals for punitive colonies for the 'won't works'.[127] As discussed later, the Webbs clung to the idea of some sort of compulsory national labour service throughout the late 1930s.

Ian Packer argues that the attack on the municipal colonies, and Lansbury's response, effectively foreclosed further attempts to use the land as a solution to unemployment.[128] This was not so, but it certainly weakened the case for municipal rural communitarianism. Voluntary agencies continued to produce new labour colonies. The Church of Scotland purchased a 35-acre farm in 1907 at Cornton Vale, near Stirling, and the Kirk's Committee on Social Work hoped to open a second colony, for Glasgow prostitutes, in the country-side near Uddingston, with a large garden where the women could work.[129] The CUSS expanded its system, purchasing Turners Court at Wallingford, in Oxfordshire in 1911.[130] And away from Burns's influence, local government collaborated with charities to promote farm colonies for public health purposes (see Chapter 3). But as a response to unemployment, the municipal movement had run its course, leaving behind the three large London colonies.

Working bodies

Norman Vanner Moore, who served as a brother at Wallingford in the early twentieth century, saw the colony's main aim as being to 'inculcate workfulness'. To 'take a man into the fresh air, bathe him in sunshine, expose him to wind and weather, subject him to the healthy discipline of regular habits and manual work' was, Moore wrote, the best 'of all prescriptions for a mind diseased'.[131] To complement hard work, the labour colonies generally offered a solid diet. The Midlocharwood men had two cooked meals a day, with porridge for breakfast every day except Sunday when the men were treated to fish or ham and eggs; for dinner, the men ate meat and potatoes, with vegetables when available; they had a more meagre meal of bread, margarine and tea or jam for supper.[132] When Henry Rider Haggard visited Hadfield, he was impressed to see the men breakfasting on oatmeal porridge, bread, butter, tea and either corned beef or 'German sausage'. Lunch consisted of meat, parsnip, boiled potatoes, bread, tea and either tart or pudding. In the late afternoon, the men were served bread, butter, and preserved or fresh meat, with tea.[133]

To provide evidence of improvement, bodies were measured. The Cambridge settlement students measured the Garden City trainees, claiming 'noticeable' improvements in the physical condition of the men 'after a very short time'.[134] In 1904, Beveridge reported that 'work on the colonies, carried out under good conditions, in country air, with good food, and in the absence of intoxicants, produced a marked improvement in the physique of the men', and also 'widened their horizon and stimulated their enterprise'.[135] Glasgow Distress Committee noted with satisfaction that few resident colonists left Palacerigg 'without being 7 lbs to a stone heavier'.[136] Not all were able to persuade the colonists to submit: Bolton Smart judged the visible 'improvement in physique' to be 'remarkable' among Hollesley Bay residents, adding wistfully that, 'I should very much like to measure and weigh, but I do not think it is wise'.[137]

Increasingly, medical expertise came into play. In an age when the poor had little access to medical care, the colonies made arrangements for local practitioners to visit the sick and injured and inspect the diet.[138] Indeed, men bound for Hollesley Bay were given a medical examination before leaving London.[139] New arrivals were put on light work; even so, Bolton Smart told the Royal Commission of one who collapsed, not having had 'a square meal for three months'.[140] In Glasgow, Dr Burges examined the men before admitting them to Palacerigg. Because the Distress Committee was deemed an employer under the Workmen's Compensation Acts, Burges turned down those likely to pose a risk to the Distress Committee 'on the ground of general weakness and unfitness'. Others he treated before sending them to the Colony. They included several men with 'unsupported hernias', several cases of previously undiagnosed tuberculosis, and a large number with 'objectionable or infectious skin conditions'.[141] Burges expressed compassion 'rather than contempt' for his charges.[142]

Healthy bodies were also clean bodies. Colonists at Hadleigh were expected to 'wash all over' at least once weekly.[143] One new arrival described his reception at Midlocharwoods: 'the superintendent received me kindly, even cordially, told me I was expected to remain three months and work to the best of my ability, gave me some acceptable refreshment and much-needed underclothing, and then sent me for a bath'.[144] At Palacerigg, Dr Burges commented that

> In the case of a few men who were at home for a very short time and were then allowed to return to the Colony, it was disappointing to see how very dirty they had become in such a little while. On the other hand, I must say that some very dirty cases moved me more to sympathy than disgust, for the poor fellows had evidently made great efforts to cleanse themselves, but circumstances had been too many for them.[145]

At Hadleigh, the men's 'personal laundry increased quite 50 per cent'.[146]

Many contemporary observers were impressed with these results. One visitor to Hadleigh wrote that: 'Men that looked shrivelled and hungry when I saw them before are now as brown as gypsies, round of limb, jolly as sandboys.'[147] At Lingfield, Paton contrasted the colonists' bustling demeanour with that of paupers, infected by workhouse life with 'what you may call, not a sleeping sickness, but a dawdling sickness'.[148] Will Crooks, the socialist, contrasted newcomers to Laindon – 'slouching about, muscle-soft, fishy-eyed, listless, being unable to fix their minds or their eyes upon anything' – with the established colonists, who were 'real useful men on the land'.[149] So, unlike mere paupers, the colonists were men. Cleanliness and physical strength were the visible marks of what Norman Moore called 'a reclaimed manhood'.[150] Strength and manliness were also invoked by Brooks, who described nine workhouse paupers who entered Lingfield as 'physically deteriorated youths, who never had been men and never would have been'.[151] Robert F Horton, writing in *The Times*, praised the way in which Wallingford restored 'outcasts and derelicts' to 'manhood and citizenship and service', suggesting that the colony's most important product was not wheat or turnips but 'a crop of regenerated manhood'.[152] The model colonist was, in body and in mind, a man and a true citizen.

Virtually all the argument treated gender as a given. It was taken for granted that whether labour colonies were suitable or not, the question was of how to tackle male unemployment. In one of the rare contemporary discussions of unemployment among women in London, Edith Abbott thought that even if it were possible to raise public sympathy for unemployed women, it would be 'next to impossible' for women to share farm colonies.[153] Some proposals for women's colonies did come forward, though with limited progress, and usually in narrowly defined areas such as inebriacy; so far as the unemployed were concerned, CUB decided to set up a non-residential workshop where unemployed women made clothing and other items for London's labour colonies and for intending emigrants. In general, the colonies aimed at reclaiming men's bodies, as well as – sometimes – their souls.

What the men made of this is another matter. Barely any direct evidence remains of the labour colonies as experienced by those who lived and worked inside them. There is not even a body of writing by those who claimed to speak on behalf of men whose voices have left no direct trace. Those who ran labour colonies seem to have shown remarkably little interest in the lives, attitudes, beliefs and aspirations of their charges, unless for some reason they posed a challenge to the colony regime. Sometimes, though, these scattered remarks provide distant echoes of the trainees' experiences and views. For example, Moore worried over 'the exceedingly meagre idea which these men have of the high aim of this institution', and fretted at their complete failure 'to see that the Christian Social Service Union is held together by the strong desire to lift them in character to the stature of men in Jesus Christ'. Though they attended the services, they responded 'with indifference', and otherwise never spoke of religion, indeed would 'promptly close up when the subject is broached'.[154] Moore found himself at a loss to explain this indifference to manly religion, but it is hardly surprising given the circumstances facing the colonists at Wallingford and the other colonies. If they were willing to accept the demanding discipline of a labour colony, miles from their home, it was more likely to be for want of an alternative at home, rather than because they shared the founders' visions of Christian virility or a contented British peasantry.

Notes

1 S. Buder, *Visionaries and Planners: The garden city movement and the modern community*, Oxford University Press, Oxford, 1990, 14–17.

2 RCPL, *Appendix Volume XIX: Report on the Effects of Employment or Assistance given to the 'Unemployed' since 1886 as a means of relieving distress outside the Poor Laws in Ireland*, HMSO, London, 1909, 83; W. Booth, *In Darkest England and the Way Out*, Salvation Army, London, 1890, 91.

3 *Minutes of Evidence taken before the Departmental Committee appointed to consider Mr Rider Haggard's Report on Agricultural Settlements in British Colonies*, Vol. II, HMSO, London, 1906, 54.

4 *Pall Mall Gazette*, 31 January 1890; W. Hazell and H. Hodkin, *The Australasian Colonies: Emigration and colonisation*, Edward Stanford, London, 1887.

5 Rev. Dr J. B. Paton, Congregational Institute, Nottingham, 27 Feb 1895 to unknown correspondent, London Metropolitan Archives (LMA), A/FWA/C/D254/1.

6 Matthew Boyd Auld to Board of Trade, 29 May 1897, National Archives of Scotland, HH1/1351; *Glasgow Herald* (*GH*), 19 February 1897

7 *GH*, 21 May 1891, 23 May 1891, 3 June 1891.

8 *GH*, 1 April 1898.

9 Board of Trade Labour Department, *Report on Agencies*, 169.

10 Board of Trade, *Report on Agencies*, 143.

11 *Pall Mall Gazette*, 26 October 1895, Lloyd's Weekly Newspaper, 21 November 1897.

12 RCPL, Appendix Volume XIX, 89.

13 *GH*, 21 January 1897.

14 *Daily Telegraph*, 18 July 1899.
15 *Minutes of Evidence on Rider Haggard's Report*, 107.
16 Board of Trade, *Report on Agencies*, 170–1.
17 *RCPL*, Appendix Vol. XIX, 89.
18 *RCPL*, Appendix, Vol. VIII, *Minutes of Evidence*, HMSO, London, 1910, 163–5.
19 *Pall Mall Gazette*, 19 August 1891.
20 D. Lamb, 'The Labour Colony as an Agency for the Prevention of Destitution', *National Conference on the Prevention of Destitution*, P. S. King & Son, London, 1911, 504.
21 H. Rider Haggard, *The Poor and the Land, Being a Report on the Salvation Army Colonies in the United States and at Hadleigh, England, with Scheme of National Land Settlement*, Longman's, Green & Co., London, 1905, 131.
22 *Daily News*, 10 September 1891.
23 *GH*, 1 December 1898.
24 *GH*, 8 November 1900; J. Maxwell Ross, County Buildings, Dumfries, 9 December 1903, NAS HH57/70, *Parliamentary Debates*, 4 August 1919.
25 M. B. Auld to Under-Secretary for Scotland, 11 July 1906, NAS HH55/70.
26 *Pall Mall Gazette*, 19 August 1891.
27 Haggard, *Poor and Land*, 135.
28 Ibid., xvi.
29 *RCPL*, Appendix, Vol. VIII, 168.
30 W. Booth, *Darkest England*, 134.
31 Board of Trade, *Report on Agencies*, 168.
32 Ibid., 172.
33 *GH*, 3 February 1900; see also 1 December 1898.
34 *RCPL*, Appendix, Vol. VIII, *Minutes of Evidence*, HMSO, London, 1910 163.
35 *RCPL*, Appendix, Vol. VIII, 166.
36 *Minutes of Evidence taken by Departmental Committee on Vagrancy*, 178.
37 Ibid., 179.
38 *GH*, 14 April 1900, *Wanganui Herald*, 16 February 1907.
39 D. Browne, *From the Slum to the Farm Colony: An account of the social work of the Salvation Army*, Vyse and Hill, Stoke-on-Trent, 1896, 33–6.
40 *GH*, 1 April 1898.
41 *Minutes of Evidence by the Committee on Vagrancy*, 176.
42 *RCPL*, Appendix, Vol. VIII, 168.
43 Ibid., 170–1.
44 *GH*, 25 January 1898.

45 *GH*, 26 January 1900, J. J. W. Handford (Assistant Secretary, Board of Agriculture for Scotland) to Treasury, 8 August 1918, NAS E824/607; *GH*, 9 April 1900.
46 Auld to Under-Secretary for Scotland, 14 November 1903, NAS HH57/70.
47 *Census of Scotland, 1911, Vol. I*, HMSO, 1912, 764.
48 Hazell, *Walter Hazell*, 24–5.
49 See *The Graphic*, 30 July 1892; *Newcastle Courant*, 17 September 1892.
50 *Pall Mall Gazette*, 21 December 1892.
51 *RCPL*, Appendix Volume XIX, 83.
52 *Report RCPL*, HMSO, London, 1909, 208–9.
53 *Daily News*, 24 July 1888.
54 F. C. Mills (1895), 'Land and Poor Law Guardians', in J. A. Hobson (ed.), *Co-operative Labour Upon the Land*, 103; *Derby Mercury*, 25 September 1895.
55 P. Thane, 'The Working Class and State "Welfare"', *Historical Journal*, 27, 4, 1984, 884–6.
56 J. Harris, *Unemployment and Politics*, 90–5.
57 Parliamentary Debates, 11 March 1912.
58 George Lansbury, *Your Part in Poverty*, The Herald, London, 1917, 22.
59 J. Shepherd, *George Lansbury*, 54–9.
60 H. L. Samuel, *Liberalism: An attempt to state the principles and proposals*, Richards, London, 1902, 129–33.
61 London Unemployed Fund. Preliminary Statement, HMSO, London, 1905, 29.
62 *Daily Mirror*, 1 January 1904.
63 *Daily Mirror*, 4 January 1904.
64 W. H. Beveridge and H. R. Maynard, 'The Unemployed: Lessons of the Mansion House Fund', *Contemporary Review*, 86, 1904.
65 J. Harris, *Unemployment and Politics: a study in English social policy, 1886-1914*, Clarendon, Oxford, 1972, 153–5.
66 *London Unemployed Fund. Preliminary Statement*, 3–4.
67 *Municipal Journal*, 4 November 1904.
68 Fels, *Joseph Fels*, 34–7.
69 Ibid., 40.
70 *Municipal Journal*, 4 November 1904.
71 H. B. Lees Smith, 'The London Unemployed Fund, 1904–5', *Economic Journal*, 16, 61, 1906, 156.
72 G. Lansbury, *My Life*, Constable, London, 1928, 147.
73 *Clarion*, 11 November 1904.
74 Fels, *Joseph Fels*, 43.
75 Admission and Discharge Book for the Labour Colony at Sumpner's Farm, 1904, LMA PO/BG/180/1.

76 Fels, *Joseph Fels*, 44.
77 G. Haw, *From Workhouse to Westminster: The life story of Will Crooks, MP*, Cassell & Co, London, 1907, 270.
78 *Minutes of Evidence on Rider Haggard's Report*, 138.
79 Fels, *Joseph Fels*, 51–2; *London Unemployed Fund. Preliminary statement*, 36.
80 Ibid., 490.
81 Bolton Smart, 'Hollesley Bay Labour Colony', *National Conference on the Prevention of Destitution*, 484.
82 Smart, 'Hollesley Bay', 485.
83 *RCPL*, Appendix, Vol. VIII, 315–20.
84 *Parliamentary Debates*, 20 June 1905.
85 Central (Unemployed) Body for London (CUB), *Tenth and Final Report, 1905–1930*, 1930, 5, 37.
86 Ibid., 76; J. Tawney, 'Women and Unemployment', *Economic Journal*, 21, 81, 137–8.
87 H. B. Lees Smith, 'The Unemployed Workmen Bill', *Economic Journal*, 15, 58, 1905, 249.
88 *The Times*, 7 October 1905.
89 K. D. Brown, Conflict in Early British Welfare Policy: The case of the Unemployed Workmen's Bill of 1905, *Journal of Modern History*, 43, 4, 1971, 615–29.
90 K. D. Brown, 'The Labour Party and the Unemployment Question, 1906–1910', *Historical Journal*, 14, 3, 1971, 600.
91 J. Burns, *The Unemployed*, Fabian Society, London, 1893, 16–18.
92 Quoted in M. A. Crowther, *The Workhouse System, 1834–1929: the history of an English social institution*, Routledge, London, 1983, 86.
93 Quoted in Shepherd, *George Lansbury*, 63.
94 *Parliamentary Debates*, 27 March 1907.
95 Ibid., 30 January 1908.
96 Fels, *Joseph Fels*, 54.
97 *Parliamentary Debates*, 12 December 1922; see also 5 August 1925, 13 May 1926.
98 Ibid., 18 July 1938.
99 Lansbury, *My Life*, 146.
100 *Parliamentary Debates*, 7 November 1906, 15 November 1905.
101 *The Times*, 3 July 1906.
102 Harris, *Unemployment and Politics*, 193–5.
103 *Parliamentary Debates*, 18 March 1908, 19 March 1908, 23 March 1908, 26 February 1912, 28 February 1912.
104 *The Times*, 7 November 1908.
105 *Parliamentary Debates*, 26 March 1907, 27 March 1907.
106 K. Laybourn, *The Guild of Help and the Changing Face of Edwardian Philanthropy, 1904–1919*, Edwin Mellen, Lampeter, 1994, 32–3.

107 *Daily Mirror*, 23 February 1907.
108 *Parliamentary Debates*, 19 March 1907.
109 S. and B. Webb, *English Poor Law History, Part II: The last hundred years*, Longmans, London, 1929, 750.
110 *Parliamentary Debates*, 9 February 1911.
111 Ibid., 13 February 1911.
112 *Scotsman*, 18 December 1907; *RCPL: Report on Scotland*, HMSO, London, 1909, 178.
113 *Fourteenth Annual Report of the Local Government Board for Scotland (LGBS), 1908*, HMSO, Edinburgh, 1909, xlii; RCPL: Report on Scotland, 178.
114 *Report as to the Proceedings of Distress Committees in Scotland for 1908*, HMSO, Edinburgh, 1908, 5.
115 *Parliamentary Debates*, 20 July 1908, 11 November 1908.
116 R. Lodge, 'The Edinburgh Labour Colony at Murieston', *National Conference on the Prevention of Destitution*, 499–501.
117 *Fifteenth Annual Report of the LGBS*, xliv.
118 *Seventeenth Annual Report of the LGBS, 1911*, HMSO, Edinburgh, 1912, xlviii.
119 *Report as to the Proceedings of Distress Committees in Scotland for 1909*, HMSO, Edinburgh, 1909, 4; *Census of Scotland, 1911*, Vol. I, HMSO, London, 1912, 707.
120 *Report as to the Proceedings of Distress Committees in Scotland for 1912*, HMSO, Edinburgh, 1912, 4; *Twentieth Annual Report of the LGBS, 1914*, HMSO, Edinburgh, 1915, liii.
121 W. Beveridge, *Unemployment: A problem of industry*, 2nd edition, Longmans, London, 1910, 160.
122 K. Woodroofe, 'The Royal Commission on the Poor Laws, 1905–09', *International Review of Social History*, 22, 2, 137–64.
123 Beveridge and Maynard 'The unemployed', 630; RCPL, Appendix, Vol VIII, 13.
124 Besant, 'Industry under Socialism', in G. B. Shaw (ed.), *Fabian Essays in Socialism*, Fabian Society, London, 1889, 139–40.
125 S. Webb, *Socialism: True and False*, Fabian Tract 51, London, 1894, 4.
126 S. Webb, 'The Reform of the Poor Law', *Contemporary Review*, 58, 1890, 115.
127 A. H. M. McBriar, *Fabian Socialism and English Politics, 1884–1918*, Cambridge University Press, Cambridge, 1966, 98.
128 Ian Packer, *Lloyd George, Liberalism and the Land: The land issue and party politics in England, 1906-1914*, Royal Historical Society/Boydell, Woodbridge and Rochester NY, 2001, 72–4.
129 *Departmental Committee on the Operation in Scotland of the Law Relating to Inebriates. Minutes of evidence*, HMSO, London, 163.

130 Christian Union for Social Service appeal signed by J Carlisle and various others, 1895, LMA, A/FWA/C/D254/1.
131 N. V. Moore, *Problems of Brotherhood. By a Brother*, Wallingford Farm Training Colony, Turners Court, Oxfordshire, 1913, 11, 47.
132 M. B. Auld to Under-Secretary for Scotland, 30 July 1906, NAS HH57/70.
133 Rider Haggard, *Poor and Land*, 130.
134 G. C. Miller, G. Collier and E. (1905), *Report of a Temporary Colony at Garden City for Unemployed Workmen mainly from West Ham during February, March and April 1905*, P. S. King & Son, London, 8–9.
135 Beveridge and Maynard, 'The unemployed', 631.
136 *Fifteenth Annual Report of the LGBS*, 1901, xlv.
137 RCPL, Appendix, Vol. VIII, 323.
138 RCPL, Appendix, Vol. VIII, *Minutes of Evidence*, 160, 170; J. C. Dunlop, 10 October 1906, NAS HH57/70.
139 *RCPL*, Appendix, Vol. VIII, 327.
140 Ibid., 324.
141 *Seventeenth Annual Report of the LGBS, 1911*, xlix; *Twentieth Annual Report of the LGBS, 1914*, liv.
142 *Nineteenth Annual Report of the LGBS, 1913*, HMSO, London, 1914, lxiii.
143 *Daily News*, 10 September 1891.
144 *Wanganui Herald*, 16 February 1907.
145 *Twentieth Annual Report of the LGBS, 1914*, liv.
146 *London Unemployed Fund. Preliminary Statement*, 30.
147 *Pall Mall Gazette*, 15 September 1892.
148 *Evidence taken by the Committee on Vagrancy*, 182.
149 *Minutes of Evidence on Rider Haggard's Report*, 138.
150 Moore, *Problems of Brotherhood*, 47.
151 *Evidence taken by Committee on Vagrancy*, 182.
152 *The Times*, 3 November 1913.
153 E. Abbott, 'Municipal Employment of Unemployed Women in London', *Journal of Political Economy*, 15, 9, 1907, 516.
154 Moore, *Problems of Brotherhood*, 15.

3

Labour colonies and public health

As well as the unemployed, labour colonies were also directed towards those who could not work for other reasons. Large numbers of people with physical or mental disabilities or impairments found themselves in workhouses, often classed together – idiots, the feeble-minded, cripples, inebriates, or simply old[1] – as incapable of earning a living in the open labour market. Increasingly, though, the workhouse was viewed as entirely inappropriate for these groups, whose vulnerability was seen as a legitimate basis for intervention by the state or by private charity.[2] Public health debates were also fed by eugenicist fears over racial degeneration, as well as more general concern over the poor physical standards of some army recruits, and the unimpressive performance of the British army in South Africa. Balfour's interdepartmental inquiry into physical deterioration, though it focused rather narrowly on the damaging effects of habitual inebriation, further fuelled the debate.[3]

Ina Zweiniger-Bargielowska argues that after the Boer Wars, the physical deterioration debate in Britain took a strongly environmentalist turn. Even eugenicists like Meath actively supported such new initiatives as the National League for Physical Education and Improvement, formed in 1905 to lobby for health and welfare reform, while the Liberals' 1907 Education Act obliged English and Welsh local education authorities (LEAs) to make arrangements for improving the health and physical condition of children in public elementary schools; George Newman, the Board of Education's first Chief Medical Officer (MO), proved himself to be a highly effective interventionist.[4] Propelled by competent lobbying from the medical profession, particularly from those active in emerging specialisms such as mental health or tuberculosis, government was not only involved earlier but played a far more active role when it came to promoting labour colonies for the sick and infirm.

Labour colonies as protected and protecting space

From Bedlam to cottage homes for crippled children, the separation of the poor and sick was a well-established practice. Many of the poor and sick in the workhouse were kept in segregated wards. From one perspective, separation was a way of stopping sick bodies from offending and contaminating the healthy and normal. If respectable society stigmatised the poor and unemployed, then the fact of being disabled, addicted, depraved, diseased or mentally ill compounded the 'undesired differentness'.[5] Another way of looking at it would be to see the unemployed and poor as the worst offenders, for the disabled and mentally ill were rarely responsible for their own condition. Unlike the unemployed, though, the bodies of the sick were increasingly subject to the interventions of trained professionals. Local government leaders had learned in the cholera epidemics of the 1830s and 1840s that infectious diseases affected rich and poor alike.[6] It was also easier to make the case for national fitness in a mature imperial power that believed itself threatened by other advanced nations. Advances in science, and in professional training, created interest groups specialising in the care, treatment and rehabilitation of the sick and feeble, as well as the increased capacity of medical practices to cure or control a wider range of health problems.[7]

Labour colonies represented one way of tackling several health problems, while simultaneously reducing the stigma of dependency. For some, labour colonies had a further purpose. As well as providing access to labour and country ways, they were also a means of isolation. This was particularly attractive to members of two schools of thought. The first group believed that their charges had acquired their malignant habits, illnesses and some types of disability from the people around them. If the inmates could be kept apart from contagion, and placed under benign influences, then there was every chance that they would improve. These ideas are particularly visible in the thinking of Christian groups, such as the CUSS and their mentor, von Bodelschwingh, but they also permeated the work of more secular labour colony advocates. A second group believed that disabling qualities were inherited. Feeble-minded parents produced feeble-minded children, epileptics bred epileptics, and so on.

For eugenicists, the task facing professionals was to improve human heredity, ideally by eradicating disease and disability, at the very least by slowing down their spread. Eugenicists appealed frequently to popular middle-class fears about the high fertility of the poor and degenerate, often using the most lurid terms in order to persuade the beleaguered bourgeoisie to donate generously to the cause. But the mainstream appeal of the eugenicists remained limited. The majority report of the Royal Commission on the Poor Law ignored eugenicist arguments, though the same was not true of the authors of the Minority Report. Sydney Webb complained that the unreformed poor law had an 'anti-eugenic influence', notably 'in the laxity of its provision for feeble-minded maternity'. The minority proposals, by contrast, were set out 'on strictly eugenic lines', not least by recommending 'segregation, permanent or temporary, of many defective persons now at large'.[8] Yet while Webb wanted to stop the 'defective' from breeding, he also wanted to ensure that other children, however poor, were able to grow and develop as productive citizens. For Webb, eugenics was completely consistent with a truly scientific socialism. After 1918, eugenicist influence remained limited. Although such ideas could be found in the Wood Report on mental deficiency in 1929, which ascribed much poor health and poverty to 'poor mental endowment', the most important voices in the medical and scientific community were those who pressed for institutionalisation rather than sterilisation.[9] While the pauper colonies closed or stagnated after the First World War, growing numbers of colonies provided for the unhealthy.

Epilepsy

It was well known, an anonymous doctor wrote in 1894, that most epileptics lived a life of 'enforced idleness', despite overwhelming medical evidence that 'congenial occupation' was an ideal 'therapeutic agent'.[10] He mentioned approvingly the supreme example of an epileptic colony, Bodelschwingh's settlement at Bielefeld, which by the 1890s was widely known in Britain.[11] Reginald Brabazon, Earl Meath, started his own small private home of comfort for women and children at Godalming after visiting Bielefeld, and continued to campaign publicly for epileptic colonies.[12] In 1893, a number of medical specialists such as Dr David Ferrier (who had also visited Bielefeld) organised a well attended conference in the London Mansion House to promote the plans of the National Society for the Employment of Epileptics (NSEE), founded a year earlier, for Britain's first epileptic colony.[13] Even Charles Loch, despite rejecting labour colonies as a solution to unemployment, thought them entirely appropriate for epileptics.[14] Epileptics were still viewed as 'mentally inflicted', and one aim of the colony was to separate the 'only intermittently insane from the ordinary lunatic', as the Duke of Fife put it.[15] Some inmates were forcibly committed, and were likely to be promptly recaptured if they dared to 'escape'.[16]

In 1893, the NSEE purchased Skippings Farm, along with 135 acres of land, near the village of Chalfont St Peters, in Buckinghamshire.[17] The colony opened in August 1894, with the first group of eighteen epileptics living in a temporary iron building, working on the land while more permanent accommodation was erected.[18] By the time that the Duke of Devonshire performed the opening ceremony in late 1895, the men had moved into their new purpose-built accommodation, and further accommodation was being built for women.[19] Its founders hoped that the epileptics would live in cottages (strictly separated by gender) and work on market gardening, boot-making, printing and other industries, with laundry work, sewing and domestic tasks for the women.[20] The first group of colonists, reported *The Times*, were already after six months 'not only showing themselves good workmen, but good citizens'.[21] By 1906, it had a population, male and female, of 200.[22]

Meanwhile, a second epileptic colony opened its doors in 1904. Funded by the Manchester Committee of the David Lewis Trust, the colony was the creation of local philanthropists and medical campaigners; it was from the outset intended for the 'sane', who could leave if they wished; and took women as well as men.[23] By 1911, the colony had 215 adult patients, and 41 children. Dr Alan MacDougall, colony director, argued for allowing epileptics to take part in indoor and outdoor games and labour, even at the risk of injury.[24] Other colonies were founded, including a London County Council colony at Horton, near Epsom, filled by transferring male epileptics from the Council's London asylums.[25] As well as 112 acres of land and a central administrative block (with dormitories for 32 women), there were workshops, a hall for dining and recreation, and eight residential villas, each housing 36 patients and two attendants, surrounding an open green (used as a cricket pitch).[26]

By 1914, colony treatment for epileptics was by widespread. Belmont started to take epileptics in 1910, and continued to take epileptics until the war, when the institution became a hospital.[27] Lingfield by now was almost entirely an epileptic colony, the superintendent asserting confidently: 'The best place, undoubtedly, for treating the epileptic is in a colony.'[28] The CUSS had also started using Starnthwaite for epileptics, and by 1907 it had completely ceased to serve as an unemployed colony.[29] Within a few years, Lingfield's physician was reporting the results of bromide treatment, which he thought likely to be well suited to curing certain types of epilepsy.[30]

Work (along with bromide) was thought particularly suitable as a treatment for epilepsy. Alfred Hume-Griffith, who served both as its superintendent and its MO, wrote in 1914 that Lingfield functioned through a combination of fresh air, hard work, sports, good food and firm moral training – plus doses of bromide. Adults were to work the land, both men and women; and while he expected women to spend two hours a day on needlework, they were taken outside to do it in the open air, but should otherwise be freed from domestic drudgery, allowing them to enjoy 'a more rational life'.[31] George Edward Shuttleworth, an experienced medical man trained in Heidelberg, told the BMA's psychology section that if 'your epileptic' was given 'suitable employment' in the 'open air', he would avoid 'loafing and the consequent temptations of great cities – drink and sexual vices'.[32]

Habitual drunkards

Isolation and occupation appeared obvious advantages in treating the alcohol-dependent. James Sturrock, MD, MO for Perth prison and criminal lunatic asylum, told a conference in 1912 that even a 'closed building is useless', compared with a 'complete labour colony' with variety of work and a goodly distance to the nearest pub; best of all, he thought, was an 'island colony'.[33] Apart from a small retreat for inebriate women at Osea Island, Sturrock's ideal drunkards' colony was never realised.[34] But several colonies were opened for drinkers, often part-funded by the state under the Inebriates Acts of 1879 and 1898. Both pieces of legislation allowed the courts to send habitual drunks for treatment in a reformatory, usually quasi-penal institutions, most of whose inmates were female

– as were most of the leading temperance campaigners who had brought the Acts into being.[35] After the 1898 Act, though, some local authorities viewed labour colonies as a safer solution, at least for the more serious cases, reasoning that a remote rural setting offered few temptations to those who wanted a drink. From their side, a number of labour colony movements, chronically under-funded, saw the Acts as a godsend.

Female drunks attracted particular attention. Duxhurst farm colony, founded by Lady Henry Somerset in 1895, took inebriate women on its 180 acres of Sussex farmland, leased by the British Women's Temperance Association (BWTA). Here, women alco-holics were set to work at bee-keeping, poultry-rearing, horticulture, basket-weaving and other rural occupations. It also produced rugs, embroidery and other fabrics, in workshops equipped with spinning wheels and handlooms. One building was named in memory of Agnes Weston, a pioneer temperance worker among sailors, who knew her more familiarly as 'Aggie Weston'.[36] Born into the landed gentry, Isobel Somerset was a forceful and passionate Christian (she had considered becoming a nun) and a leading temperance campaigner. Her marriage, once she discovered her husband's homosexuality, was short-lived. By 1890, she was president of the BWTA, a role she took extremely seriously. England, she claimed, was 'the only nation that has a drunken womanhood'; she was also alarmed to see mothers calming their children with liquor, and young children carrying jugs of drink from pub to home.[37] Much influenced by Julie Sutter's account of Bodelschwingh's work, and viewing alcoholism as 'an evil which is not only moral, but physical', she found the best 'antidote' in 'pure air and bright sunshine', where 'hard work' could redeem the women from the 'sadness and remorse' of their previous existence.[38] She took a direct and personal interest in the colony's work, governing as superintendent with a 'rule of love'.[39]

Like a number of inebriate colonies, Duxhurst was initially a retreat for voluntary cases. The Manor House was used to house 'ladies suffering from alcoholism or narcotism', mostly sent and paid for, by their families, at rates set between 2 and 5 guineas a week. Patients of 'a less educated class' were housed 'some little distance' from the Manor House, at a weekly fee of up to 30 shil-lings. Finally, 'habitual inebriates of a still lower class', usually sent by the courts, lived in 'six prettily constructed cottages', built in a semicircle with a central building for catering and recreation, with provision for children as well as the women.[40] As usual with voluntary residential settlements, the costs were considerably higher than the income, and Duxhurst's founders decided to seek a licence under the Inebriate Acts. The Home Office duly certified the colony as suitable for inebriates, living alongside women paid for by family or friends. The colony managers soon discovered that the two groups were incompatible. While the volunteers were usually women of some respectability and status, if not always decidedly middle class, the committed cases were 'so inferior' that 'their presence interfered with the main work of the institution', and by 1902 none remained. Only after an appeal from the National Society for the Prevention of Cruelty to Children did Somerset relent, though she ensured that, as one inspector put it, Duxford undertook only 'the cream of reformatory work'.[41]

Elsewhere, the voluntary colonies moved in with speed. The superintendent at Lingfield wrote to the London County Council in early 1899 offering ten beds for inebriates, in return for a donation of £500 and a payment of 4s. per man per week.[42] The colony also took voluntary committals, so that between 1902 and 1907 more than one third of all 'private' cases were drunkards.[43] These were, Brooks said, often 'educated men' and compared with the common paupers, he found them a troublesome group, ill-suited to the discipline of a farm regime, and liable to smuggle in liquor.[44] The Salvation Army also took inebriates, housing habitual drunkards separately in Hadleigh Great House, and employing them around the colony.[45] In Scotland, Glasgow Council, somewhat unusually, opened its own colony for women at Girgenti House, in east Ayrshire, in 1900.[46]

As at Duxford, some colony managers had second thoughts about their inebriate inmates. The Church Army obtained a certificate for the care and reform of up to twelve inebriates for its Newdigate colony in June 1901. At first, things went well and during the first eighteen months, not one of the inebriates tried to escape. At precisely that point, an inmate vanished, and others followed; far from helping with the finances, the inebriates were raising costs, and Newdigate decided to take no more. R. Welsh Branthwaite, the Home Office inspector, concluded that the average committed inebriate was 'too degraded, or too mentally diseased' to be dealt with 'by moral and religious influences alone, without the initial enforcement of strict discipline'.[47] Glasgow's inebriate women, meanwhile, posed a continuing challenge at Girgenti, whose managers apologised in 1903 for the high number of escapes.[48] Twenty-four escaped in 1907, two of whom were never recaptured.[49] According to its MO, the Glasgow women were hardened whisky drinkers, with many occupying 'the "borderland" between sanity and insanity'.[50]

Elsewhere, drunkards posed less of a challenge. The SLCA, which obtained a licence in1904, saw their new role as partly an extension of existing activities, for many of the unemployed suffered from addiction.[51] With the proviso that inebriates should be housed in the main building, James Crauford Dunlop, the government's medical inspector, recommended that the colony be licensed for two years for up to ten men.[52] In 1906, two men arrived from Dundee Sheriff Court: William Gallacher and John Boyd had been sentenced to eighteen months and two years respectively, and were the first men to enter Midlocharwood following a court sentence.[53] Alexander Kater, the supervisor, then complained that Gallacher, a 35-year-old labourer and ex-serviceman from Dundee, and Boyd, a 46-year-old fish processor from Dundee, had 'incited the other men not to work and generally stirred up discontent among the inmates'.[54] David Cant, a former joiner and another Dundonian, was, it seems, 'deeply interested in Ladies and he thinks they should have an interest in him'.[55] In its publicity material, the SLCA glossed over these problems, claiming in their annual report for 1906 that the inebriates were working hard, and 'express themselves as having no desire for liquor while there'.[56]

Most of the inebriate colonies were in decline before the Great War removed many of their potential clients. SLCA closed its colony in 1916, by which time a mere three inmates – all inebriates – remained.[57] Glasgow Corporation closed Girgenti colony, which was eventually purchased by the SLCA. Langho, in Lancashire, was in sharp decline by 1914, and in 1920 was converted into a mental asylum.[58] A number of factors led to their demise, including the usual concerns over costs (particularly as the government steadily reduced the grant paid for those who had been sentenced). After the introduction of severe controls on public houses during the war, drunkenness had almost vanished as a public concern.[59] But the greatest problem was simply a lack of any evidence that labour colonies had any impact on the problem of habitual drunkenness. Even those who admitted that the labour colonies improved the inmates' health doubted whether the 'moral effect' was worth the cost.[60]

Tuberculosis

Tuberculosis colonies, by contrast, survived to form a part of the post-1945 welfare state. At the start of the twentieth century, tuberculosis was one of Britain's largest killers, accounting for roughly one death in eight, and was the largest single cause of death among men. It was particular a disease of the working class, associated with poverty, urban overcrowding and factory work.[61] By this time, the causes of the disease were relatively well understood, and as the editor of the *Poor Law Magazine* put it, it was now possible to 'stamp out a plague from our midst which has too long been permitted to injure the virility of the British race'.[62] Public health campaigners and national efficiency enthusiasts were united in pressing for limits on the sale of infected milk, bans on public spitting, and access to the benefits of fresh air. Clean, dry air was a popular remedy, and those who could afford it travelled to private sanatoria; public housing campaigners reminded their supporters that those who could not afford a lengthy Alpine retreat could benefit from 'hygienic' accommodation.

The first public fully 'open-air' treatment centre opened in 1889, as part of Edinburgh's Royal Victoria Hospital. Within twenty years, around a hundred similar institutions had sprung up around Britain.[63] Work was not yet normally part of the treatment until Dr Marcus Paterson, medical superintendent at Frimley Sanatorium from its opening in 1904, developed a system of graduated labour. Noticing that some tubercular patients did well while working, Paterson introduced a staged approach to exercise: after a period of absolute quiet, the patients were sent out walking; once they could manage ten miles a day, they were asked to spread mould across the sanatorium lawns, then take on short bursts of spadework, followed by longer bursts, then periods with larger shovels, followed by pickaxe labour, and finally sustained heavy labour with pick and shovel. This was followed, of course, by regular and careful examinations of the patients, with Paterson and his staff carefully measuring their weight and muscle development. He duly reported positive benefits, not only in health but also in turning 'sullen and apathetic' sufferers into men with 'a lively and cheerful mental attitude'.[64]

Frimley received many visitors, and Paterson's ideas were widely discussed, not least in the wider context of public health reform and the campaign over 'national efficiency'.[65] Sir Robert Phillip, of Edinburgh University and the Royal Victorian Hospital, opened the first colony for tubercular patients in 1910, at Polton, a hillside village to the south of the city. Affiliated with the Hospital, Polton was based on a 50–acre estate some 280 feet above sea level. Consistent with Paterson's scheme, the work was 'graduated to the condition of each patient', starting with absolute rest, followed by easy walking, then light work in the open air, until it was possible to complete a three- to six-hour working day. Where Polton diverged from Paterson was in the work itself, which was organised around the colony farm, and involved potato growing, fruit farming and poultry-rearing.[66] In 1914, control of the colony – along with the Royal Victoria Hospital and Dispensary – passed to Edinburgh Town Council. As part of the transfer, the University and Town Council also reached an agreement on teaching and research into tuberculosis.[67]

Polton inspired other medical specialists to develop similar plans. Its opening and early developments were widely reported in the medical press, and it was cited as an example when later colonies were founded.[68] The prevalence of tuberculosis in the trenches provided further impetus. Lanarkshire County Council started work on accommodation for discharged tuberculous servicemen at Hairmyres in summer 1916.[69] Hairmyres had earlier served as the Lanarkshire Inebriate Reformatory, setting women to work at market gardening. Eight miles from Glasgow, the 200 acres provided, in the words of one proud local MP, 'a very well-equipped sanatorium and farm colony'.[70] By early 1918, similar colonies were being opened in Dorset, Cambridgeshire, Cheshire and North Wales, and the government was considering further developments in Edinburgh, Northumberland, Durham, Norfolk, Suffolk, Worcestershire and South Wales.[71]

Mental health

In 1909, Dr Reginald Langdon Down addressed the conference of the National Association for the Feeble-minded on the subject of colony treatment. As he saw it, mental defects were a 'permanent condition', and rather than trying unsuccessfully to adapt the patient to the labour market, the colony provided an environment suited to the patients. Medical specialists could classify the patients into different sub-groups, from 'low grade imbeciles' to the 'fairly able feeble-minded'. Provided that the colony was large enough, it would provide a variety of work, so that each individual performed tasks appropriate to their condition. He praised the work of Darenth, Sandlebridge and Starcross for their 'industrial work'. At the conclusion, the meeting carried a resolution urging the government to act.[72]

Down was a specialist of some standing. In his mid-forties at the time, he was the eldest son of Dr John Langdon Down, the man who first identified the condition known as Down's Syndrome. The son followed his father's interest in mental deficiency, and indeed directed the mental home at Teddington which his father had founded. He was a leading member of the British Medical Association (BMA), in which he held a number of offices, taking a particular interest in ethical issues.[73] He was also a eugenicist, contributing a chapter on 'The Feeble-Minded' to a book called *Human Derelicts*.[74] His interest in colony treatment was bound to attract attention across the medical profession.

Of course, there had been earlier proposals for housing the feeble-minded in colonies. A Mr E. J. Stout, of the Birmingham Board of Guardians, told a London poor law conference in 1896 that a 'little colony' would be helpful in segregating child and adult 'pauper imbeciles and idiots'.[75] But the movement only really took off after the Mental Deficiency Act 1913, which empowered local authorities to establish specialist institutions including colonies, overseen by a newly created Board of Control.[76] This Act has attracted abundant criticism from historians. Sheila Rowbotham presents it as a reflection of 'eugenic attitudes', while Matthew Thompson describes it as 'the last major attempt to solve a social problem by locking it away from the rest of society'.[77] It had certainly been preceded by a concerted campaign for what one leading eugenicist called 'restrictive eugenics', or the prevention of the unfit from breeding, by segregating them in institutions such as colonies.[78] Winston Churchill, as Home Secretary, circulated the Cabinet with an article by Alfred Tredgold, who had advised the Royal Commission on the Feeble-Minded, calling for such people to be sent to colonies, where they would contribute to their own upkeep, enjoy protection from 'a certain section of society', and avoid 'the danger of their propagation'.[79] Tredgold himself had called for 'compulsory detention in suitable colonies or institutions' of the feeble-minded, together with more extreme eugenic interventions such as limits on marriage and sterilisation for the graver cases of mental deficiency.[80]

Yet if the Act was inspired partly by eugenicist thought, its implementation was a more nuanced and complex process. Different local authorities took different approaches, not least because some had no spare money, and others resented spending the rates on a costly land colony. Nor was this simply a matter of political choice: in poorer districts, councillors knew that local ratepayers were not going to provide the sums needed for a new residential institution. In such cases, mental defectives were sent to the workhouse, unless they came before the courts, who could send them to prison. In several respects, the 1913 Act built on and helped to consolidate existing trends. The major voluntary body in the field, the National Association for the Care of the Feeble-Minded, had in 1911 opened the Princess Christian Farm Colony, at Hildenborough in Kent, catering for people with 'such severe mental defects as practically to cut them off from the rest of the world'.[81] As usual, the colonists were expected to work, partly in order to reduce the running costs of the whole operation. As well as Princess Christian herself, Dr Down was also actively involved in the initiative.

Hildenborough was a voluntary initiative, but local government was also active before 1913. In 1912, the MP for Tavistock told Parliament that in the South-West, 'we are moving on the voluntary principle' to 'provide an institution for the feeble-minded of these counties'.[82] By 1916, the idea of labour colonies for the mentally defective was sufficiently well-rooted for a group of feminists to deny that their own plans involved the 'feeble-minded', emphasising that their proposed colony was 'for women of minds sufficiently normal to respond to training'.[83] Moreover, we should note that the 1913 Act was only actively implemented after 1918. The Board of Control, an agency of the Ministry of Health, favoured the use of large institutions for mental defectives, partly on grounds of economy, and partly because they allowed classification. In 1919, the Board reported that it was considering some nineteen proposals from local authorities, 'mostly in the direction of buying an estate on which a Country House or Workhouse is situated, with the idea of using the existing building as the nucleus of a colony'.[84]

A number of proposals duly came forward. Leeds City Council established Meanwood Park Colony in 1919, for example. In 1924, the Edinburgh Women Citizens' Association raised funds for a colony for the 'permanent care' of the feeble-minded, hoping that segregation would 'stop the reproduction of feeble-minded people to a certain extent'.[85] The Royal Scottish National Institution for Mentally Defective Children duly opened an industrial colony for adults at Larbert, near Stirling, in 1935. Its aim was to provide aftercare for 'mentally defective' children after they reached adulthood. As well as an existing mansion house, which was given over to private patients, the colony comprised five large villas for inmates, nurses' homes, a recreation hall, workshops and poultry sheds, on 750 acres of land.[86] Meanwhile, a committee representing five local authorities in south-western England submitted proposals for a colony at Langdon Farm. Having purchased the site, the committee then set about drafting its plans and seeking funds. Its aim was to provide 'for the care, treatment and training of defectives of all grades and ages, including those who are also epileptic, paralytic, tuberculous, blind and deaf'. The plan was for around 100 adult patients, living in six two-storey villas, grouped around a village green, and working on a farm and market garden, affording 'useful and profitable work', and thus training 'lower grade patients' for 'positions under the kindly supervision of selected employers as well as the Voluntary Association'. The 'higher-grade patients', meanwhile, would be kept at the existing asylum in Starcross, which in 1914 had been renamed the Western Counties Institution.[87]

As with other groups, work was a central feature of colony life for the 'feeble-minded'. Most frequently, it took the form of relatively light routine tasks, including gardening, handicrafts and housework, but with sufficient variety to allow for grading of tasks. Moreover, as in other colonies, the patients helped reduce costs by producing their own food. More unusually, the colonies for the feeble-minded tended to be actively promoted, and sometimes led, by women. This pattern was noted by Willoughby Dickinson, assiduous supporter of women's suffrage and chair of the National Association for the Care of the Feeble-Minded, who thought that virtually all 'the pioneers of this movement have been women guardians and women educationists', a pattern he attributed to the contacts they had with the poor in their everyday lives.[88]

While most other forms of labour colony went into decline in the interwar years, colony treatment for mental defectives continued to attract interest. A joint committee of the Board of Education and Board of Control on mental deficiency advocated colonies as a way of 'socialising' mental defectives in 1929. Shortly afterwards, the Board of Control published a report on colonies for mental defectives, mainly with the aim of ensuring that new proposals met its standards while reducing costs in the light of the economic crisis.[89] Less than a year later, labour colonies were recommended in a report from the British Medical Association's mental deficiency committee as a way of combining treatment and segregation with opportunities for research and training. In an appendix, the committee described 'an ideal colony' as one that provided up to 1,500 places for 'persons of both sexes and of all ages, grades and varying types'.[90] Local authorities continued to bring plans forward, so that by the end of the 1930s there were twenty colonies in England and Wales for mental defectives, eighteen of them managed and owned by local government, and the Board of Control had given permission for a further five.[91] Many continued largely unaltered through the war, though Redmires colony, near Sheffield, became a prisoner-of-war camp.

Abnormal bodies

Asked in 1909 what he offered inebriates by way of training, Alexander Kater described the Midlocharwood regime as a combination of 'good wholesome food, fresh air, and plenty of work to keep their minds and bodies employed and exercised'. As for educating the inmates on the evils of alcohol, he offered just the occasional lecture and 'private conversation'.[92] A few years later, during the First World War, a group of prominent Britons launched an appeal on behalf of a labour colony for tubercular ex-servicemen, aimed at helping them to 'work out their salvation under proper conditions, training those who require it in some open-air, healthy occupation suited to their condition, especially fitting them for a life on the land, so that they may become once more self-supporting citizens'.[93] Work and fresh air were also central to the Board of Control's continuing support for labour colonies as a way of treating mental defectives.

Work and fresh air, though, were common features of the labour colony. In the case of the unhealthy and abnormal, there was also a particular interest in the colony as a place of sequestration. This was particularly marked among eugenicists, some of whom, such as Alfred Hume-Griffith, superintendent of Lingfield, believed that colony life and sterilisation were entirely compatible.[94] For others, such as the south-western councils trying to found a colony at Langdon, segregation offered a humane and acceptable alternative to sterilisation.[95] Later on, several enthusiastic eugenicists took an interest in the colony's potential contribution. In a book published in 1931, the director of medical services and the consulting neurologist at Stoke Park Colony put forward an ambitious plan involving a combination of segregation, in a colony, with a policy of sterilisation through male vasectomy. 'The Model Colony', they proposed, according to their plans, would provide facilities for work in the fresh air, meeting 'the necessity of an abundant provision of air, light, and oxygen for the under-developed brain'.[96] In a grading scheme that anticipated Aldous Huxley's *Brave New World*, they anticipated that 'cheap labour' would be provided by 'inmates above the level of the idiot-imbecile class, who are largely useless for any purpose whatsoever', while the 'defectives of both sexes' would undertake out-of-door employment.[97] Meanwhile, they noted – without further comment – that it had been suggested that an overdose of morphine might be the kindest treatment for 'the perfectly hopeless, degrading and degraded idiot-imbecile'.[98]

In fact, euthanasia was illegal in Britain (the administration of a lethal overdose to King George V was successfully kept secret for half a century).[99] Nor did labour colonies ever play a major eugenic role, at least not of the sort envisaged by committed eugenicists. While some of the colonies were established primarily for children, most were targeted at adults, with the dual view of providing therapeutic work in an isolated and health-promoting (but not completely closed) setting. Gender played, as ever, an interesting and significant role. Many of the public health colonies accepted both men and women, albeit into separate buildings, though the inebriate colonies were an important exception, with the majority recruiting women. Even in this area, though, while both sexes worked, women were more likely to be undertaking handicrafts and domestic tasks with some light gardening, while men worked at farming and heavy labour. Nevertheless, their public health role grew in the interwar years, particularly in respect of epilepsy, tuberculosis and mental deficiency.

At this stage, it is tempting to confront the ideas of Michel Foucault, one of the most influential social thinkers of the late twentieth century. Particularly in his more Marxist phases, Foucault thought that docile bodies were the product of 'discipline', exercised by punitive institutions and practices that sought to turn the flawed and feeble into useful human beings.[100] Foucault's thinking has inspired some important analyses, particularly in the field of disability studies, where his idea of disciplinary power has contributed to an understanding of inmate labour as a form of bodily training.[101] But to be honest, I doubt that Foucault's notion of normalisation and the panopticon can add much to our appreciation of the way that labour colonies developed in late Victorian and Edwardian Britain. Power is not an abstraction; it is the result of human agency, including the agency of emerging groups of experts, voluntary and professional, who are seeking to establish their place (and perhaps that of their 'clients') in what they see as a hostile world. Certainly, I view the public health labour colonies as instruments of regulation and control, more liberal, rational and scientific than the old workhouse regimes that they partially displaced and partially amended. At the same time, of course, they should be understood in their own context, in relation to ideas and practices of work and nature as these related to the developing sciences and professions of public and mental health.

Notes

1 I follow standard historical practice in using these terms where contemporaries would have done so.
2 H. G. Simmons, 'Explaining Social Policy: The English Mental Deficiency Act of 1913', *Journal of Social History*, 11, 3, 1978, 387–403.
3 *Report of the Interdepartmental Committee on Physical Deterioration*, HMSO, London, 1904.
4 I. Zweiniger-Bargielowska, *Managing the Body: Beauty, health and fitness in Britain, 1880–1939*, Oxford University Press, Oxford, 2010, 81–7.
5 E. Goffman, *Stigma: Notes on the management of spoiled identity*, Prentice Hall, Englewood Cliffs, NJ, 1963, 5.
6 R. J. Morris, *Cholera 1832: The Social Response to an Epidemic*, Croom Helm, Beckenham, 1976.
7 P. Thane, *The Foundations of the Welfare State*, Longman, London, 1982, 36.
8 S. Webb, 'Eugenics and the Poor Law', *Eugenics Review*, 2, 3, 233–41.
9 G. Jones, 'Eugenics and Social Policy Between the Wars', *Historical Journal*, 25, 3, 1982, 722–5.
10 *BMJ*, 23 June 1894.
11 *BMJ*, 16 July 1892.
12 *The Times*, 14 July 1892.

13 *Standard*, 26 January 1893.
14 Loch to Dr Paton, 6 August 1902, LMA A/FWA/C/D254/1.
15 *The Times*, 2 July 1903.
16 *The Times*, 23 January 1912.
17 *Daily News*, 30 January 1894.
18 *Daily News*, 7 November 1894.
19 *Birmingham Daily Post*, 26 November 1895; *Standard*, 27 November 1895.
20 *Daily News*, 5 August 1892.
21 *The Times*, 1 February 1895.
22 *The Times*, 29 November 1906.
23 A. McDougall, 'The David Lewis Manchester Epileptic Colony', *Journal of Mental Science*, 52, 1906, 87–8.
24 *BMJ*, 16 December 1911.
25 *The Times*, 20 December 1898, 2 July 1903.
26 *BMJ*, 4 July 1903.
27 S. Webb and B. Webb, *English Poor Law History, Part II*, Longmans, London, 1929, 750.
28 A. Hume-Griffith MD, 'The Epileptic', in T. Kelynack (ed.), *Human Derelicts: Medico-sociological studies for teachers of religion and social workers*, Charles H. Kelly, London, 1914, 109.
29 *RCPL*, Appendix, Vol. VIII, *Minutes of Evidence*, HMSO, London, 1910, 172.
30 A. J. McCallum, 'The Colony and Bromide Treatment of Epilepsy', *BMJ*, 14 March 1908, 616–18.
31 Hume-Griffith, 'The Epileptic', 109–11.
32 *BMJ*, 16 September 1899.
33 J. P. Sturrock, 'Inebriety and Feeble-mindedness', *National Conference on the Prevention of Destitution*, P.S. King & Son, London, 1912, 537.
34 *Report of the Inspector under the Inebriate Acts for 1903*, HMSO, London, 1904, 112.
35 P. McLaughlin, 'Inebriate Reformatories in Scotland: An institutional history', in S. Barrows and R. Room (eds), *Drinking: Behavior and belief in modern history*, University of California Press, Berkeley, 1991, 288–93.
36 *Nursing Record & Hospital World*, 9 November 1895.
37 Lady Henry Somerset, 'The Duxhurst Industrial Farm Colony for Female Inebriates', *British Journal of Inebriety*, 10, 2, 1912, 81.
38 Lady Somerset, 'The Story of Our Farm', *North American Review*, 175, 692–3.
39 *British Journal of Nursing*, 7 May 1904.
40 *Journal of Mental Science*, 1896, 42, 684.
41 *Report of the Inspector under the Inebriate Acts for 1903*, HMSO, London, 1904, 10.

42 *BMJ*, 1 July 1899.
43 *RCPL*, Appendix, Vol. VIII, *Minutes of Evidence*, 163.
44 *Minutes of Evidence taken by Committee on Vagrancy*, 177.
45 *Bristol Mercury*, 2 September 1899.
46 *Parliamentary Debates*, 29 June 1903.
47 *Report of the Inspector under the Inebriate Acts for 1903*, 11.
48 *Glasgow Herald*, 3 September 1903.
49 *BMJ*, 23 November 1907.
50 *Poor Law Magazine (PLM)*, 12, 1902, 222.
51 *Departmental Committee on the Operation in Scotland of the Law Relating to Inebriates. Minutes of evidence and appendices*, HMSO, London, 16.
52 Dr James C Dunlop, 12 December 1903, NAS HH57/70.
53 Kater to Sec for Scotland, 21 April 1906, NAS HH57/70.
54 Auld to Under-Secretary for Scotland, 24 June 1907, NAS HH57/70.
55 Ibid.
56 Tenth annual report of the SLCA, 1906, NAS HH57/70.
57 M. B. Auld to Dr J. C. Dunlop, 26 April 1916, NAS HH57/70.
58 D. Beckingham, 'A Historical Geography of Liberty: Lancashire and the Inebriates Acts', *Journal of Historical Geography*, 36(3), 2010, 400.
59 McLaughlin, 'Inebriate Reformatories', 302–8.
60 *BMJ*, 19 January 1907.
61 L. Bryder, *Below the Magic Mountain: A social history of tuberculosis in twentieth century Britain*, Oxford University Press, Oxford, 1988, 1–4.
62 *PLM*, 12, 1902, 413.
63 Bryder, *Below the Magic Mountain*, 23.
64 *Lancet*, 23 March 1907; also *BMJ*, 18 January 1908.
65 Searle, *Quest for National Efficiency*, 63–4.
66 *BMJ*, 26 March 1910.
67 *BMJ*, 1 April 1921.
68 *BMJ*, 26 March 1910, *BMJ*, 8 January 1921.
69 *Parliamentary Debates*, 8 August 1916.
70 *Report of the Inspector under the Inebriate Acts for 1903*, HMSO, London, 1904, 23–4, *Parliamentary Debates*, 6 March 1917.
71 *Parliamentary Debates*, 21 March 1918.
72 *BMJ*, 6 November 1909.
73 *BMJ*, 11 June 1955
74 R. L. Langdon Down, 'The Feeble-Minded', in Kelynack (ed.) *Human Derelicts*, 74–98.
75 *Daily News*, 5 March 1896.
76 G. Chester and P. Dale, 'Institutional Care for the Mentally Defective, 1914–1948: Diversity as a response to individual needs and an

indication of a lack of policy coherence', *Medical History*, 51, 1, 2007, 60–1.
77 S. Rowbotham, *Dreamers of a New Day: Women who invented the twentieth century*, Verso, London, 2010, 89; M. Thompson, *The Problem of Mental Deficiency: Eugenics, democracy and social policy in Britain, c.1870–1959*, Oxford University Press, Oxford, 1998, 113.
78 *The Times*, 6 May 1910.
79 A. F. Tredgold, 'The feeble-minded: a social danger', *Eugenics Review*, 1, 2, 1909, 104; see also M. Gilbert, 'Churchill and eugenics', 2009, at www.winstonchurchill.org/support/the-churchill-centre/publications/finest-hour-online/594–churchill-and-eugenics (accessed 5 January 2011).
80 A.F. Tredgold, *Mental Deficiency (Amentia)*, William Wood, New York, 1908, 359–60.
81 *BMJ*, 10 February 1912.
82 *Parliamentary Debates*, 11 March 1912.
83 *Prospectus: Women's Training Colony*, no date [1916?], Modern Records Centre MSS 16C/3/W.
84 *Annual Report of the Board of Control for 1919*, HMSO, London, 1920, 56.
85 *BMJ*, 20 December 1924. For a feminist account of the EWCA, see S. Innes, 'Constructing women's citizenship in the interwar period: the Edinburgh Women Citizens' Association', *Women's History Review*, 13, 4, 2004, 621–47.
86 *BMJ*, 21 September 1935.
87 Western Counties Institution to Board of Control, 3 November 1932, Devonshire Records Office MSS/118/1/6/11/7, Report by the Committee to the Local Authorities of Devon, Somerset, Dorset, Exeter and Plymouth, 4 May 1929, DRO MSS/118/1/4/3/1.
88 W. H. Dickinson, 'Homes and colonies for the feeble-minded', *National Conference on the Prevention of Destitution*, King & Son, London, 1911, 638.
89 *BMJ*, 7 November 1931.
90 *BMJ*, 25 June 1932.
91 *Annual Report of the Board of Control for 1938*, 50–1.
92 *Departmental Committee on the Operation in Scotland of the Law Relating to Inebriates. Minutes of evidence and appendices*, 126.
93 *BJN*, 3 November 1917.
94 Hume-Griffith, 'The Epileptic', 112.
95 Chester and Dale, 'Institutional Care', 66.
96 R. L. Berry and R. G. Gordon, *The Mental Defective: A problem in social inefficiency* McGraw-Hill, New York, 1931, 178.
97 Ibid., 179.
98 Ibid., 188–9.

99 *BMJ*, 28 May 1994.
100 M. Foucault, *Discipline and Punish: The birth of the prison*, Vintage Books, New York, 1979, 137.
101 For example, L. Carlson, 'Docile Bodies, Docile Minds: Foucauldian reflections on mental retardation', in S. Tremain (ed.), *Foucault and the Government of Disability*, University of Michigan Press, Ann Arbor MI, 2005, 133–52.

4

Alternative living in the English countryside
Utopian colonies

In April 1892, Herbert Vincent Mills led two friends to their new home on small plot near Starnthwaite, in the Lake District. Encouraged by the artist and critic John Ruskin as well as the Liberal MP John Morley, their aim was to create a permanent cooperative settlement. By 1893, the group had expanded to 11 men, 5 women and 6 children, and occupied over 130 acres.[1] All being well, they hoped to pioneer a new way of living, replacing what they saw as the blighted existence of Britain's city-dwelling, industrial working class. Yet before a year passed, the Starnthwaite socialists were arguing among themselves, and Mills was losing patience. A handful of colonists struggled on for a few more years, before handing the estate over to the Christian Union for Social Service. It is easy to mock Mills and his friends as wild-eyed, woolly-minded idealists, but secular, utopian labour colonies appealed to a variety of those who felt life had more to offer than factory work and city life.

A little piece of England

Idealistic notions of land settlement thrived in the 1870s, often under the influence of John Ruskin's romantic critique of industrial capitalism and the orthodox political economy that underpinned it. Ruskin founded the Guild of St George in 1871, to serve as a league of agricultural 'companions', who would live on the land and meet their needs by the labour of their own hands, watched over by a hierarchy of 'marshalls'. Five years later, he invested £2,025 in a small estate at Totley, near Sheffield, where a group of socialist working men were planning to settle on the land. Ruskin was delighted: 'here is at last', he wrote, 'a little piece of England given into the English workman's hands, and heaven's'.[2]

But Ruskin, unlike many of the early settlers, was no democrat. When the settlers proved mediocre farmers, Ruskin brought in a professional farm manager, John Harrison Riley, a former Chartist. Riley first argued with the settlers, and then fell out with Ruskin, who claimed that Riley enjoyed smoking more than digging. The community broke up, with Riley emigrating to the United States and several settlers bankrupted.[3]

Despite this setback, Ruskin's ideas exerted a continuing influence on practical utopianism. As well as encouraging Edward Carpenter, who settled for a time near Totley, Ruskin's thinking shaped Patrick Geddes' ideas on town planning. He also continued to inspire followers in the northern cities who drew on his trenchant critique of industrial urban society. His ideas also blended well with socialist historical narratives of earlier utopian land settlements. For many radicals in the 1880s, these ideas had also found practical expression within living memory. In the late 1840s, the Chartist orator Fergus O'Connor had enthused crowds with eloquent descriptions of an English 'peasant republic', with 70,000 of his followers investing in the Chartist Land Company. Against ferocious odds, the company created five communal settlements before it was wound up in 1851 by Act of Parliament, amid wild allegations of embezzlement and maladministration.[4] Over time, the allegations started to look like a smear campaign, and by the 1880s O'Connor's plans were being fondly recalled by a new generation of land campaigners.[5]

By the 1880s, the movement had a harder, more political edge. Both the Land Nationalisation Society and the Land Restoration Society campaigned for punitive land taxes on large holdings and support for smallholdings. And it is possible to see the Highland crofters who undertook the land wars of the 1880s and 1890s, as well as the Irish tenant farmers who supported the Land League's campaign during the 1880s, as in some ways isolated from the radical land reformers of urban society.[6] Certainly they were distinctive movements with their own roots, and no pale reflections of the movement in England, lowland Scotland and the Irish cities. But connections there certainly were.

Irish and Scottish land tenure had attracted radical attention for decades, helping fuel interest in the ideas of the American economist and writer Henry George, whose *Progress and Poverty* appeared in a British edition in 1881. George's arrest in Ireland made him a hero on the popular lecture circuit, but he also had a lasting influence on the Liberal Party, producing new legislation on smallholdings and allotments.[7] Radicals of a more socialist tinge could draw inspiration from Robert Blatchford and his *Clarion* newspaper. For Blatchford, the issue was clear-cut. As he saw it, 'There is neither justice nor reason in private ownership of land, any more than there would be in the private ownership or class monopoly of the sea or the air.'[8] When Mills and his comrades took charge at Starnthwaite, they were entering political terrain that was both deeply familiar and hotly contested.

Christians, cooperators and campaigners

A Unitarian minister and critic of the factory system, Mills was a popular lecturer and writer on the idea of the self-supporting 'industrial village'. In 1886 he published his ideas in book form, claiming that he had come to realise the failings of contemporary capitalism in Liverpool when he saw three unemployed men – a baker, tailor and shoemaker – each lacking decent shoes, clothing or food. Mills presented himself modestly, as merely a campaigner against the workhouse, but he was equally clear about his view of the rich, who were increasing in wealth and numbers while the poor were cast into the workhouse.[9] He was also a reader of Carlyle, quoting his savage attack on the 'Bastille' (workhouse).[10] He rejected emigration – and denounced Hadleigh – as 'a remedy which drains the country of its industrial strength'.[11] He shared Ruskin's view of the inherent value of labour, and envisaged that the colonists would meet their own needs by dint of their own craft skills. His model for the future was a form of rural and craft cooperation, such as found on the island of St Kilda, where independent-minded Hebrideans existed by trading goods and services with one another. For Mills, the islanders represented a 'survival of all that was wholesome in the life of the working class in the pre-commercial days, mingled with a strong flavour of communism'.[12]

Mills can be understood, then, as a Christian who detested poverty and a cooperator who saw salvation on the land. In 1888, he was invited to present his case to the Select Committee of the House of Lords on the Poor Law. He took the opportunity with relish, telling their lordships that the Local Government Board (LGB) should sponsor 'four or five experimental colonies' where unemployed men would have 'a little allotment of land by means of which they could make a beginning if they chose towards getting money'. Vagrants and the 'idle', by contrast, would be sent to a separate class of punitive working colonies, as in Holland.[13] Their lordships were unconvinced, but Mills continued to travel through England and Scotland, urging poor law reformers and land reformers to pursue his goal of communal land settlement. Among many others, his apparent combination of eloquence and hardheadedness won over the prominent land campaigner and eminent natural scientist Alfred Russel Wallace, best known today as Darwin's co-developer of the theory of natural selection. Long interested in the work of Robert Owen, by the late 1880s, Wallace was an avowed socialist, and was fascinated by Mills's proposals for communal land settlement. In 1889, he told the Land Nationalisation Society – of which he was president – that if implemented, his proposals would 'prove that poverty and want of work are wholly landlord-created, and that, whether as individual independent workers or in *co-operative association*, our labouring classes, if permitted, can support themselves upon the land'.[14]

Mills's plans were indeed put into practice. Initially, his group bought a small four-acre plot at Starnthwaite, near Kendal, where two settlers started work in April 1892.[15] The Society extended their holdings to 131 acres over the next six months; the site also contained a corn mill, stables, oilcake mill, sawmill, joiners' shop and blacksmiths, as well as three dwellings.[16] Much of the work was on the land, including forestry and the raising of pigs, breaking horses, and extracting peat from a few acres of moss. Others worked at weaving, tailoring, shoemaking, fruit-bottling, jam-making, and smithing.[17] From the outset, Mills believed that women and children should live on the colony along with men, seeing this as being 'in harmony with human nature and Divine law', and denouncing male-only colonies as 'unnatural'.[18] Of the 22 settlers in residence in September 1893, 11 were men, 5 women and 6 children. The women included a milliner, a dressmaker, and two servants, while the men included an ironworker, two clerks, an insurance agent and a butcher, as well as three labourers. A civil servant noted that some did not come from 'the ordinary unemployed class', but had 'been attracted to the colony by the expectation of taking part in a communal experiment'.[19] A number were vegetarians.[20]

Mills described the life at Starnthwaite as idyllic:

> We have worked harmoniously together on the peat land, in the harvest field, on the pig farm, in the corn mill, and on the erection of our new house; and the variety and healthy nature of the work during the day, and the music and talk and rambles of an evening have made life satisfactory and complete.[21]

Within a year, though, divisions had opened among the colonists. A group of socialist colonists challenged the idea of appointing foremen to oversee the work as excessively hierarchical, or worse. Miss Enid Stacey, a Bristol schoolteacher, socialist and women's rights campaigner who was still in her twenties, described Mills before a crowd in Accrington as an 'autocrat' and 'absolute dictator' who was imposing his own rules and values on the colonists.[22] Stacey was not the only colonist to complain of Mills's authoritarianism. Shortly after Stacey's attack, six colonists appeared at Kendal courthouse, charged with malicious damage to the colony and its property; the men claimed that while Mills had excluded them for failing work, they had done no more than break open the door on returning in the evening.[23] Mills viewed the rebels as keen on preaching but not on tilling the soil, and fourteen were expelled.[24]

Starnthwaite struggled on for a few years. Twenty colonists remained on the farm in 1895, living largely on a vegetarian diet; most had previously been unemployed.[25] Four members of Edward Carpenter's Norton Socialist Colony joined it for a couple of months, before judging it 'advisable to continue our effort at Norton'.[26] In 1900 Mills transferred the estate to Paton's English Land Colonisation Society (ELCS), which in turn handed control to CUSS, who announced that Starnthwaite would henceforth take disabled ex-servicemen returning from South Africa.[27] Up to 20 men were accommodated in dormitories of 4–6 beds, and taught such crafts as cobbling, sandal-making, knitting, net-making, basket-making and cooking. Most of the costs came from the soldiers themselves, probably out of their pensions.[28] But this was a limited pool from which to recruit and by 1907 Starnthwaite was an epileptic colony, a role in which it continued for some years.[29]

Mills, presumably losing heart, appears to have played little further role in the land colonisation movement. Had it not been for Alfred Russel Wallace, Mills would probably have been quietly forgotten. In 1893, the veteran socialist land campaigner and naturalist leapt to Mills' defence, arguing that his ideas were as relevant as ever. The long-term aim of Starnthwaite and similar ventures, Wallace wrote, should be to train 'a body of men and women fit to carry out successfully a truly co-operative life'. And he outlined detailed plans for a series of worker co-operative land colonies across Britain, each with a population of around 800 families.[30] Unfortunately, this would, Wallace admitted, be a very long-term plan indeed. Living in 'perfect freedom' was impossible until 'a fresh generation had grown up under the new conditions, and each community had been weeded by the voluntary departure of all whose too independent and aggressive natures preferred the excitement and the risks of individual struggle with the world'.[31] In 1908, he returned to Mills' proposals. In two articles, later reissued as a *Clarion* pamphlet, Wallace praised Mills for combining 'the most important, and at the same time the least disputable methods of both Socialism and Individualism'.[32] Reflecting on the Starnthwaite rebellion, Russell insisted that while the ultimate aim was a 'self-governing community', the early phases required 'an official director, whose rule must necessarily at first be autocratic', while such 'serious offences as repeated drunkenness, immorality, or violence should be punished by absolute dismissal or expulsion'.[33] Discipline and freedom, democracy and control: these tensions were to dog the history of utopian settlements in Britain.

Kropotkin and Tolstoy: anarchism and the land

While never a mass movement, British anarchist groups had attracted a number of members, many local and some immigrants who had brought their political beliefs from Italy, Spain, Russia or France. They were a very heterogeneous group, politically as well as culturally, ranging from those who believed in violent attacks on the rich and powerful ('anarchism of the deed') to those who foreswore all aggression against man or beast and strove to live a life of peaceful community with all beings. Some, egged on by government agents, resorted to violent direct action; the bomb plots, while isolating anarchism from the rest of the left, also led many British anarchists to turn their backs on physical force, reflecting instead on the long and hard pathway to radical social change.[34]

In the turn towards experimental communal living, Prince Peter Kropotkin was particularly influential. Ever since the Owenite and Chartist settlements, mainstream British socialism had become increasingly sceptical about the value of alternative land colonisation, and Mills' venture had done nothing to persuade them of its merits. The painter and socialist Evacustes Phipson complained in 1896 that orthodox socialists always 'ridicule and denounce' cooperative colonisation, arguing that what was needed was one successful example, using 'every possible labour-saving contrivance' along with 'scientifically organised' labour.[35] Kropotkin spoke clearly to this modernising tendency, deploring the more nostalgic and backward looking land settlement movements, and favouring modern techniques such as intensive market gardening, using artificial heating and fertilisers, underpinned by education based on 'a reasoned, scientific knowledge of Nature's laws'.[36]

With a long record of anarchist writing, punctuated by incarceration and expulsion, Kropotkin had moved to Britain in 1886, embarking on a lecture tour and becoming friendly with socialist intellectuals such as William Morris, George Bernard Shaw and Edward Carpenter. His ideas were firmly based on localism, mutual self-help and cooperation, combined with a principled anti-statism, and an interest in the latest developments in natural science. In 1895, a small group of Northern anarchists announced their intention of putting Kropotkin's ideas into practice, following a debate led by John Coleman Kenworthy at the 1894 cooperative congress in 1894.[37] Undeterred by the Prince's refusal to serve as treasurer (he claimed that communities founded under capitalist conditions were doomed to fail), his followers founded Clousden Hill Co-operative and Communist Colony on a 20–acre farm near Newcastle.[38] According to its founding statement, the work was 'to be done on the most advanced principles of scientific research and instruction; machinery to be used wherever possible so soon as the funds of the Society permit'.[39]

Clousden survived for six years. At its peak, some twenty-six people lived in the colony, with Germans, Danes and Belgians working and living alongside Geordies. Like Frank Capper, a tailor and Czech refugee, most were manual workers, though one was apparently a professor of literature at the University of Brussels, another a professional golfer from Scotland.[40] They grew fruit, vegetables, poultry and flowers, using glass frames to nurture tomatoes, cucumbers and orchids. Men and women worked, though in different domains. The colony's statement of founding principles laid down that housework should be done on 'the most improved system, to relieve the women from the long and tiresome work which unduly falls as their share today'.[41] In practice, the division of labour was conventional, with women cooking and washing, and men working the gardens.[42] On Sunday afternoons, the entire community – male and female – met to discuss the work, examine the balance sheet, and allocate tasks for the week ahead.[43]

Though short-lived, Clousden had its successes. Sunderland Co-operative Society arranged to buy any surplus produce (the tomatoes were particularly popular).[44] The colony entertained a steady trickle of visitors, including the celebrated trade union leader Tom Mann and Kropotkin himself.[45] By 1898, the colony was in decline, mirroring the broader collapse of British anarchism.[46] Moreover, as at Starnthwaite, some colonists apparently took a fairly relaxed view of the common workload, there were squabbles over leadership, and the colony was chronically under-funded. Frank Starr, the young compositor who served as treasurer of Clousden Hill, 'thought that the cause of its non-success was our poor human nature. All wanted to lead, and none would follow.' One man, a tailor, had insisted on working the gardens, a job he was bad at; others spent their days writing papers for socialist journals. Starr thought the experience promising for the future – 'say 5,000 years hence' – but meanwhile, 'we were a bit too previous'.[47] Most of the colonists drifted away, until only three remained: Frank Starr, a compositor by trade, his wife and Hans Rasmussen, a young Dane.[48] The three tried their hands at commercial market gardening but failed, filing for bankruptcy early in 1902.[49]

The second colony to follow Kropotkin was both smaller and shorter-lived. In 1896, seven Sheffield idealists – followers of Kropotkin, Thoreau and Edward Carpenter –founded Norton Socialist Colony. Led by Hugh Mapleton, a shop manager, and Herbert Stansfield, a young art student, the group occupied a cottage in the grounds of Norton Hall, growing lettuces, mushrooms and tomatoes and making sandals; while they lived communally, without any formal rules, they were strict about their lifestyle, forbidding all meat, alcohol, tobacco and salt, and wearing cloaks. As well as selling fruit and vegetables from door to door, the Norton colonists sold sandals and cloaks, both of which Carpenter saw as important in liberating the body from artificial restrictions. Norton Socialist Colony survived until its lease ran out in 1900, when its members turned to other projects.[50]

If Kropotkin's disciples had limited success (the Prince turned down the role of president at Clousden Hill), followers of Nikolai Tolstoy enjoyed rather better fortunes. Tolstoy's simple Christianity, his pacifism, his emphasis on everyday contact with nature, and his privileging of physical labour tended to appeal more to middle-class anarchists than the northern workers who had founded Clousden. Purleigh developed out of Croydon Brotherhood Church, whose pastor was John Coleman Kenworthy. As a young man, Kenworthy belonged to the Liverpool Ruskin Society, participating in its discussions about an 'industrial colony'.[51] He then settled in Canning Town, working for the Mansfield House university settlement in London's East End, helping local people to set up cooperatives, and launching the Brotherhood Trust to serve as a practical example of cooperation and buy land for rural settlement.[52] Inspired by Herbert Mills, he became secretary to the ELCS, where he wrote a report on farm colonies with Paton and Harold Moore, and lectured on land reform.[53] Through the Fellowship of the New Life, of which he was an active member, he encountered Carpenter and Ramsay MacDonald.[54] In 1896, Kenworthy took a small plot of land at Purleigh, where he was joined in 1897 by other Tolstoyans, including two Russian families from the Dukhobor movement.[55]

According to one sympathetic reporter, the Purleigh colonists thrived in their new home. In his view, 'from a hygienic point of view this unconstrained existence seems peculiarly felicitous if the fresh and ruddy complexions of the colonists are a criterion'.[56] The colonists farmed and gardened, passed their evenings with discussion and music, and like Tolstoy, were vegetarians. In 1898, though, the colonists split, and a small group left to found the new Whiteway colony at Sheepscombe, near Stroud, leaving Kenworthy to reflect on how few true Tolstoyans there were: 'The entrance to the good life is strait and narrow; few there be that find it. But those few are the salt of the earth, the light of the world, the city, the society set on a hill.'[57] Aylmer Maude, a Purleigh settler and Tolstoy's translator, later recalled that at least five of his fellow settlers 'were subsequently put under medical supervision on account of their medical condition', while even 'those of us who kept our sanity did not always keep out tempers'.[58] Meanwhile, with Kenworthy's resources drying up, the Purleigh colony closed in 1900.

The Whiteway colonists began by publicly expressing their contempt for private property, ceremoniously burning the title deeds to the estate.[59] Led by Samuel Veale Bracher, a journalist from Gloucester who had largely funded the purchase, the settlers included a group from Purleigh, intent on running the new settlement 'on a broader and less selfish basis. Between twenty and thirty men and women, most of them highly educated, cultivated their own food, planted fruit trees, made bricks, and opened a small quarry for stone.[60] Their radicalism extended to their dress: one visitor described the 'Russian Communists' as wearing 'the smallest amount prescribed by decency'. While men wore an open necked shirt and knickerbockers or linen trousers and sandals, the women had adopted very short pinafore dresses.[61] Both sexes went bareheaded, and bare-legged. Nellie Shaw, a founder who was still living there in 1937, claimed that women certainly experienced greater freedom than in conventional society.[62] The Communists continued to trade by barter, and to shun money. Their refusal to pay taxes led to the seizure of their piano and a fourteen-day prison sentence for one of their members, while another absconded with £20 cash and a box of sailors' clothing.[63] After two years of experimenting with a shared workload, they abandoned communal farming for individual plots.

While disputes about workload were common in the anarchist communities, Whiteway was also shaken by disputes over sexuality. Samuel Veale Bracher and his wife became alarmed when some of the Communists espoused the principle of free love. Kenworthy travelled down from London to support Mr and Mrs Bracher, though once he had gone the free love advocates were as active as ever.[64] Nor was this the only issue where Tolstoyan principles and British sexual values clashed. In 1900, Platon Drahoufes, formerly an Oxford tutor, was fined for sun-bathing naked in public view.[65] Whether cloaks, sandals and bare legs or heads, or outright nudity, the utopian colonies were spaces where new freedoms of the body could be explored. It was easy to attack Whiteway as a haven of 'indolence and licence'.[66] According to Nellie Shaw, though, the main problem was that the original colonists found that they did most of the work, while the newcomers simply tilled their own plot, so that community life became 'almost impossible'.[67] Yet Whiteway continued – if less collectively, as a group of smallholdings – and still has a strong community identity today.

Whatever its failings and challenges, Whiteway survived longer than any other Tolstoyan community. The Daisy colony in Lancashire blossomed in 1904 but had closed by 1906.[68] Tolstoyan colonies at

Leeds, founded in 1897, and Braunstone, founded in 1899, were said in 1900 to be struggling, but have otherwise sunk without trace.[69] The reasons by now are familiar. All were under-capitalised and struggled to meet their running costs; they were riven by internal conflicts, especially over work; few of the colonists had much experience of farming; and frequently, local businesses were hostile. Moreover, as Michael Thomas points out, anarchist communities rarely enjoyed widespread popular support.[70] Clousden is a partial exception, given its ties to the cooperative movement, but otherwise the communities were isolated within the wider labour and socialist movement. The wonder is that they survived as long as they did.

Work camps as protest movement: The Triangle Camp

Utopian colonies were designed to build a new world by withdrawing from this world. Such asceticism appealed to the select few, baffling the majority whom the socialist and labour movement were trying to lead. The Triangle Camp at Plaistow, in what is now the London Borough of Newham, attracted hundreds of supporters, but it did so by mobilising around the issues of unemployment and the land, building an urban farm camp as a vehicle of protest rather than as an advance towards a new communitarian life. In the event, the Triangle Camp had an even shorter life than any of the anarchist colonies, though its memory is still honoured in the urban horticultural experiment known as the Abbey Gardens.[71]

Early in the morning of 13 July 1906, Ben Cunningham and William King led a group of fourteen unemployed men onto five acres of derelict land. Cunningham, a man of substance, was a coal agent and a member of West Ham council, the first Labour-controlled borough in Britain, and was irate over claims that the unemployed were idlers who were unwilling to work. Inspired by a land-grab in Manchester, the men met at a nearby church, then marched down Northern Road armed with picks, forks and shovels. Flinging open the gate, they ran up a red flag and put up a tent. After lighting a brazier, setting out a collection tin for visitors to give material support, and passing a resolution stating their intentions, they started to dig the land. The original group was joined by others until they became 21 in total, aged between 25 and 66, and all but two were married. They called their little settlement the Triangle Camp, their tent the Triangle Hotel.[72]

Triangle Camp presented an opportunity for the East End unemployed to challenge lazy assumptions about their readiness for work. There was a roll-call at 5 a.m. and again at 10 p.m., and the working day lasted from 7 a.m. until 5 p.m.[73] The founders agreed to accept any man who was unemployed and of 'good character'; alcoholic drinks were banned entirely; and they would stay until removed by the police.[74] They breakfasted on bread and butter with cocoa, then planted Brussels sprouts and cabbages and dug a 20–foot well for water. On their first weekend, the campers were entertained by a concert under canvas, with songs such as 'Sailor Jack' and Longfellow's 'The Village Blacksmith', following a speech by Charles Mowbray, veteran anarchist orator and tailor. Donations of food included a box of haddock, pots of marmalade, and fresh butter and cheese.[75]

Within a few days, the campers received a message of support from their local MP, Will Crook.[76] They received a similar, if guarded message from George Bernard Shaw, who reminded them to stay within the law, and were visited by Wilson Carlisle, founder of the Church Army.[77] Shortly afterwards, lawyers acting for West Ham Corporation sought a writ from the High Court to evict the men. When the Mayor communicated the Corporation's decision to the campers, Cunningham ceremonially burnt his letter in front of a crowd of 3,000, who reportedly shouted 'Cheers for the social revolution' and 'Are we down-hearted?'[78] When the Corporation sent its officers, with a police escort, to remove the tent and flag, and evict the men, George Blain, the Corporation's road foreman, started by clapping Cunningham on the back and putting a shilling into the collection box. While the Triangle Band played, Cunningham told the men to 'be orderly' and to 'be your own police'.[79]

Yet while the Corporation hesitated to enforce its injunction, divisions were emerging between the leaders. Although both were now banned from entering the Camp, King continued to live in the Triangle Hotel and work the land, while Cunningham carefully made his speeches from a neighbouring plot of land. King denounced Cunningham, telling him that, 'Instead of being under a red flag, you should be under a white one.'[80] On the day that this was reported, the Corporation sent in its staff, supported by the police. Faced down by the authorities, the other land-grabbers took their bedding to a neighbouring plot, offered by a sympathetic landowner. Another group of unemployed occupied the land again in the afternoon, but were chased off by evening, with three arrests. Cunningham spent the weekend addressing street meetings, surrounded by policemen, and by the Sunday evening the camp was deserted.[81] The Corporation then secured a further injunction against Cunningham and King, forbidding them to enter the triangle again.[82]

That might have seemed the end, but three weeks later Cunningham was back. This time he held a meeting outside Upton Park station, denouncing the Corporation for failing to produce deeds proving its title to the land. Evading some thirty police officers and Corporation officials, and watched by a large crowd, Cunningham and four other land-grabbers made their way back onto the land, where two were promptly arrested. Thomas Evans, a 45-year-old labourer from Canning Town, received fourteen days' gaol for assault; 35-year-old George Pollard, an unemployed gardener and father of six, told the court he was an Anarchist-Communist and a volunteer ambulance man with a gold medal for life-saving. Receiving a sentence of six weeks for assaulting a foreman from the Corporation's roads department, Pollard said: 'Well, I shall have some work.'[83] Cunningham was arrested after a further incursion on the land, and gaoled for contempt of court.[84]

That was not quite the last of Cunningham, who served his sentence, announcing that he wanted no favours from the prison governor or 'the class whom he acts for'.[85] While in prison, he wrote appeals to public figures that he thought likely to be sympathetic, including George Bernard Shaw and Henry Rider Haggard.[86] Rider Haggard wrote to *The Times*, distancing himself from the land-grabbers' methods, but expressing sympathy with their goal.[87] After his release, Cunningham anticipated the pantomime appearances of Ken Livingstone, a prominent later London socialist, by taking part in staging of the Triangle land-grab at the Bow Palace Music Hall while sporting a gold chain across his waistcoat and a panama hat.[88]

The Plaistow land-grabbers were working the land as a protest against unemployment, rather than a serious attempt at settlement. Initially, the Triangle Camp represented a visible way of showing their willingness and ability to labour, precisely in order to challenge prevailing ideas about the 'demoralisation' and 'idleness' of the unemployed. Yet although Cunningham and King were able build a popular movement around the Triangle Camp, the small colony itself was short-lived, and the demonstrators were easily dispersed.

But if the camp was quickly forgotten, the ideas behind it were not. Rider Haggard, commenting on Triangle Camp, proposed that unused land in 'our great cities' should be leased to 'poor persons who genuinely desire to cultivate them'.[89] A year later, Toynbee Hall settlement invited the West Ham Unemployed Society to address a meeting on their 'successful experiment in market gardening', and shortly afterwards, supported by Joseph Fels and Patrick Geddes, a number of land reform activists formed the Vacant Land Cultivation Society.[90] In 1910, the Society claimed that it had secured some 60 acres of land for allotments, and reckoned that the capital had another 10,000 acres of waste land that might be put to good use.[91] By this time, a sister society had been formed in Dublin, largely by philanthropic well-wishers.[92] Both societies continued for a number of years, combining campaigning activities with the more prosaic business of trying to secure allotments for the poor in the capital cities, coming briefly into the limelight during the First World War.[93] As well as highlighting the human damage of unemployment, the whole episode is reminiscent of the contemporary guerrilla gardening movement, not least in the way that initially hostile authorities have found ways of living with those who cultivate neglected public spaces, from waste land to roundabouts.

Feminism and the Women's Training Colony

Overwhelmingly, the labour colony movement in Britain was male. This might at first seem odd. Women played a prominent role in many voluntary movements that aimed to tackle social problems in late nineteenth century Britain, and dominated many philanthropic institutions.[94] But poverty and unemployment was rarely perceived as a female issue, at least in a direct way. Edith Abbott, one of the first writers to comment on unemployment among women, complained in 1907 that most schemes for employing the unemployed 'presuppose that all of the unemployed are men'.[95] An American who had been influenced by the Webbs while studying at the London School of Economics, Abbott thought it 'next to impossible' for women to enter a farm or labour colony, where they would be required to share facilities with men.[96]

The idea of a labour colony for women alone apparently never occurred to Abbott, nor to many other proponents of the labour colony. Lansbury and Bondfield were involved in plans for an unemployed women's colony, only to have it rejected by the LGB (see above), and a number of eminent women helped to found the inebriate women's colony at Duxhurst (pp. 62–3). Specifically feminist plans only emerged during the First World War, when a group of women's suffrage campaigners and Christian philanthropists came together to propose a women's training colony. Its aim was largely remedial; most of the founders had a long-standing interest in prostitution, and came from the social and moral purity wing of the feminist movement. Their aim was two-fold: to reclaim fallen women from the male-dominated world of the sex industry, and to practise the self-government of women by women.

Based at Cope Hall near Newbury, the Women's Training Colony (WTC) opened in 1917. Its moving spirits included old labour colony hands like William Henry Hunt, superintendent of the CUSS colony at Wallingford and Commissioner Adelaide Cox of the Salvation Army, but most were feminists. Millicent Fawcett, leader of the National Union of Women's Suffrage Societies, had protested against the double standards of Britain's Contagious Diseases Acts, which required prostitutes to be examined for sexually transmitted infections but left their male clients alone, and had campaigned for the closure of Britain's brothels.[97] Dr Helen Wilson, a Sheffield GP and president of the Sheffield Women's Suffrage Society, was also a campaigner against the one-sided nature of the law on prostitution, arguing vehemently that:

> The ultimate remedy is the acceptance of a single standard for men and women, and the recognition that man is meant to be the master and not the slave of his body.[98]

Jane Walker, MD, was medical superintendent of a tuberculosis sanatorium, founder and later president of the Medical Women's Federation, and treasurer of the Association for Social and Moral Hygiene.[99]

The colony recruited 'women whose lack of character and training renders them ineligible for other institutions', and aimed to 'train the women in a sense of responsibility and independence', and encourage 'perseverance and self-control', by isolating them in the colony and offering work.[100] Miss Wakefield, honorary secretary to the committee, went into slightly more detail about the intended 'colonists': while the 'more docile and less virile girl' could benefit from being placed in a home, the colony aimed at recruiting women

with a 'more emotional and headstrong nature, with a keener appreciation of the good things of life and less patience with drudgery'.[101]

The women, aged between 14 and 40, lived in cottage homes,
undertook work on the gardens and farm as well as in the houses,
and were trained in handicrafts.[102] There was a small chapel room
in the main house for Anglicans, but with freedom for others to
worship according to their denomination. So far so familiar, but the
WTC also had a second role: practical enfranchisement of women,
in a world where their political and social participation was severely
circumscribed. The committee proclaimed themselves believers in
'the *system* of self-government', who aimed at 'restoring to normal
citizenship delinquent and difficult women and girls, especially those
of some refinement and education', as well as preparing them for
what they hoped would be an enlarged franchise after the war. They
therefore decided that 'much of the administration [will be] left in
the hands of the colonists'.[103] While acknowledging the risks in
creating a democracy whose citizens consisted largely of 'women and
girls who need a fresh start in life', the alternative was 'an unnatural
condition of things which are not strengthening to the character'.[104]

Ideas of democracy should, of course, be understood against the
background of women's claims to citizenship. These were hotly
contested, not least within the feminist movement of the time.
Miss Shaw, WTC superintendent, was thinking of something that
combined participatory democracy with Christian social work. As
she wrote to Helen Wilson shortly before the colony closed,

> Speaking vaguely, I feel the Colony ought to be on the lines of a
> Settlement, with people working, praying, living, & girls coming &
> going as it suits them, just a body of people willing to live community
> life of work & prayer (I purposely put the work first), & to a very
> large extent being self-supporting. It is all misty yet, but I see some
> outlines quite clearly, but only during these last few days.[105]

This was tied in with ideas about citizenship and belonging. As Christians and women's suffrage campaigners, the Colony's promoters
understood citizenship as connected to the 'spirit of common weal',
encouraging the women to attend collective worship, making
arrangements with a number of churches in the locality.[106] New
entrants were required to serve a period of probation before earning
the title of 'colonist', accompanied by the right to wear a red ribbon
and participate in the weekly meetings.[107] And while they learned

the skills of citizenship and the spirit of common weal, the women had to work.

Work was both redemptive and practical in value. The founders proclaimed that 'these women need work, which by its artistic and creative interest can offer them scope for their individuality, they also need industries which offer not only training but permanent employment'.[108] As well as market gardening, they were to learn domestic and country crafts such as toy-making and hand-weaving. While handicraft work was viewed as particularly therapeutic, the founders also emphasised the value of outdoor experience: As Maude Royston wrote in a suffragette magazine, 'For sick bodies and shattered nerves, nature herself is the greatest restorer.'[109] For Lilian Hay-Cooper, Christian feminist and biographer of Josephine Butler, work, citizenship and personality were inseparable: the Colony's aim was to train 'women of wholesome character, capable of being good home-makers, or of entering the industrial world as competitive and independent wage-earners'.[110]

After three years of fund-raising, the WTC opened in February 1917. Like so many other utopian communities, though, the initiative was short-lived, closing in 1919. Its promoters publicly blamed the warden's resignation to take up other forms of social work, the unsuitability of the building, and lack of time and funds.[111] Moreover, by 1919 the brand of feminism embodied in the WTC looked decidedly old-fashioned. Existing divisions within the suffrage movement were concealed for as long as women were denied the vote; after 1918, the sexual purity wing of the movement seemed conservative when set beside those who campaigned for birth control and sex education, let alone those radical spirits who sought to break altogether with conventional definitions of sexuality.[112] I have found no evidence that the WTC was riven by factionalism and feuding, perhaps because its democratic practices, important though they were, were subordinated to a clearly laid down hierarchy of managerial responsibilities, and perhaps because the founders, however enthusiastic about the role of colonies in promoting women's citizenship, had no intention of living in one themselves. Hay-Cooper portrayed the women colonists as 'human wreckage' living 'waste lives'.[113] These were utopian communities for others, with the middle-class promoters remaining firmly in the committee room.

Glorious failures?

With the possible exception of Whiteway, all of the utopian colonies can reasonably be described as failures. Few survived more than a few years, and those that did, like Starnthwaite and Whiteway itself, underwent considerable change in the process. But if they failed, they did not all fail in the same ways. Some of the underlying problems were similar, of course, such as dealing with those who refused to work, an inability to fund capital investment, and hostility from the authorities or local businesses. These tended to be more acute the greater the colonists departed from accepted norms and practices. But as Dennis Hardy notes of other utopian movements, the colonies faced two even more profound problems, partly of their own making: a reluctance to engage with political processes and organisations, combined with the very small level of support that the utopian colonies enjoyed.[114] Even though their core beliefs were connected to wider, more popular concerns – women's suffrage, the land, unemployment – the retreat from industrial capitalism or patriarchy also removed the colonists from the social movements that promoted and advanced these interests. George Bernard Shaw once said of the split between the Fellowship of the New Life and the Fabian Society that one group chose to 'sit among the dandelions, the other to organise the docks'.[115] Shaw, as ever, had a talent for coining a memorable phrase.

Notes

1 Board of Trade, *Report on Agencies and Methods*, 179–80.
2 J. Ruskin, *Fors Clavigera: Letters to the workmen and labourers of Great Britain*, vol. 2, G. Allen, London, 1907, 16.
3 S. Rowbotham, *Edward Carpenter: A life of liberty and love*, Verso, London, 2008, 66–7.
4 D. Hardy, *Alternative Communities in Nineteenth Century England*, Longman, London, 1979, 44.
5 M. S. Chase, 'Wholesome object lessons: The Chartist Land Plan in retrospect', *English Historical Review*, 118, 2003, 59–85.
6 M. Winstanley, *Ireland and the Land Question, 1800–1922*, Methuen, London, 1984, 27–30.
7 A. Howkins, 'From Diggers to Dongas: The land in English radicalism, 1649–2000', *History Workshop Journal*, 54, 2004, 13–14.
8 R. Blatchford, 'Land Nationalisation', *Co-operative Wholesale Societies Annual for 1898*, CWS, Manchester, 1898, 244.

9 H. V. Mills, *Poverty and the state, or work for the unemployed: an inquiry into the causes and extent of enforced idleness*, Kegan Paul & Tench, London, 1886, 2–6, 14.

10 Ibid., 16.

11 *Bristol Mercury and Daily Post*, 29 October 1892.

12 Mills, *Poverty*, 165–9.

13 *Report from the Select Committee of the House of Lords on Poor Law Relief*, 254–5.

14 *Report of the Land Nationalisation Society, 1888–9*, London, 1889, 21.

15 Board of Trade, *Report on Agencies*, 179.

16 *Pall Mall Gazette*, 1 April 1892.

17 *Leeds Mercury*, 15 February 1895.

18 Ibid.

19 Board of Trade, *Report on Agencies*, 180.

20 *Manchester Times*, 18 January 1895.

21 *Bristol Mercury*, 29 October 1892.

22 *Bristol Mercury*, 4 April 1893.

23 *Lancaster Gazette*, 12 April 1893.

24 Board of Trade, *Report on Agencies*, 180.

25 *Manchester Times*, 18 January 1895.

26 W. H. G. Armytage, *Heavens Below: Utopian experiments in England, 1560–1960*, Routledge & Kegan Paul, London, 1961, 312.

27 *Manchester Times*, 14 December 1900.

28 *The Times*, 17 February 1903.

29 RCPL, Appendix, Vol. VIII, *Minutes of Evidence*, HMSO, London, 1910, 172.

30 *Daily Chronicle*, 26 December 1893.

31 Ibid.

32 A. R. Wallace, 'The Remedy for Unemployment: Part 1', *Socialist Review*, June 1908, 314.

33 Ibid., 'The Remedy', 316–17.

34 M. Thomas, 'Paths to Utopia: anarchist counter-cultures in late Victorian and Edwardian Britain, 1800–1914', PhD Thesis, University of Warwick, 1998, 35–40.

35 *Labour Annual*, 1896, 58.

36 P. Kropotkin, *Fields, Factories and Workshops*, Nelson, London, 1912, 411–13.

37 N. Todd, *Roses and Revolutionists: The story of the Clousden Hill Free Communist and Co-operative Colony, 1894–1902*, People's Publications, London, 1986, 8–9.

38 *North Eastern Daily Gazette*, 25 February 1895; M. Bevin, 'The Rise of Ethical Anarchism in Britain, 1885–1900', *Historical Journal*, 69, 1, 1996, 158.

39 Quoted in Howkins, 'From Diggers', 15.
40 Armytage, *Heavens Below*, 312–14.
41 Reproduced in Todd, *Roses*, 27.
42 *Northern Echo*, 7 August 1896.
43 *Northern Echo*, 11 August 1896.
44 *Northern Echo*, 7 August 1896.
45 *Northern Echo*, 11 August 1896.
46 Todd, *Roses*, 46.
47 *Belfast Newsletter*, 22 September 1898.
48 Ibid.
49 *Sunderland Daily Echo*, 18 April 1902.
50 Rowbotham, *Edward Carpenter,* 250–1; Thomas, *Paths to Utopia*, 156–7.
51 Armytage, *Heavens Below*, 302–3.
52 Ibid., 344.
53 J. C. Kenworthy, 'The Work of the English Land Colonisation Society', in Hobson (ed.), *Co-operative Labour*, 117–18; ELCS, *Report upon farm labour colonies and farm settlements*, ELCS, London, 1893.
54 Armytage, *Heavens Below*, 334–7.
55 Bevin, 'Rise of Ethical Anarchism', 159; Thomas, *Paths to Utopia*, 144–7.
56 *Morning Post*, 13 January 1899.
57 J. C. Kenworthy, 'Leo Tolstoy', in Arthur [Compton-]Rickett (ed.), *Prophets of the Century*, Ward Lock & Co, London, 1898, 302.
58 A. Maude, *The Life of Tolstoy: Later years*, Dodd and Mead, New York, 1911, 546–7.
59 *Reynold's Newspaper*, 15 October 1899.
60 *Reynold's Newspaper*, 26 August 1900.
61 *Scotsman*, 2 August 1899.
62 N. Shaw, 'Whiteway Colony – the story of a pioneer experiment', *Community in Britain: A survey of community thought and activity,* Bruderhof Press, Ashton Keynes, 1938, 35–7.
63 *Reynold's Newspaper*, 26 August 1900.
64 *Reynold's Newspaper*, 15 October 1899; N. Shaw, *Whiteway: A colony in the Cotswolds*, Daniel, London, 1935, 129.
65 *Reynold's Newspaper*, 29 July 1900.
66 W. C. Hart, *Confessions of an Anarchist*, Richards, London, 1906, 80.
67 Shaw, 'Whiteway Colony', 36.
68 P. Salvesen, 'Getting Back to the Land: The Daisy Colony experiment', *North West Labour History Society Journal*, 10, 1984, 31–6.
69 *Labour Annual*, 1900, 115.
70 Thomas, *Paths to Utopia,* 174.
71 See www.whatwilltheharvestbe.com/about (accessed on 25 May 2012).
72 *Daily Mirror (DM)*, 14 July 1906.

73 *DM*, 16 July 1906.
74 *DM*, 14 July 1906.
75 *DM*, 16 July 1906; 17 July 1906; 18 July 1906.
76 *DM*, 21 July 1906.
77 *DM*, 23 July 1906.
78 *DM*, 25 July 1906.
79 *DM*, 27 July 1906.
80 *DM*, 4 August 1906.
81 *Daily Express*, 6 August 1906; *DM*, 6 August 1906.
82 *Evening Post*, 3 September 1906; *Scotsman*, 6 August 1906; *Times*, 10 August 1906.
83 *The Times*, 3 September, 4 September 1906.
84 *Daily Express*, 3 September 1906; *Daily Mail*, 6 September 1906.
85 *DM*, 10 September 1906.
86 *The Times*, 5 September 1906.
87 *The Times*, 19 July 1906.
88 *Daily Express*, 26 October 1906.
89 *The Times*, 19 July 1906.
90 J. A. R. Pimlott, *Toynbee Hall: Fifty years of social progress, 1884–1934*, Dent, London, 1935, 139–40.
91 *Evening Post*, 10 September 1910.
92 *Parliamentary Debates*, 2 March 1911.
93 *Parliamentary Debates*, 20 July 1916.
94 J. Lewis, *Women and Social Action in Victorian and Edwardian England*, Stanford University Press, Stanford CA, 1991.
95 E. Abbott, 'Municipal Employment of Unemployed Women in London', *Journal of Political Economy*, 15, 9, 1907, 515–16.
96 Ibid., 518.
97 L. Bland, '"Purifying" the Public World: Feminist vigilantes in late Victorian England', *Women's History Review*, 1, 3, 1992.
98 *The Times*, 19 February 1917.
99 *BMJ*, 26 November 1938.
100 *Proposed Scheme for a Women's Training Colony*, leaflet, no date [1915/1916], Modern Records Centre (MRC) MSS 16C/3/W/1.
101 *Globe*, 10 August 1917.
102 *Proposed scheme*; *Prospectus: Women's Training Colony*, no date [1915?], MRC MSS 16C/3/W/1.
103 *The Women's Training Colony* no date [?1917], MRC MSS 16C/3/W/2.
104 W. Clarke Hall, *The State and the Child*, Headley Brothers, London, 1917, 170–1.
105 Miss M. Shaw to Dr H. Wilson, 19 November 1918, MRC MSS 16C/3/LC.
106 *Prospectus: Women's Training Colony*, no date [1916?], MRC MSS 16C/3/W/2.

107 *Globe*, 10 August 1917.
108 *Proposed scheme*, MRC MSS 16C/3/W/1.
109 *Common Cause*, 27 April 1917.
110 *A Women's Training Colony*, 1916, MRC MSS 16C/3/W/3.
111 *Women's Training Colony*, leaflet, November 1919, MRC MSS 16C/3/W/7.
112 S. Rowbotham, *Dreamers of a New Day*, 71–80.
113 *A Women's Training Colony*, 1916, MRC MSS 16C/3/W/3.
114 D. Hardy, *Utopian England: Community experiments, 1900–1945*, Routledge, London, 2000, 271–3.
115 Cited in ibid., 209.

5

'The landless man to the manless land'
Labour colonies and the Empire

While most radicals and land reformers wanted to settle Britain, others defined their nation more broadly. For William Booth, the colonies were 'pieces of Britain distributed about the world'.[1] And if, as one provincial English journalist confidently asserted, 'town life is gradually producing a feebler type of physique in the English race', then the 'greater Britain over the seas' would warmly welcome citizens with 'strong arms and stout hearts'.[2] Economically, politically and militarily, then, were there not abundant reasons to train those who were unwanted in Britain, and resettle them on the lush pastures of the Empire or perhaps the United States?

Until the 1920s, most labour colony training for emigration was conducted by voluntary bodies. Government involvement was limited to local support for pauper emigration under the poor laws; most of the many British and especially Irish emigrants travelled with no state support; at most, they were financed by their families, or at a pinch by a local philanthropist. The Empire Settlement Act 1922, which allowed central government to support training and other activities, changed this balance. While the government continued to work with voluntary colonies, and most migrants went with limited formal preparation, the state opened a number of residential training centres for farming and domestic service overseas. Only with the world economic crisis of 1929 did the flow of Britons to the Dominions slow to a trickle, but by that time the principle was established that central government might provide training – including residential training – for the unemployed, including unemployed women.

Voluntarism and the state: the evolution of policy

Until the early 1920s, with a small number of exceptions, such as the Scottish crofters who were sent to Canada in 1889–90, national government took little part in emigration, and the role of local government was largely limited to the poor law bodies. Nationally, British governments were also anxious to avoid unwanted controversy in the Dominions, where local labour organisations resented the influx of immigrants competing with local labour.[3] In 1888, the House of Lords Select Committee on Poor Relief heard from several witnesses who supported state labour colonies. The Reverend Charles Henry Turner, of St George's-in-the-East, declared that the 'ordinary labourer' in London knew nothing about farm work, so that would-be emigrants needed to be prepared 'in home labour colonies'.[4] Their lordships were unimpressed, seeing any proposals for state intervention as the thin end of a long and horribly socialist wedge. The House of Commons Select Committee on Colonisation was no more sympathetic to the principle of state aid.[5] Charitable individuals and organisations, on the other hand, played an active role, particularly in the area of child emigration.

Until 1918, the field was largely left to the voluntary sector, though the South African experience gave greater impetus to the idea of state action. British attempts to settle a 'loyal' population on land seized from the Boers proved disappointing, with many of the new settlers hot-footing it for jobs in the towns and mines.[6] Earlier failures had simply reinforced government in its laissez-faire views.[7] This time, however, the government agreed to proposals from the Salvation Army and the Rhodes Trustees to launch an inquiry to investigate training for the land, led by the adventure writer, agricultural reformer and enthusiastic imperialist Henry Rider Haggard. In the short term Haggard's report had little direct influence, but its author was a celebrity, whose novels were read out loud to public schoolboys, and whose writings on farming were quoted by Kropotkin.[8] He followed his report by a speaking tour, in Britain and overseas, and used his considerable social and political networks to promote his views to the middle-class public at home and in the Dominions.

Haggard's report was largely taken up with descriptions of existing overseas settlement initiatives. As well as visiting Hadleigh, he toured Salvation Army settlements in the United States, finding himself troubled by the thought that proud Britons might turn into patriotic Americans. His own proposals focused instead on preparing the poor to occupy either 'the depopulated lands of the United Kingdom' or 'the fertile and uninhabited wastes of the Empire overseas'.[9] He presented Empire settlement not as charity but enlightened self-interest, for if nothing were done, the next recession would bring the 'desperate, ominous shapes of Misery and Want, and in their hands the sword of Socialism'.[10]

Still government held back. As we have seen, the 1905 Unemployed Workmen Act had given local distress committees increased powers to fund emigration, and also gave them the power to establish farm colonies.[11] But not all of those who supported labour colonies for land settlement at home shared Haggard's enthusiasm for Empire settlement. Supporting the Unemployed Workmen Bill in 1905, Keir Hardie complained that Laindon men had been sent to Canada, expressing the hope that future labour colonies would be used to 'grow food for the people of England from English soil … Those who were born in England should not be called upon to leave so long as one rood of it lay waste and untilled.'[12] Will Crooks attacked Haggard for urging that the unskilled be sent 'away to the colonies to be a burden to the colonies', rather than settled on the land at home.[13] The London Trades Council denounced William Booth and Wilson Carlisle for transporting 'for life thousands of the lower of the working classes as a pretended relief for the unemployment difficulty', while diverting attention from socialist proposals for social and economic change.[14]

Despite opposition, Haggard pursued his ideas for the rest of his life, exploiting colonial insecurities. He warned the Canadians that unless they accepted well-trained labourers from Britain, their land would succumb to the 'yellow peril'.[15] Canada, after recruiting Chinese labourers to build the national railroad, had passed legislation imposing prohibitive head taxes on further immigrants from China, and several provinces tried to ban Chinese migrants from owning land or even voting.[16] Similar fears tormented white Britons in Australia. In 1913, Haggard served as a member of the Dominions Trade Commission, along with his friend and fellow social imperialist Christopher Turnor, pressing for imperial migration and settlement.[17] In 1916 he was warning a lunchtime audience of the New South Wales branch of the Colonial Institute that 'another 200 years might see the western races "out"'.[18] Such arguments were designed to persuade his audience – white and British – to abandon any prejudice against unemployed cockneys. Nor were racial fears confined to the dominant elites: in 1892, the Australian Labour Federation, after attacking Booth and the Darkest England scheme, also called for an end to Italian, Chinese and kanaka (Pacific Island) immigration.[19]

Racial considerations, of course, worked both ways. From the British side, some feared the loss of good men and women. One London MP, for instance, lamented that instead of 'the unemployed or the ne'er-do-wells' it was 'the strong and the healthy' who emigrated; somewhat illogically, he then complained that Britain itself attracted 'the worst class of immigrant'.[20] Haggard, presumably with such criticism in mind, had prefaced his report with a eugenic insistence on keeping 'our best blood within our shores'.[21] He continued to press his proposals during the war, joining Turnor on a Royal Colonial Institute delegation to ask Bonar Law, as Colonial Secretary, to plan for peacetime land settlement in the Dominions.[22] An Australian newspaper enthusiastically praised Haggard and Turnor for remembering that the country's future security depended on 'a wider distribution of the Anglo-Saxon race, which has shown itself to be specially adapted for vigorous colonisation'.[23]

The real turning point came with the 1918 Khaki election. Lloyd George knew Haggard, and respected his ideas on agricultural reform, and appointed the enthusiastic imperialists Leo Amery and Viscount Milner to the Colonial Office, the former as Under-Secretary, the latter as Secretary of State. Haggard by now was more worried about the threat of communism, though Lloyd George had him knighted for his services on the Empire Settlement Committee. But Haggard was ageing, and had never been much of a political force. Amery by contrast was an adept and energetic politician who used his position to steer the Oversea Settlement Committee (OSC) into areas where the state might extend its support, such as the emigration of veterans, and leading the Empire Settlement Act 1922 through Parliament.[24] By allowing the government to support land settlement and emigration, through training and subsidised passages, the Act provided the legislative basis for a subsequent administration to introduce a programme of farm training in Britain for unemployed men. Voluntarism by no means disappeared, and the Christian labour colonies continued to train emigrants, but from the early 1920s the state was ever more active, as a partner and in its own right.

The Christian labour colonies

Walter Hazell, founder of Langley colony, had a long track record of campaigning over public health, poverty and electoral reform. He served for a time as Liberal MP for Leicester, helped create the Fresh Air Children's Mission, and supported Home Rule for Ireland, Scotland and Wales. He admired Ruskin as a social thinker, publishing his work, while earning a reputation as a fair employer who encouraged employee shareholding in the company.[25] Along with John Brown Paton and the radical journalist Andrew Mearns, in 1884 he founded the Self-Help Emigration Society (SHES). Starting work in 1885, with strong support from the Congregationalist Union and funded largely by charitable donations, SHES set itself the task of helping Britain's poor to resettle the 'new English-speaking countries' of the colonies.[26] With branches in a number of urban centres, the Society concentrated on publicising opportunities, helping fund would-be migrants, providing letters of introduction to employers, and lobbying for state-aided emigration.

SHES' first annual report cited an eight-stanza poem inspired by Froude's vision of Oceania, weaving virility and racial strength together:

In the great England over seas,
Where, giant-like, our race renews
Its youth, and stretched in sinuous ease
Puts on once more its manhood's thews.[27]

Impressed by the Reverend Andrew Mearns's 1883 pamphlet, *The Bitter Cry of Outcast London*, Hazell toured Canada, the United States, Australia and New Zealand. This convinced him that 'men of an inferior type' needed 'some kind of test and training in this country' to 'weed out' the unsuitable and prepare the suitable.[28] While he still hoped to settle at least some colonists in Britain, preferably as part of a thorough reform of land ownership, most of SHES' effort was on emigration overseas: by 1888 it had helped over 1,000 Britons settle in Canada.[29] In January 1890, he organised a meeting in Russell Square, London, to outline plans for a small training farm; Langley was the result.[30]

Initially, Hazell recruited mainly through the COS or SHES, or poor law connections. In London, the Whitechapel Guardians sent a small number of men to Langley, on the understanding that they would emigrate to Canada. Unfortunately, no one asked whether the Canadians would accept the East End unemployed, and the High Commission rejected them as paupers. The men duly went to New Zealand instead.[31] Despite this setback, the SHES continued to work with other bodies, and between 1892 and 1900, when Hazell closed his colony, it was estimated that almost half of the men 'emigrated and made a successful fresh start in the New World'.[32] By this time, the Congregationalist labour colony movement was focused on the CUSS colonies at Starnthwaite and Lingfield.

Hadleigh was a much larger operation and it was very well funded. The Salvationists also had good international connections, having expanded into Australia, Canada and the United States in the early 1880s, partly because some members had emigrated and taken its ideas with them.[33] Booth had ambitious plans for labour colonies as a conduit to the New World, depicting the labour colony as a stepping stone in transferring 'the entire surplus population of this country'.[34] Hadleigh was to test the suitability of potential emigrants and train the best in general agricultural skills, in a suitably Christian environment, before paying their passage to a new land. As Captain Clibborn reminded critics, Salvation Army emigrants would be 'the cream', selected only after a 'strict testing time' reinforced by a 'good moral training'.[35]

Haggard shared the Army's optimism about the quality of its Hadleigh emigrants.[36] The economist James Mavor, who had himself emigrated to Canada from Scotland, was sceptical, believing that 'knowledge of agriculture gained in this country is useless in Canada'. Moreover, he told a government inquiry, 'there is an assumption that you can take people who have been useless here and make them useful in Canada'.[37] While some might be trained beforehand, Mavor thought it likely to be on a small scale. This did not deter the Army which sent its Hadleigh superintendent, Commissioner David Lamb, to Canada to investigate the possibilities of large-scale emigration. By 1905, Salvationists had also built three colonies in the United States to take immigrants from Britain, one specialising in inebriates, one in farm workers, and one for the general unemployed.[38]

Others followed where the Salvationists led the way. The Anglican-inspired Church Army, the nonconformist CUSS, and the Presbyterian Church of Scotland all ran sizeable schemes, based on their farm training colonies in Britain. The CUSS saw emigration as a natural extension of its existing activities, and it had close ties to the SHES. Between 1902 and 1907, 286 men left Lingfield, of whom 96 went to Canada and one 'coloured man' to America.[39] Most Church Army emigrants initially sailed for Canada, where the Army maintained a base in Montreal, with an agent who helped them find work with farmers who were known through the church.[40] In 1905, the Church Army extended its interests to Australia, after an anonymous benefactor donated Hampstead Hall, in Essex, with 740 acres, for use as a farm colony.[41] Wilson Carlile announced that he could now send 3,000 families and 2,000 single men to Australia, provided the government helped fund passage and maintenance. The Church Army, though, viewed emigration as a 'desperate remedy', preferring home colonisation.[42] Few such schemes helped single women, for whom there was a ready demand in the colonies, though the British Women's Emigration Association opened a Colonial Training Home at Leaton, in Shropshire, in 1893 to provide domestic training to young women from workhouses, along with occasional private pupils, at a cost of 15 shillings per week.[43]

The early poor law colonies were also active. The SLCA sent Midlocharwood trainees to Canada, as did the Kirk colony at Cornton Vale.[44] The CUB sent men to Canada from Hollesley Bay during the depression of 1904–5 and afterwards, and also sent occasional groups from its Fambridge colony.[45] The Victoria League, founded in response to the South African War, gave encouraging lectures in Hollesley Bay.[46] However, the poor law authorities were hampered, not merely by Burns's hostility, but also by disagreements among municipal activists over the value of using emigration to tackle unemployment. State involvement remained limited, even at local level, while at national level it was almost unthinkable, until after the First World War had ended and unemployment reappeared.

Emigration and training under the Empire Settlement Act

Under Amery and Milner, British emigration policy reflected a blend of strategic imperial thinking, sentimental loyalties and domestic electoral concerns. Tactically, after the losses incurred during the war, state aid for settlement might be the price of continuing loyalty. After the war, the government set up an Oversea Settlement Department (OSD). With a staff seconded from the Colonial Office, advised by its newly created OSC, its initial role was to help facilitate emigration by veterans to the Dominions, men going to the land and women into service.[47] Its creation marked a new and direct role for the state, but voluntarism still dominated the field: the OSD worked with some forty societies, including the YMCA and Salvation Army, to encourage emigration.[48]

Meanwhile, government faced rising unemployment. In 1920, the British government invited its Dominions counterparts to a conference on empire settlement, arranging a parallel meeting whose purpose, according to Milner, was to develop 'an enduring policy of oversea settlement which should bring about the best distribution of the man power of the Empire and so to develop and strengthen the whole Empire'.[49] The assembled representatives largely endorsed Amery's proposals for a scheme of selective assisted passages for adults (child migration would continue as before), combined with systematic land settlement policies in the Dominions. The exception was South Africa, whose premier made it clear that 'the limited demand for white labour' was a non-negotiable block on any involvement.[50] Official British emigration policies were therefore directed at Australia, Canada and New Zealand.

Amery's Empire Settlement Act, which came into force in May 1922, allowed the government to help migration through assisted passages, initial allowances, and training, in partnership with approved voluntary agencies as well as the Dominions governments. Between 1922 and 1931, around 885,000 Britons emigrated to other parts of the Empire, at least a third of whom were assisted under the Act, mostly through subsidised passages.[51] Analysis of passenger lists shows that most emigrants to the Dominions were young adults and a majority were male; a particularly large number came from the coalfields, and in the 1920s at least, a disproportionate number were Scots.[52] Though still a minority, increasing numbers had at least some preliminary training. Initially, government turned to the labour colonies, and in 1921 the Ministry of Health wrote to London Boards of Guardians, urging them to make greater use of the CUB's resources, particularly for single long-term unemployed men.[53] By 1922, sixteen London boards were sending men to Hollesley Bay. Reportedly, rather than sending the most able, guardians sent their hardest cases, so that 'those who arrive at the Colony are probably those least likely to derive permanent benefit from the instruction'.[54] Belmont was even worse: one inspector found a 'stifling atmosphere of boredom', with able-bodied young men, in mid-morning, 'standing at the windows or lying on their beds'.[55] With many in the Dominions suspicious of 'pauper labour', using poor law colonies to train emigrants could do more harm than good. New training institutions were required if Dominion governments were to welcome the new migrants.

Government and the oversea training centres

On 4 November 1925, a group of young men jumped down from a lorry parked in front of a three-storey red brick building in rural Suffolk. The building had an institutional feel: erected in the 1760s, it had served until 1920 as the Bosmere and Claydon workhouse, then for three years was used to train unemployed ex-servicemen in basic industrial skills. The new inmates were to live there for six months, working the land and learning rudimentary agricultural techniques, before sailing for a new life in Canada or Australia. T. W. Ledger, a young unemployed miner from Walkley, in Sheffield, was among the group. After six months he had put on 11 lbs in weight, describing the food as 'very good', and had 'nothing but praise for the course', having spent some 'jolly evenings' listening to the piano, radio and gramophone; he commended the experience as 'a fine thing for any young fellow'.[56]

Although the previous administration had considered opening training centres for overseas emigration, Claydon Training Centre was largely a product of the 1924 minority Labour government. George Plant, secretary to OSC, later wrote that before 1924,

> everyone had the impression that the Labour Government and orga-nized labour would be opposed to a policy of Empire migration and settlement in principle. But as soon as Labour Ministers got to grips with the problem they saw the great possibilities of Empire settlement and development, and were no whit behind their political opponents in pressing on with the policy of State aid under suitable conditions.[57]

It was true that Margaret Bondfield and other leading Labour figures were sometimes critical of conditions facing British settlers, but they supported the principle. Bondfield, who had visited Canada to see for herself the lives of child migrants, advocated improved education for those who were to be sent to the Dominions. As under-secretary at the Ministry of Labour, she actively supported government training for emigration, as did her Cabinet colleague Jimmy Thomas at the Colonial Office.

Claydon actually opened in 1925, after Bondfield and her party had fallen from power, and a second centre opened at Brandon in 1926. The programme was aimed at single unemployed men between 19 and 25, extended to 29 in the case of ex-servicemen. Trainees applied through local labour exchanges, and had to provide two references. Robert Beddall, a Sheffield labourer who hoped to settle in Manitoba, started at Fermyn Woods in 1929, with the blessing of his headteacher, who commented that 'it is like him to desire to strike out and if he is successful all I can say is Canada will be richer and England poorer'.[58] Beddall and Ledger were expected to undertake heavy manual work as a form of 'testing', then train on Canadian equipment. Seven instructors, according to the Minister of Labour, had direct experience of farm work in Canada.[59] The day began with reveille at 7 a.m., with work starting at 8 and finishing at 5 in the afternoon.[60] The four-week testing period comprised 'log felling and splitting, clearing and stumping land, erection of fences, road making', followed by a month with the dairy herd, a month at ploughing, wagon driving and horse care, sessions on seeding, and periods of workshop instruction in rough carpentry and tool repairs.[61] It almost goes without saying that the men were weighed: in its first year, men at Claydon were said to have gained an average of 14 lbs each.[62]

If the main purpose of the centres was to train the men and harden their bodies, the Ministry of Labour quickly discovered that it was also thought responsible for their leisure. Lights out was at 10.30, leaving a long five-hour evening. Men stayed indoors or formed their own football and cricket teams, while some spent Saturday evenings in Ipswich.[63] Otherwise, opportunities were limited, and local residents complained that the trainees made 'an undue amount of noise and cause disturbance in other ways outside the Training Centre', causing the minister to make a personal visit.[64] At Brandon, camp manager Major Hall thought the problem was less the impact of the trainees on villagers than the other way round, writing to the Chief Constable of Norfolk to complain of 'the undesirable moral effect of the village on the trainees'.[65] The Ministry duly decided to appoint welfare officers.

More unexpectedly, the Unionist government in Northern Ireland got in on the act, though characteristically it promptly made a mess of things. The Ministry of Labour purchased Richhill Castle and 200 acres in County Armagh with a view to training batches of

75 unemployed men under the Empire Settlement Act 'in the rudiments of farm labour, rough carpentry, iron work, etc.'[66] Officials in Belfast had not thought to mention this to their counterparts in London, who learned about Richhill from a newspaper report.[67] Nor had they done their sums: within a month, Stormont discovered that it could not afford the passages to Canada.[68] Given the politics of Northern Ireland, this may have been as well.

With unemployment stubbornly stuck at over one million and a crisis in the coal industry, British policy makers looked at the Dominions with hope. In 1926, with the mine-owners' lockout at its height, the OSC sent its deputy chair to Canada to discuss emigration. Wilfrid Eady, a senior official in the Ministry of Labour, briefed the delegation beforehand to depict Britain's migration policy as primarily designed to deal with the under-population of the Dominions.[69] This was a classic piece of spin. Desperate to resolve a growing unemployment crisis, the government placed training and other migration issues high on the agenda of that autumn's Imperial Conference. Initially, the signs were encouraging. Stanley Bruce, Australia's prime minister, called for 'a true and co-ordinated development of the resources of the Empire and a better distribution of the white population' as ways of tackling 'the great problems that face us today as British people'.[70] When it came to detailed discussion, though, New Zealand was interested in training only as a way of 'testing boys', Canada wanted 'the trainee to be regarded as an experienced worker on arrival', South Africa only wanted skilled tradesmen and professionals, while Australia saw training as both 'eliminating unsuitable types, and providing the settler with an elementary acquaintance of farm life'.[71] Only when it came to women was there unanimity: all would take anyone healthy, young and able to bear white children.[72]

Recruitment of trainees lay largely with the Ministry of Labour, who controlled the labour exchanges, and also possessed a small but energetic training division. Recruitment was voluntary, though the Ministry instructed exchanges to report all who refused a place, adding that those who asked what would happen 'should be informed that it is necessary that they shall be genuinely seeking work and that the Chief Insurance Officer may require to consider whether refusal of the opportunity of training is consistent with the satisfaction of this condition'.[73] In other words, local officials could use considerable pressure. All applications were scrutinised by an interviewing panel consisting of the exchange manager and a representative of the training department. If selected, they were then told to undergo a medical examination before entering, covering not just health but also 'personal cleanliness'.[74] Surviving candidates were then considered by immigration officials from the Dominions, before finally being approved for training.[75]

As the mines started to reopen in 1927 after the long and bitter lockout, it rapidly became clear that the industry would not absorb all the male unemployed in the coal communities. As a stop gap, the OSD and Ministry of Labour agreed with the Canadian Government to arrange for 10,000 men, mainly from the coalfields, to emigrate as harvest workers. Unable to find enough shipping to take the full number, the British authorities sent 8,449 men, over 2,000 of whom stayed on in Canada after the harvest, while some returnees intended to emigrate in future. The main lesson that Osmond drew from the experience, though, was that in future, men would need proper 'testing' and selection well in advance.[76] With Canadian support, the Ministry decided to expand its facilities for training single men, with the aim of training or testing 6,000 harvest workers during spring 1929.[77]

Up to that point, Brandon and Claydon had only been filled 'with difficulty'. Nevertheless, Noel Barlow, then head of the Ministry of Labour's training department, reached agreement with the Army that an intake of 100 miners would be trained at its vocational training centre.[78] Even this was judged inadequate in light of the Industrial Transference Board (ITB) report in 1928. Created to advise the Government on how best to transfer 'surplus' labour out of the coalfields and other distressed areas, the ITB started with the 'fact' of 'surplus labour in certain industries' – a surplus which it calculated at around 200,000 workers, who would need to be transferred to other areas. While the ITB generally avoided measures that might increase government spending, it recommended a limited expansion of emigration, and proposed that the Ministry of Labour should open new farm training centres and women's hostels.[79] The Cabinet promptly referred the ITB's report to a committee, chaired by Winston Churchill as Chancellor of the Exchequer. Churchill's committee endorsed many of the ITB's proposals for training, and also suggested buying land in one of the Dominions for use as an 'Empire Colony', an interesting notion that the Cabinet did not adopt.[80]

In the short term, the Ministry added tented summer camps, offering twelve-week training courses on Forestry Commission land in Norfolk.[81] Five testing camps were also added: two in the English Midlands, at Fermyn Woods, Brigstock, near Kettering, and Bourne, Lincolnshire, two on the Welsh border, at Presteigne in Radnorshire and Shobdon, in Herefordshire, and one at Swanton Novers, in Norfolk.[82] Subsequently, the Ministry of Labour opened four new hutted centres to deal with the planned 6,000 trained men who had been promised. The new centres were at High Lodge, Cranwich and West Tofts in Norfolk, and Carstairs in Scotland.[83] Carstairs centre, for example, at Lampits Farm, in North Lanarkshire was a half-hour walk from Carstairs Junction railway station and with good road connections; there was also a dismantled railway line, which could be turned into a spur link. The hutted camp was on some 500 acres of farmland. There was also a two-storey stone dwelling house, with electric lighting from the camp generator, which was put to use as the administration building.[84] Some 4,456 men completed courses at the training and testing centres in 1929 – more than in all previous years together.[85]

Running the new centres posed unusual challenges for civil servants. Advertising the post of centre manager to its civil servants, the Ministry made it clear that this was not a routine administrative position:

> Applicants must have had experience of handling large numbers of men and of organizing and running camps. The Centre Manager will be responsible for the efficient conduct of the work at the camp and for the control of the men and of the staff. His duties will, therefore, call for the exercise of initiative, resourcefulness and tact. Most of the centres are situated in remote country districts and the Manager must be prepared for long hours of duty and rough conditions of living.[86]

Despite this demanding job description, there were 140 applicants in 1928.[87] Colonel Hogarth, centre manager at Bourne, came from the Ministry's Glasgow Division and was the only manager with a military title.[88] J. H. Owen, a third-class officer, was appointed camp manager at Presteign partly because he was 'a Welsh-speaking Welshman' who would manage the largely Welsh recruits.[89] Camp managers initially received the salary of a third-class officer (between £200 and £400 annually), and a monthly allowance of £5. Like all camp staff, they also received free board and lodging, valued by the Ministry at 15 shillings weekly.[90] As well as oversight of the trainees and responsibility for administration, they had to direct a sizeable and sometimes specialised staff, including drivers, cooks, and a team of instructors. Brandon even employed a warrener.[91]

Managing the trainees posed distinctive challenges. Discipline was a constant pressure: of 144 men whose course was terminated summarily in 1926, 69 were dismissed for 'unsatisfactory conduct', 15 for 'unsuitability', and 50 on grounds of health.[92] In three of the testing centres – Bourne, Fermyn Woods and Swanton Novers – welfare officers were appointed and paid by the YMCA to help relieve tensions.[93] The OSC produced a welter of publicity materials including books, pamphlets, posters and a number of films, one of them on the training centres.[94] Royal visits inevitably followed. The Prince of Wales visited Claydon in February 1926, accompanied by Sir Arthur Steel-Maitland as Minister of Labour, Noel Barlow from the Training Department, and the camp manager, Mr Steward. At the close of the visit, the Prince congratulated the men on their 'jolly good spirit'.[95] After returning to power in 1929, the Labour Government sent the heavyweight Secretary for the Dominions and former union leader Jimmy Thomas to visit Brandon. Addressing the trainees in the dining hall, Thomas reminded them that 'as they were of the same stock as those who had gone out and succeeded, there was no reason why they also should not succeed', sentiments apparently received with wild cheering.[96] Imperial identities were not merely rooted in British genes; they had to be created and maintained.

Politically, the overseas centres enjoyed a range of support, though some Conservatives were likely to criticise the training centres, mainly on the grounds that they were publicly funded. Sir Joseph Nall, a Manchester MP, thought that people who wanted to migrate should be responsible for preparing themselves, asking 'why spend public funds on the training of such individuals?'[97] If there was to be any new training, Churchill argued, then much of it should be paid for by the Dominions governments who would benefit.[98] In Scotland, Nationalists feared that state-sponsored migration would deplete the Scottish race. The Reverend Duncan Cameron, author of the spectacularly named report to the Kirk on *The Menace of the Irish Race to our Scottish Nationality*,[99] denounced emigration policy at a luncheon meeting of the City Business Club in Glasgow, telling his audience that 'unless drastic measures were taken to safeguard the

Scottish race in their native land', the Irish would be able 'to dictate the lines of policy'.[100] At its annual meeting, the Elgin Branch of the National Party heard Charles Davidson complain that: 'The finest went overseas, and were replaced by others not of the same stock, class or quality.' In case his audience missed the allusion to the Irish, Davidson added that 'Glasgow could tell us something of this.'[101] Fears of racial deterioration also worried nationalists in England, where Rider Haggard had tried to placate fears that the best would leave while the worst remained.

Strengthening voluntarism

The Empire Settlement Act led to the creation of a new, central training sector, but it also had consequences for the labour colonies. Existing colonies soon spotted a way of raising income, and such activity intensified after 1926, and particularly after the Imperial Conference. The Church of Scotland's committee on social work undertook to train approximately 100 men a year at Cornton Vale, sharing costs for maintenance, testing and transport within the UK, as well as providing an 'outfit for overseas', with the OSD.[102] A number of new labour colonies opened, with the aim of training poor Britons for emigration. First off the mark was Dr George Cossar, who in 1922 purchased a farm at Craigielinn, on Glennifer Brae near Paisley. In the subsequent decade, Cossar's Training Farms tested some 1,600 lads, and over a thousand emigrated.[103] Cossar was a multiply-talented and energetic man with a history of charity work among young people, who had served with the Royal Army Medical Corps, was wounded twice, and in 1918 received the military cross for bravery under fire.[104] He secured funding for Craigielinn under the Empire Settlement Act, and was able to offer free courses to any Scottish lad aged between 14 and 17 who undertook to settle overseas. In the first year's operation, sixty-five went to Australia and forty to Canada.[105] By 1928, Craigielinn was being funded to 'test' 100 lads a year with a view – and Cossar also had his own reception farm in Canada – to help lads settle in their new country.[106]

Cossar's operation faced a number of challenges. Tasmanian farmers complained in 1923 that the lads were 'tight-knit and aggressive'; worse, five reportedly committed suicide in the same year, suggesting that life in Australia was not what they had expected.[107]

Then the Dominions authorities rejected a high proportion of his young charges. In 1926, Cossar complained to Sir John Gilmour that he was 'much annoyed' when Australian representatives turned down five lads whom he had trained at Craigielinn.[108] As Secretary of State for Scotland, Gilmour took matters to the OSC secretariat, who refused to intervene in what they saw as an Australian policy matter, suggesting that Cossar redirect his complaint to Australia House.[109] Canadian immigration authorities also took a dim view of some Cossar lads; several were deported as unsuitable, including several young Scots who had served prison sentences back home.[110] The British Government was also reluctant to challenge internal Canadian decisions, despite lobbying from Cossar.[111]

Cossar repeatedly complained of challenges in sending Scottish lads 'from the poorer parts away because of the standard of physique required'.[112] Marjory Harper suggests, reasonably, that Cossar neither accepted nor understood the principles of selective migration; he was interested in improving not the Empire but the boys' lives.[113] An inveterate lobbyist, Cossar persuaded the New Brunswick Provincial Government to let him bring out, 'as an experiment, twenty boys a year who did not reach the present high standard of physique'.[114] Australia posed a more difficult challenge. Entry was simplest for those who took an assisted passage, after being 'nominated' by a responsible person in Australia, who assumed liability for their upkeep until they started work. The authorities in Australia could also 'requisition' boys and young men to work on the land, but claimed the ITB, 'a physical standard so severe is exacted as to result in the rejection of a large proportion of applicants'.[115] Cossar never did crack the Australians' resolve.

Cossar's was not the only new initiative. In 1927, the Hudson's Bay Company approached the OSD with a proposal for a labour colony on a 250–acre farm at Brogborough, in Bedfordshire, where it planned to train 100 men, aged 16–35 – half bound for Australia and half for Canada – for periods of 4 to 10 weeks.[116] The OSD was willing to meet half of the operating costs, but was anxious to know from the Ministry of Labour whether it was likely to run on a comparable standard to Claydon.[117]

The Empire Settlement Act also encouraged existing labour colonies to align their emigrant training with government policies. The Salvation Army was naturally at their head, negotiating with the OSC to secure funding for its emigration activities, including the training provided at Hadleigh.[118] While men learned basic farming, women were trained as servants or housewives. Young men were taken in for a programme of eight or so weeks, learning rough carpentry, basic cooking, boot repair and other handicrafts at one of the Salvation Army's London homes, then transferring to Hadleigh where they were introduced to horse handling, dairy work and other farm tasks. After this confessedly 'rudimentary training', the Army sent them to Canada.[119]

In 1926, the YMCA reached agreement with the Church of Scotland to send single men and young married men to Cornton Vale for training. It also announced plans to use Cossar's training farm at Craigielinn for lads of 14–19, as well as for a larger preparation centre in England, using Osborne College on the Isle of Wight. With these facilities, the YMCA hoped to send out 2,000 young men and lads a year.[120] Glasgow Parish Council decided in 1927 that it would also send unemployed young men to Cornton Vale for training, and Govan Council followed suit, with the Kirk's social work department paying for an outfit, fares for the passage, and landing money.[121] In exchange for its grant, the Kirk agreed to give its Cornton Vale trainees 'careful instruction in general farm work, wood cutting and grubbing, milking and dairy work, care of horses, poultry and pigs and other similar work together with technical training in carpentry, harness making and blacksmithing'.[122] Between thirty and forty men were still being trained for emigration at Cornton Vale in spring 1929.[123]

As with the state centres, activities were expanded again after the ITB report was published. Amery's OSD reached agreement with a number of voluntary agencies to provide hostels for training boys and young women, including a small summer camp at Witney in Oxfordshire for jobless Boy Scouts from County Durham, while Glasgow Parish Council was funded to place young lads on private farms.[124] The Ministry also funded family training through the Catholic Emigration Society, telling the Treasury that it trained the men while the Society supported their dependants.[125] In the period up to 1929, the Empire Settlement Act permitted the creation of state training farms, while also providing state support to the voluntary labour colonies. But in 1929 the onset of the depression brought adult emigration shuddering to a halt.

The deepening crisis

1929 saw Labour back in power. The party manifesto promised a range of measures to deal with unemployment, including 'Training and assistance by agreements with the Dominions for those who wish to try their fortunes in new lands'.[126] Australia was first to experience problems, at least so far as men were concerned, announcing the suspension of its assisted passages scheme in November. By the early 1930s, more people were leaving Australia than were coming in.[127] Canada was a better prospect, though the 1929 harvest was a poor one and the Dominion government decided to exclude single men from its assisted passages scheme, causing the Ministry of Labour to fund the journey for single men who were unemployed. Demand fell further in 1930, with Australia limiting its requirements to young single women for domestic work and lads for farm work.[128]

The Ministry of Labour closed its five testing centres in June 1929, while recruitment to the five training centres fell when potential applicants learned of difficulties overseas.[129] John Reginald Passmore noted in September that Fermyn Woods and Presteigne were being used for 'reconditioning purposes', beefing up unemployed men for public works jobs at home, and would do so 'for some time'. Bourne, Swanton Novers and Shobdon were closed, and although he planned to re-open them for training purposes in December, they would be training emigrants for no more than three months during the coming winter.[130] Nevertheless, the Ministry was bullish in its discussions with the Treasury, reporting in February 1930 that 5,291 men – mostly unemployed – had applied to train for farm work in Canada, of whom 3,119 had been interviewed by Canadian authorities and 1,324 approved.[131] Yet a mere 1,138 completed their courses in 1930, barely a quarter of what it had been in 1929, and in the winter the Ministry brought the programme to a close. The training centres were henceforth to be used for 'reconditioning', though the Ministry decided to sell Columbie Farm at Carstairs.[132] Purchased in 1928 for training emigrants, Columbie offered few opportunities for heavy manual work of the kind required for 'reconditioning'.[133] In a weak agricultural market, the farm and woods were sold separately between 1931 and 1933.[134]

Voluntary agencies too were inevitably affected. At Cornton Vale, the Kirk was still training some 30–40 men when the Canadian Government announced the end of its £2 passages. Although the trainees came from across Scotland, and not solely from the depressed areas, the Ministry agreed to treat the men as though they were its own trainees, and give them additional support to compensate for the increased cost of migration.[135] In 1931, the OSD withdrew its support from a number of the training centres, as part of the government's policy of retrenchment.[136] The Kirk proved remarkably reluctant to accept that its emigration work was over; as late as 1938, it held a sum of £2,000 in its budget at Cornton Vale, in readiness for a new emigration programme.[137] Cossar's work proved less durable and in 1932, the Cossar Boys' Training Farms were wound up. At the final subscribers' meeting, a sorrowful Cossar confessed that 'circumstances were going dead against them'. He hoped that Craigielinn Farm could continue to help 'unemployed lads and boys on probation to receive training for farm work', but in Britain rather than overseas.[138] Shortly afterwards, the farm was handed over to the Kirk, whose social work committee had effectively shared the management with Cossar for a number of years.[139]

Government policy in Britain was slow to respond to this deepening crisis. Initially, the government believed that the block on migration was temporary. Then, in April 1930, the Ministry of Labour told the Treasury that the Australians and Canadians were acting on simple prejudice against 'assisted' men. Nevertheless, the Ministry claimed, 'a man migrating for farm work is better with training than without it; and any future demand for men with work on the land is almost certain to resolve itself into a request for men trained and tested, as they have been at the centres'.[140] Passmore, the Ministry of Labour's director of training, was still maintaining in June 1931 that 'it would appear to be unsafe to assume that migration will not be resumed in the course of a year or two'.[141]

In 1930, the government appointed a Committee on Empire Migration to consider the matter. Its members included G. D. H. Cole, Oxford economist, political theorist and libertarian socialist; Alexander Carr-Saunders, eugenicist and professor of social sciences at the University of Liverpool, with a background in the settlement movement; Captain Lionel Ellis, a veteran of the trenches and secretary to the National Council for Social Service; and Haggard's old friend the agricultural expert and English patriotic socialist Christopher Turnor.[142] Viscount Astor, Unionist politician, newspaper owner and friend of David Lloyd George, took the chair.

The committee concluded that many of the traditional arguments in favour of Dominions migration had weakened as living standards in Canada and Australia had fallen. They also took a eugenicist view of emigration as 'a highly selective process' which 'draws unduly upon those elements in the population of which this country has most need'.[143] The main remaining argument for emigration was, they thought, its contribution to Britain's strategic interests.[144] So far as training young men was concerned, the Committee believed that while the centres helped eliminate the unsuitable and build 'the morale and physique of would-be migrants', they should only be paid for by public money if confined to the unemployed.[145]

As the committee's report was published after the collapse of the Labour government in August 1931, its influence was minimal. Nevertheless, it gives some insights into the mindset of senior policy thinkers, and its emphasis on the strategic value of emigration reappeared periodically through the 1930s. As late as 1938, the Oversea Settlement Board was urging the Dominions governments to 'take into account not only considerations of internal policy but also their responsibilities in relation to other members of the Commonwealth'. An 'adequate and homogeneous populations in the oversea Dominions' would require replenishment, 'as far as possible by people of British stock'. Parliament even extended the Empire Settlement Act in 1937, allowing government to support agreed schemes of migration, and the Board was keen to assist, including through 'training or testing in this country or overseas'.[146] But nothing came of this enthusiasm.

Looking back at the history of state supported emigration, the OSC reflected in 1928 that 'the results so far achieved have fallen far short of the hopes'. The main problem, in their view, arose from the 'industrial habits and townward bent' of the British, and their 'consequent unwillingness, and, without training, unfitness, to take advantage of openings overseas'.[147] In retrospect, George Plant thought his department's experience of 'all these schemes of testing and training' showed that 'those which operate in the United Kingdom do not add materially to the actual numbers of assisted migrants'. Between 1922 and 1934, he calculated, people tested or trained in UK amounted to no more than 15 per cent of boys, 0.8 per cent of single men, 2.3 per cent of single women and 0.2 per cent of families assisted under the Empire Settlement Act. He added, sourly, that this was at an average cost 'per unit of £8, £18, £11 and £31 respectively'.[148] The residential farm training programme had been particularly expensive. Contrary to the claims of some Australian historians today, such training was simply not possible 'at minimal cost', requiring as it did a sizeable outlay on land, buildings, transport, equipment, people and – usually – animals.[149] Maintaining the white settler population in the Dominions was expensive, requiring political effort and financial investment, as well as a degree of sheer faith.

Notes

1 Booth, *In Darkest England*, 144.
2 *Liverpool Mercury*, 14 March 1894.
3 *Brisbane Courier*, 5 February 1892; *Argus*, 5 March 1904; *Western Mail*, 30 September 1905.
4 *Select Committee of the Lords on Poor Law Relief*, 191.
5 K. Williams, '"A Way out of our Troubles": The politics of Empire settlement, 1900–1922', in S. Constantine (ed.), *Emigrants and Empire: British settlement in the Dominions between the wars*, Manchester University Press, 1990, 22.
6 Ibid., 28.
7 E. Richards, *Britannia's Children:Emigration from England, Scotland, Wales and Ireland since 1600*, Continuum, London, 2004, 191.
8 P. Kropotkin, *Fields, Factories*, 95.
9 H. Rider Haggard, *The Poor and the Land, being a report on the Salvation Army Colonies in the United States and at Hadleigh, England, with a scheme of national land settlement*, Longman's, Green & Co, London, 1905, xxvii–xxviii.
10 Ibid., xxix.
11 *Parliamentary Debates*, 20 June 1905.
12 Ibid.
13 *Minutes of Evidence on Rider Haggard's Report*, 139–44.
14 *The Times*, 2 October 1905.
15 *The Times*, 18 April 1905.
16 N. Gogia and B. Slade, *Immigration*, Fernwood, Halifax NS, 2011.
17 *Brisbane Courier*, 2 April 1913.
18 *Sydney Morning Herald*, 29 April 1916.
19 *Brisbane Courier*, 5 February 1892.
20 *Parliamentary Debates*, 20 June 1905.
21 Haggard, *Poor and the Land*, xviii.
22 *Royal Colonial Institute Yearbook, 1916,* London, 1916, 46.
23 *Queenslander*, 10 July 1920.
24 Williams, "A Way Out", 35–41.

25 *Leicester Chronicle*, 25 August 1894.

26 *Here and There: First report on the work of the SHES*, 1886, 2.

27 Ibid., 16.

28 R. C. Hazell, *Walter Hazell, 1843–1919*, Hazell, Watson & Viney, London, 1919, 23.

29 *Liverpool Mercury*, 23 March 1888.

30 *Pall Mall Gazette*, 31 January 1890.

31 F. C. Mills, 'Land and Poor Law Guardians', in J. A. Hobson (ed.), *Co-operative Labour,* 103–7.

32 Hazell, *Walter Hazell*, 24.

33 M. Langfield, 'Voluntarism, Salvation and Rescue: British juvenile migration to Australia and Canada, 1890–1939', *Journal of Imperial and Commonwealth History*, 32, 2, 2004, 88.

34 W. Booth, *In Darkest England*, 148.

35 *Birmingham Daily Post*, 12 September 1892.

36 *Minutes of Evidence on Rider Haggard's Report*, 18.

37 *Minutes of Evidence on Rider Haggard's Report*, Vol. II, 19.

38 J. Harris, *Unemployment and Politics*, 130.

39 *RCPL*, Appendix, Vol. VIII, *Minutes of Evidence*, HMSO, London, 1910, 163.

40 *Minutes of Evidence on Rider Haggard's Report*, 54.

41 Ibid.

42 E. Rowan, *Wilson Carlile and the Church Army*, Hodder & Stoughton, London, 1905, 302.

43 J. Bush, '"The Right Sort of Women": Female emigrators and emigration to the British Empire, 1890–1910', *Women's History Review*, 3, 3, 1994, 392.

44 *Tenth annual report of the Scottish Labour Colony Association*, 1906; *Thirteenth annual report of SLCA,* 1909, NAS HH57/70.

45 H. B. Lees Smith, 'The London Unemployed Fund, 1904–5', *Economic Journal*, 16, 61, 1906, 156, *RCPL*, Appendix, Vol. VIII, 61.

46 E. Riedi, 'Women, Gender and the Promotion of Empire: The Victoria League, 1901–1914', *Historical Journal*, 45, 3 (2002), 590.

47 G. F. Plant, *Oversea Settlement: Migration from the United Kingdom to the Dominions*, Oxford University Press, London, 1951, 64–73 .

48 A. C. C. Hill and I. Lubin, *The British Attack on Unemployment*, Brookings Institution, Washington DC, 1934, 118.

49 *Conference of Prime Ministers and Representatives of the United Kingdom, the Dominions and India*, HMSO, London, 1921, 59.

50 *Conference of Prime Ministers, 1921*, 8.

51 R. L. Schnell (1995) 'The Right Class of Boy: Youth training schemes and assisted emigration to Canada under the Empire Settlement Act, 1922–39', *History of Education*, 24, 1 73–90.

52 M. Harper and N. J. Evans, 'Socio-economic Dislocation and Inter-war

Emigration to Canada and the United States', *Journal of Imperial and Commonwealth History*, 34, 4, 535 and 540–2.

53 H. W. S. Francis, Circular 253 to Metropolitan Boards of Guardians, 7 October 1921, NA MH63/7.

54 CUB, Report in relation to activities in operation at Hollesley Bay Colony, 3 July 1922, NA MH63/7.

55 E. C. Blight to C. F. Roundell 29 February 1928, NA MH68/134.

56 *Sheffield Daily Independent*, 17 February 1926.

57 Plant, *Oversea Settlement*, 131–2 .

58 Cited in B. Simon, 'Rebert Beddall at Brigstock Camp', *Bygone Brigstock*, 12, 2011, 12.

59 *Parliamentary Debates*, 27 June 1928.

60 *Sheffield Daily Independent*, 17 February 1926.

61 Ibid.

62 *The Times*, 1 February 1926.

63 *Sheffield Daily Independent*, 17 February 1926.

64 J. A. Barlow to G. C. Anderson, 28 June 1926, NA LAB2/1775/SE729.

65 E. R. Parminter, 30 December 1926, NA LAB2/1775/SE729.

66 C. H. Blackmore, Cabinet Secretary, Belfast, to S. J. Baker, Home Office, 30 September 1926, Conacher to Blackmore, 29 September 1926, PRONI CAB/9C/20.

67 Baker to Blackmore, 25 September 1926, PRONI CAB/9C/20.

68 C. M. Martin-Jones to Blackmore, 20 October 1926, PRONI CAB/9C/20.

69 Eady to T. C. Macnaghten, July 1926, NA DO/57/13.

70 *Imperial Conference, 1926. Appendices to the summary of proceedings*, HMSO, London, 1927, 20.

71 Minutes of meeting, 25 October 1926, NA CAB/32/62B.

72 Ibid.

73 Circular to all Divisional Controllers and Exchange Managers and Branch Manager, Brandon, 13 October 1926, NA LAB2/1260/ED4126.

74 Ibid.

75 *Parliamentary Debates*, 10 February 1926; Circular to all Divisional Controllers and Exchange Managers and Branch Manager, Brandon, 13 October 1926, NA LAB2/1260/ED4126.

76 *Report of the OSC for 1928*, HMSO, London, 1929, 22.

77 *Report OSC 1928*, 27.

78 J. A. N. Barlow, note, 25 August 1927, NA LAB2/1275/ET5924.

79 *ITB Report*, HMSO, London, 1928, 48–9..

80 Unemployment Policy Committee, 10 July 1928, Report of Unemployment Policy Committee, 21 July 1928; Interim Report of the Migration Sub-Committee, 20 July 1928, NA CAB24/374.

81 *Report OSC 1928*.

82 Ministry of Labour (MoL), *Annual Report, 1928*.

83 MoL, *Annual Report, 1929*.
84 Note by J. Watt, Chief Valuer, Scotland, 15 October 1932, NA LAB2/2034/2F/1572.
85 MoL, *Annual Report, 1929*.
86 General Vacancy Circular, 23/9/29, NA LAB2/1778/CEB202.
87 Selection of Officers for Posts of Managers of Testing Camps, 20 December 1928, NA LAB2/1778/CEB202.
88 Ibid.
89 A Norman, Note of meeting with Passmore on future of Testing and Transfer Centres, 9 May 1929, NA LAB2/1778/CEB202.
90 MoL to Treasury, 1 October 1929, NA LAB2/1778/CEB202.
91 Hill? to Steward and Hall, 23 January 1928, NA LAB2/1775/SE729.
92 *Parliamentary Debates*, 6 April 1927.
93 A. K. Yapp, YMCA, to Passmore, 9 May 1929, NA LAB2/1778/CEB202.
94 *Sheffield Daily Independent*, 14 February 1928; *Report of the OSC 1928*, HMSO, London, 1929, 29.
95 *The Times*, 10 February 1926.
96 *The Times*, 9 December 1929.
97 *Parliamentary Debates*, 14 April 1927.
98 The Empire Settlement Act Amendment Bill – note by the Chancellor of the Exchequer, 26 March 1928, NA CAB24/193.
99 *Scotsman*, 15 May 1923.
100 *Stirling Journal and Advertiser*, 15 April 1926.
101 *Scotsman*, 1 April 1935.
102 Agreement between HM Secretary of State for Dominion Affairs and the Convener of the Church of Scotland Committee on Social Work, 10 November 1926, NA LAB/2/1236/ED0307.
103 *Scotsman*, 19 March 1932.
104 *BMJ*, 21 September 1918.
105 *Parliamentary Debates*, 28 May 1924.
106 Young Men's Christian Association, *Opportunities Overseas for the Youth of To-day*, Migration Department, YMCA, London, no date [1928?].
107 M. D. Prentis, *The Scots in Australia*, University of New South Wales Press, Sydney, 2008, 94.
108 Cossar to Sir John Gilmour, Scottish Office, 1 February 1926, NAS AF51/174.
109 G. F. Plant, Oversea Settlement Committee, to Cossar, 16 February 1926, NAS AF51/174.
110 M. Harper, *Emigration from Scotland between the Wars: Opportunity or exile?*, Manchester University Press, Manchester, 1998, 172.
111 Geoffrey Whiskard, Oversea Settlement Department, to David Milne, 9/4/1930, NAS AF51/174.

112 G. C. Cossar to Hon. Wm Adamson, Secretary of State for Scotland, 26 March 1930, NAS AF/51/174.

113 Harper, *Emigration from Scotland*, 184.

114 Cossar to Hon. William Adamson, Secretary of State for Scotland, 25 April 1930, NAS AF51/174.

115 ITB, *Report*, 41.

116 Col. O'Kelly, Canada Building, to Passmore, 31 Dec 1925, NA LAB/2/1279/ET425.

117 Eady to Barlow, 27 July 1927, Draft agreement between Secretary of State for Dominion Affairs and Hudsons Bay Company Overseas Settlement Ltd, 1927, NA LAB/2/1279/ET425.

118 *Parliamentary Debates*, 26 March 1923.

119 *Inverness Courier*, 7 October 1924.

120 *Scotsman*, 11 December 1926; *The Times*, 11 December 1926.

121 Harper, *Emigration from Scotland,* 170–1.

122 Agreement 10/11/1926 between Secretary of State for Dominion Affairs and Convener of the Church of Scotland Committee on Social Work, NA LAB2/1236/ED0307.

123 F. G. Bowers to Sydney Turner, HM Treasury, 8 March 1929, NA LAB2/1236/ED0307.

124 L. S. Amery, Oversea Settlement – Recent Developments, 6 November 1928, NA CAB24/198; Note by J. A. Barlow, Ministry of Labour, 22 August 1928, NA LAB2/1236/EDO574; *Children's Newspaper*, 14 September 1929.

125 Passmore to Bindloss, 2 March 1928, NA LAB2/1237/EDO700.

126 *Labour's Appeal to the Nation*, Labour Party, London, 1929, 5.

127 Langfield, 'Voluntarism, Salvation and Rescue', 102.

128 MoL, *Annual Report 1930*.

129 MoL, *Annual Report 1929*.

130 Passmore to Norman, 17/9/29, NA LAB2/1778/CEB202.

131 J. W. Todd to Treasury, 25 February 1930, NA LAB2/1778/CEB202.

132 Labour Emergency Expenditure Committee, Proposal, 28 April 1930, NA LAB2/1384/8.

133 Passmore to Bindloss, 17 March 1930, NA LAB2/2040/ET6119.

134 [Illegible] to Watson, Treasury, 5 March 1931, NA LAB2/1275/ET6041; Passmore to Allen, 6 June 1933, NA LAB2/2040/ET6119.

135 Bowers to Sydney Turner, Treasury, 8 February 1929, NA LAB/2/1236/ED0307.

136 W. G. Ives, OSD, to Passmore, 29 December 1931, NA LAB/2/1279/ET425.

137 *Stirling Journal and Advertiser*, 16 June 1938.

138 *Scotsman*, 19 March 1932.

139 *Glasgow Herald*, 10 June 1933.

140 Labour Emergency Expenditure Committee, Proposal, 28 April 1930,

NA LAB2/1384/8.
141 Passmore to Reid, 15/6/31, NA LAB/21271/2/F2255.
142 R. Douglas, 'The National Democratic Party and the British Workers' League', *Historical Journal*, 15, 3, 1972, 544–5.
143 Economic Advisory Council, *Committee on Empire Migration. Report*, HMSO, London, 1932, 11–12.
144 *Committee on Empire Migration. Report*, 29.
145 Ibid., 48.
146 *Report of the Oversea Settlement Board, May 1938*, HMSO, London, 1938, 2, 4–5, 19.
147 *Report OSC1928*, HMSO, London, 1929, 10–12.
148 Plant, *Oversea Settlement*, 145–6.
149 E. Daniel, '"Solving an Empire Problem": The Salvation Army and British juvenile migration to Australia', *History of Education Review*, 36, 1, 2007, 33.

6

Transference and the Labour government, 1929–31

'On the whole', Beatrice Webb confided to her diary in 1929, 'we are satisfied with the result of the General Election.' On 1 June, Beatrice and Sydney sat up with their friends Harold and Frida Laski until 2.30 a.m. to listen to the results. Beatrice found herself 'almost hysterical' at 'the flowing tide of Labour victories' and 'the final collapse of the Liberal Party'.[1] She had little to say about the Conservatives, who gained more votes than Labour but won twenty-seven fewer seats. Under Britain's first-past-the-post system, Ramsay MacDonald found himself leading a minority Labour government for the second time; a week after the election, Sydney became Colonial Secretary, sitting in the upper house as Lord Passfield. Margaret Bondfield, the former shop assistant and union leader, replaced Sir Arthur Maitland-Steel as Minister of Labour.

Bondfield, who had been Tom Shaw's parliamentary secretary in 1924, was in her mid-50s when she became Britain's first female Cabinet minister. Brought up a Congregationalist, she had a long track record of political and union activity. As an active suffragist – that is, arguing for complete equality in voting for all men as well as women, she spoke out against the privileged property franchise being claimed by what she saw as the middle-class leaders of the suffragette movement.[2] As secretary of the Women's Labour League, she had campaigned for unemployed women, and was involved in plans for a women's labour colony. By 1918, she was a formidable figure in the British labour movement, becoming president of the Trades Union Congress (TUC) general council in 1923, as well as MP for Northampton; losing her seat after the 1924 crisis, she was back in 1926 as MP for Wallsend.

MacDonald's second government came to power barely four months before the Wall Street crash. MacDonald's Cabinet relied on

Liberal MPs to get its legislative programme through. It inherited high levels of unemployment, and faced massive social tensions. It also inherited a deeply problematic set of compromises over unemployment relief. While there was a national unemployment insurance system, it did not cover all workers, and it combined the principle of insurance with elements of the poor relief system. In particular, once the great unrest of the post-war years had disappeared, the government, in 1921, introduced a clause requiring claimants who had exhausted their insured benefits to demonstrate that they were genuinely seeking work before they could claim 'uncovenanted' benefit. If in doubt, labour exchange officials could refer a claim to the local employment committee, who had power to reduce or even disallow the claim entirely. Thus those who were uninsured or had exhausted their insurance could face the rigours of a poor law that had been amended and adjusted but never fully overhauled, with all the stigma of pauperism attached. Little wonder that the Communist-led activists of the National Unemployed Workers' Movement (NUWM), combining local casework with imaginative public campaigns, found an audience.

While the Communist Party had little influence outside London and Glasgow, Wal Hannington was a popular and effective leader of the NUWM. In 1929, the Party picked Hannington to fight Wallsend, and 'expose' Bondfield as a 'social fascist'. Bondfield had the satisfaction of seeing Hannington come bottom of the poll, but the NUWM was not so easily dealt with. Fresh from a lively campaign against the Canadian harvesters programme in 1928, the NUWM held its second hunger march early in 1929, and followed up with what Richard Croucher describes as a 'major mobilisation' in the summer over the impact of the 'not genuinely seeking work' clause.[3]

Bondfield faced more serious challenges in Parliament, where her party lacked a majority, and in Cabinet, where she had to fight for what the Treasury presented as a spendthrift ministry. Beatrice Webb described this tough and forceful woman along with two other Labour MPs, Susan Lawrence and Ellen Wilkinson, as 'distinctly celibates', pouring energy into ceaseless political activity and giving no thought to 'emotional companionship'.[4] Having publicly opposed the Great War, Bondfield was no stranger to controversy, and in 1927 the TUC denounced her for serving as a member of the Blanesburgh Committee on Unemployment Insurance.[5] As Rodney

Lowe points out, Bondfield was perfectly able to fight the Treasury when she wanted, but she was hardly an economic radical.[6] Nor was there any obvious reason why she should have opted for a radical rise in public spending to stimulate economic growth. Most contemporaries saw the British depression as comparatively gentle by international standards, and anyway there was no consensus on the best way of lifting the economy out of depression.[7]

Bondfield also faced a tough public relations battle. Sympathy for the unemployed could all too easily give way to contempt for social parasites. As Jimmy Thomas told trainees at Brandon, British public opinion all too easily forgot that 'the so-called "dole" was an unemployment insurance fund to which the workers had contributed'.[8] MacDonald's government had relaxed many of the restrictions facing claimants, and in January 1930 Bondfield increased benefit rates. The National Insurance Act 1930 also amounted to an acceptance by government that unemployment benefits could no longer be funded under the insurance principle. As unemployment rose, so the costs of unemployment benefits soared, from £12 million in 1928 to about £125 million in 1931, triggering widespread and ultimately fatal criticisms of Labour's alleged extravagance.[9] Facing such monumental challenges, how would Bondfield handle the training programmes and institutions that she had inherited?

Transfer and residential training

Bondfield's ministry in 1929 was responsible for a patchwork of training institutions. As well as the five oversea training centres, and the mothballed testing centres, it still had links with the Army vocational training centre, and with Glamorgan County Council's demonstration farm at Pencoed. It also had three residential training centres for women and eight non-residential training centres which were used for handyman training. It ran eighty or so juvenile instruction centres, as well as supporting training for young people in centres belonging to local authorities and voluntary agencies, and also 39 home training centres belonging notionally to the Central Committee for Women's Training and Employment (CCWTE). Days before the election was held, the Ministry of Labour had responded to the ITB report by opening, what it called, five Transfer Instructional Centres (TICs), aimed at physically 'reconditioning' men to suit them for transfer to work away from the depressed areas. Two were hutted camps, previously used as 'testing centres', at Presteigne and Fermyn Woods. The other centres, at Carshalton, Poole and Blackpool, were non-residential, with the men accommodated in lodgings.[10]

Bondfield also had an interest in those labour colonies that were still training unemployed men. In England, with the abolition of the much hated poor law under the Local Government Act 1929, local authorities took over a range of institutions in March 1930, including farm colonies. In London, the Public Assistance Committee of the London County Council (LCC) acquired responsibility for three so-called 'residential training colleges'. Overall, it now controlled 1,409 places at the London Industrial Colony at Belmont, by far the largest, with accommodation for 899 men, as well as Dunton – also known as Laindon – Farm Colony (150) and Hollesley Bay Labour Colony (360). The men sent to the colonies were, according to London's chief officer of public assistance, the 'less hopeful' of the unemployed, a 'residue' whose unemployment was 'due, not so much to economic circumstances, as to their own weakness of character, mind or physique'. In taking over the colonies, the LCC would help 'combat the demoralisation of months, or even years, of idleness' through 'a tonic regime' of open air exercise and regular work.[11] Elsewhere, municipal unemployed colonies barely existed. Glasgow Corporation still owned its colony at Palacerigg, for example, but had not used it since 1927 owing to lack of funds.[12] Bondfield took an interest in the colonies, and occasionally promoted their activities, but formally they came under Arthur Greenwood, her Cabinet colleague at the Ministry of Health, which absorbed the LGB in 1919.

In the political circumstances of 1929, the question of training the long-term unemployed was tricky. Bondfield's initial reaction in office was to accept that the previous government's strategy of training men for transference was 'fundamentally sound', and simply needed 'overhauling and extension'.[13] While consistent with Bondfield's economic conservatism, this was politically risky. In its Report, the ITB had warned that long-term unemployment was often '"frozen" by its close concentration in or about the coalfields'.[14] Yet the coal regions were a Labour heartland, whose voters took a dim view of any scheme that transported the most active and productive youngsters from their communities. Joseph Batey, MP for Spennymoor since 1922, representing constituents hit particularly hard by the collapse of coal mining, was one of several mining MPs who repeatedly challenged the Board's conclusions.[15] Even the Treasury weighed in to discourage the minister from proposing any new powers in legislation, on the ground that it 'would widen the field of attack'.[16] Worried about the implications, the Cabinet created a small committee, chaired by J. R. Clynes, to look into 'the question of transferred labour'.[17] This was by no means the first time that Bondfield was given 'help' to develop and present policy on labour matters, and it would not be the last.

Nevertheless, Bondfield was well placed to press the potential of training as a policy instrument. She was a long-standing and committed member of the CCWTE, and had represented the Labour interest on the Oversea Settlement Committee. She was among the TUC delegates who met Steel-Maitland to discuss unemployment insurance in late 1928, taking the opportunity to press him on training and specifically calling for the expansion of the TICs.[18] She shared Congregationalist enthusiasm for training men to settle the land, albeit preferably in Britain rather than for emigration.[19] While insisting that she did not believe that training offered an easy solution to the problem of unemployment, she did 'believe that it is one of the things that the Government can do to prevent deterioration. It is one of the things that the Government can do to save our young people from a kind of dry rot.'[20] Shortly after taking office she published an article on unemployment, arguing that training was particularly vital for those 'handicapped' by the experience of long-term unemployment.[21]

Bondfield was not alone among Labour policy thinkers in finding training camps broadly to her liking. Writing shortly before the 1929 election, the Webbs reflected that existing provision for training the unemployed was 'ludicrously small', especially in comparison with 'the aggregate number of men, women and youths receiving Unemployment Benefit'.[22] Cecil Wilson, MP for Sheffield Attercliffe, was among a number of Labour members who demanded expansion of the existing training centres.[23] Others praised Brandon and Claydon, and urged that recruitment be extended to cover all unemployed men. If there were criticisms from the Labour side before the election, it was that progress was far too slow. The Conservative government, proclaimed Manny Shinwell in opposition, had gone into painful labours and produced merely 'this futile, puny, meandering mouse'. The maverick Clydeside socialist had no objection whatever to the training, which struck him as 'the proper thing to do' for 'men who appear to have become unemployable, to rescue them from social ostracism'.[24] A few days later, Shinwell was attacking the government for urging unemployed Scots to find work in the south of England, rather than fulfilling its 'bounden duty' by 'setting up labour colonies' to give men 'that self-respect which is so often necessary when a man has been a long time unemployed'.[25]

A number of unions had also supported the government training programmes before the 1929 election. In 1928 the Durham Miners Association (DMA) had cooperated with local labour exchanges to recruit 100 miners for training for the Dominions.[26] In the following year, Peter Lee, leading light in the DMA and future president of the Miners' Federation of Great Britain, told a conference in Newcastle that government should provide training for the unemployed, along with schemes for afforestation and road-making.[27] Ben Tillett, legendary dockers' leader of 1889, had led a TUC delegation in 1928 to the Minister of Labour, telling Steel-Maitland that 'workers who could not be offered vacancies should be provided with educational or instructional centres where they would spend their time to good account'.[28] Like many in the Labour Party, these union leaders were keen to expand training for the male unemployed.

Whether by accident or design, such thinking was also very much in tune with the ideas of Bondfield's civil servants. Five months before the election, Frederick Gatus Bowers, accountant general in the Ministry of Labour, had written to his opposite number in the Treasury about plans for promoting transference through training. 'I think I ought to warn you', he said, that the Ministry was proposing a training scheme for 'those, especially among the younger men, who, through prolonged unemployment, have become so "soft" and temporarily demoralised that it would not be practicable to introduce more than a very small number of them into one of our ordinary training centres without danger to the morale of the centre'. The government's transference policy would only succeed if employers believed that they were being sent 'the best material available', and 'the class of whom I am speaking cannot be considered by our local officers for transfer until they are hardened'. Bowers, a somewhat puritanical figure who was close to the Treasury, was considering an eight-week course, either in market gardening or on forestry land, but at this stage he emphasised that the idea was not a full proposal.[29]

This was probably an example of civil service economy with language, for Bowers submitted the worked up proposal a mere nine days later. The paper came formally from the Labour Emergency Expenditure Committee, a group composed of senior officials in the Ministry of Labour.[30] The Committee used similar language to Bowers, writing of 'soft' young men who needed to be 'reconditioned', but rather than market gardening, it proposed to use the men on heavy labour, and extended the proposed period of training to twelve weeks. It placed a limit on the numbers to be trained, which were to be no more than could be placed at the end of their time in the centre, and added that

> The progress of reconditioning will be quicker and more effective if carried out away from the distressed areas, so that men live away from the depressing atmosphere of the coalfields.

The Treasury confirmed its approval rapidly, within a week, though typically it emphasised that the scheme 'should be regarded as experimental and subject to review at the expiration of twelve months'.[31]

One Treasury official, while supporting the proposal, added that the government was probably hoping 'to make some kind of splash at Christmas'.[32] He was right to detect party spin: months before the election, Steel-Maitland had been worrying that voters did not know 'of the relief which transference is giving to the finances of the worst areas'.[33] The first TIC opened in April; based in Blackpool, it offered an eight-week course of heavy outdoor work, preparing a field for use as a municipal aerodrome. Most of the men were accommodated in local guest houses, with the exception of a handful of locals who stayed at home. Four more TICs opened later in the year. Non-residential TICs were opened at Carshalton in Surrey and Poole in Dorset, where the men helped lay out playing fields, while the testing centres at Presteigne and Fermyn Woods were converted into hutted camps, where the men could work on Forestry Commission land. *The Times* welcomed the new centres, praising their 'limited aim of toughening the fibre of men who have got out of the way of work'.[34]

Once in power, Bondfield also supported the TICs, which she thought 'of great value to the depressed areas'.[35] Brandon and Claydon were still training handymen, and she now had the task of deciding what to do with their spare capacity as well as the other three oversea training centres. By 1929, the Ministry of Labour had developed a small but significant role in training the unemployed, and the residential farm training centres could claim a reasonable track record. Passmore, the Ministry's director of training, wrote in confidence to Major Hall and Mr Steward, managers at Brandon and Claydon respectively, asking for their advice on what to do with their centres when the Canadian training scheme came to an end.[36] Passmore was unimpressed with their response – Steward came up with a scheme for retraining unemployed miners as chauffeur-gardeners – and continued to search for creative new ways of using the old farm training centres. Bondfield promptly contributed her own idea, of sending young city lads to the centres for summer holidays, but the civil servants put a stop to this once they learned that it would mean handing the centres over to local education authorities.[37]

Meanwhile, Bondfield risked being outflanked by her colleagues. In June 1929, George Lansbury and Sir Oswald Mosley visited a number of the Ministry's training centres. Both men, who were preparing for a Cabinet meeting, held loosely defined ministerial positions, Lansbury as First Commissioner of Works and Mosley as Chancellor of the Duchy of Lancaster, and they had joined a small Cabinet committee on unemployment, chaired by Jimmy Thomas, the railwaymen's union leader who now served as Lord Privy Seal.[38] Thomas's committee mainly concerned itself with public works (among other ideas, it considered a channel tunnel and a road bridge across the Firth of Forth) and reducing working life by raising the school-leaving age and improving pensions.[39] However, on 6 November 1929, the Cabinet authorised Thomas to consult law officers on whether a short Bill was required to give 'the Government compulsory powers in certain matters with a view to avoiding the large number of Bills required to implement the Unemployment Policy announced in the House of Commons on the previous day'.[40] This was code: 'certain matters' referred to the power to instruct the unemployed to attend a prescribed course of training. In May 1930 this was precisely what came about.

The introduction of compulsion

In early 1930, Bondfield put a new proposal before the Cabinet. She did not require new legislation, as Jimmy Thomas had anticipated; rather, she wanted the Cabinet to back her in using use her powers of compulsion under existing unemployment insurance legislation to recruit young unemployed men into training. In her paper for the meeting, she expressed alarm at the number of men, chiefly young men, in the distressed areas who were unlikely to obtain work locally or elsewhere 'without some reconditioning or training, but who refuse to avail themselves of the offer'. Bondfield was unsentimental about the next step, concluding that 'the stage has been reached in the process of "draining the waterlogged areas" when such men should have their benefit disallowed if they refuse without good reason to take a course of instruction'.[41]

At first, it might seem surprising for a Labour minister, from a modest background herself, to be so exercised about requiring the unemployed to attend training. But Bondfield's views on 'demoralisation' and 'reconditioning' were not so unusual. In 1927, for example, one Labour front-bencher complained that the unemployed were losing their 'dignity and virility' along with their 'character'. J. R. Clynes, an Irish labourer's son and trade union activist who had entered Parliament in 1906, was promptly supported by Dr Drummond Shiels, a Labour MP from Edinburgh, who stated that 'the so-called dole is entirely inadequate to maintain a proper standard of nourishment and health among the working people', leading to serious 'physical deterioration'.[42] Fear that long-term unemployment was damaging working-class bodies, particularly men's bodies, was something Bondfield shared with many other socialists. And able bodies were often associated with membership of the wider social community. Clynes had feared that unemployed men were losing 'their usefulness as serviceable citizens' because of 'the continuity of their unemployment'.[43] The question, then, was how best to restore these idle bodies to the 'dignity and virility' that were supposed to be fundamental to the character of the idealised worker.

Initially, attendance at TICs was voluntary. Men from depressed areas, aged between 19 and 35, were able to apply for a TIC course if they had been unemployed for at least six continuous months. Labour exchange officers then picked those they thought suitable in terms of 'physique and general intelligence', sending those judged as brighter to a government training centre (GTC) and the strong but dim to a TIC. Of course, local officials in the exchanges may well have used pressure to persuade the reluctant, but men could and did refuse, without risking their benefit. Reviewing the first year, the Ministry publicly noted that while many had refused for good reasons, others – no precise number was offered – declined 'for reasons which cannot be regarded as sufficient'.[44] Alan Barlow, who as principal assistant secretary was an influential figure, later told the Royal Commission on Unemployment Insurance that he saw refusal to volunteer for a TIC course as in itself evidence of 'that deterioration of morale which it was one of the purposes of the training scheme to remedy'. Compulsion, it followed, was in the best interests of the men themselves.[45] But there was a further factor, in the number who entered the TICs only to withdraw. Well over a third of the 2,783 men who left the centres during 1929 did so before completing the course, though the published official figures do not distinguish between those who walked out and those who were dismissed.[46] As the Ministry explained to the TUC, sanctions were particularly required against those who attend voluntarily then 'leave after a short time on inadequate and indeed ridiculous grounds'.[47]

Such arguments helped to build a policy consensus in favour of compulsion, but this still left the risks of defeat in Parliament. As Jimmy Thomas had quickly learned from the Cabinet's legal advisers, new legislation was unnecessary: powers of compulsion already existed under the 1921 Unemployment Insurance Act. This came as an enormous relief to politicians and officials who feared the risks of trying to change the law, but there were still the unions to consider. The Cabinet accordingly decided that Bondfield should consult Walter Citrine, secretary of the TUC 'with a view to ascertaining whether it would be advisable to consult the TUC or any of its committees before submitting proposals to the Cabinet'.[48] As so often, she had a minder: she was accompanied by her old boss Tom Shaw, an experienced union official who was serving as Secretary of State for War, under whom Bondfield had served as Minister of Labour in 1924.

After meeting Citrine, Bondfield duly reported that the TUC General Council 'fully approve in principle'. Bondfield and Barlow had sent their plans to Citrine, spelling out the Ministry's proposals in detail, including measures for local exchanges to require men to attend or lose their benefit; they also planned sanctions against those who attend voluntarily then 'leave after a short time on inadequate and indeed ridiculous grounds' or were expelled for gross misbehaviour.[49] Citrine in turn referred the matter to the Social Insurance

Committee, who declared that they approved fully of the scheme, 'subject to the reservation that the training referred to would not be training for a trade or as a handyman'.[50] In turn, Bondfield reassured Citrine that while she had 'no hesitation in feeling that strong pressure ought to be put on the class of men whom I have in mind' to attend the TICs, the 'numbers are not large'. She also confirmed that she would only invoke her powers in respect of the unskilled men entering TICs; they would not be used to recruit men into the GTCs.[51]

In fact, Citrine had made it clear to Barlow a week previously that this was the TUC's position.[52] But for Bondfield, it was clearly important to commit the TUC irrevocably before proceeding, and for Citrine it was important to ensure that the TUC would be consulted on as the plans developed. Trade union agreement mattered for Labour's sense of its place in the great family of the labour movement, and it also helped in heading off potentially awkward questions from the Labour left.

The idea of compulsory labour service had also been discussed, favourably, by some distinguished Labour intellectuals. Writing shortly before the 1929 election, Sydney and Beatrice Webb denounced voluntarism and called for a national Government Labour Corps, a suggestion that Sidney had originally made in 1886.[53] Young unemployed men who refused to serve, they recommended, should be committed to a penal detention colony.[54] Beatrice Webb returned to the topic in her evidence before the Royal Commission on Unemployment Insurance, calling for a 'National Labour Corps', recruited from unemployed 'navvies or miners', who would 'be sent about in detachments, equipped with tents, lorries and tools ... to execute works of coast protection, embanking and draining land, and other improvements'. She also thought government should have powers to order the unemployed to perform 'Swedish drill'.[55]

The socialist political theorist, economic historian and adult educator G. D. H. Cole similarly favoured what he called a 'National Labour Corps'. In *The Next Ten Years*, which the prolific left-wing thinker published in the hope of influencing the 1929 Labour government, Cole advocated allowing unemployed men the 'option of enrolment in a national organised body of workers available for any useful form of national service'. Nor was this a mere fancy of opposition, for Cole subsequently restated this proposal in his evidence before the Royal Commission on Unemployment Insurance in 1931. His aim was to bring together 'a great body of civil engineers, with the task of making the country as a whole both a pleasanter place to inhabit, and a more efficient productive concern'. While normally living at home, its members would be ready to move into hutted or tented camps as the work required, ready 'to take light-heartedly a certain amount of "roughing it" under somewhat primitive conditions'. And while he was mainly concerned with men, he thought unemployed women should not be excluded from the scheme. Unlike the Webbs' proposal, Cole's plan was voluntary, at least initially, requiring 'no more militarisation than exists in any body of Boy Scouts or Girl Guides, in any Fire Brigade, or in any body of men who agree to accept a common discipline'.[56]

Implementing compulsion

In May 1930, the Ministry of Labour issued Circular ML104/29. As official circulars go, it was clear and to the point. Managers of local labour exchanges read that under Section 7(I) (v) of the Unemployment Act 1921, the Minister of Labour already had the power to withdraw benefit from any unemployed person who refused to accept a place in a training centre. Exchange managers should therefore note that henceforth, the minister had decided to exercise this power with respect to any unemployed man refusing to enter a TIC, and they should therefore treat any such case accordingly.[57] Regardless of whether the man had applied for a TIC course or not, those who refused a place were now to be denied benefit for the duration of the course.[58] Men judged eligible for a TIC by the insurance officer in their local exchange, and who refused to attend, were duly reported to the local Board of Assessors, who had been appointed to advise the local labour exchange on disputed claims, and could therefore decide to withdraw benefit.

The net result was that, under a newly elected Labour Minister of Labour, attendance at a TIC was now potentially compulsory for all young, long-term unemployed men. The situation regarding GTC courses was more complicated. While local exchanges could not refuse benefit to men who refused a course in a GTC, they did have the power to sanction men who had applied for a GTC course and accepted a place, and then failed to attend for no acceptable reason. They could also refuse benefit to men who had started a course in either a TIC or GTC and walked off, as well as those who were dismissed for misconduct if they suspected that the misconduct was deliberate. Unsurprisingly, local officials normally came to the conclusion that men had intended to offend, making their case 'one of voluntary leaving'. In all such cases, the sanction normally lasted for the duration of the course.[59]

In the short term, this produced an increased flow of recruits, leading the Ministry to open the Brandon Annexes as TICs in their own right.[60] Between 5 March 1930 and 1 December 1930, well over 31,000 men had an appointment to attend a selection panel for entrance into a TIC. Of these, just over half had volunteered, while the remaining 47 per cent had been sent under threat of losing benefit. Interestingly enough, it was the volunteers who were slightly more likely to turn up to the panel meeting. Even more interestingly, over a third of those who did attend the panel were then rejected, usually on grounds of health.[61] Some 884 men in 1930 – over one in ten of that year's intake – agreed to attend a TIC after refusing an earlier offer from the exchange and then losing an appeal to the Board of Assessors; unrecorded others went reluctantly after being threatened verbally with loss of benefits.[62]

Compulsion also reduced the number of early leavers. In 1929, 1,029 of the 2,783 trainees were either dismissed or left voluntarily before completing their course. In 1930, the 'wastage' rate was still high, at 3,516 out of 12,585 trainees, but was still lower in proportional terms than in 1929. By 1931, the wastage rate was down to 689 out of 14,755 men.[63] From the Ministry's perspective, compulsion helped increase recruitment and reduce wastage from 37 per cent in 1929 to 5 per cent in 1931.

As with the earlier overseas scheme, the labour exchanges sent all candidates for a medical examination before accepting them for training. Conducted by a general practitioner selected by the exchange manager and paid by the Ministry, the check-up was duly recorded on form TIC46, which posed a number of questions about the applicant's health, including their record of infectious diseases. It also asked:

> Is he, in your opinion, suitable to be placed in a Residential Hostel in respect of:
> (a) Personal cleanliness.
> (b) General Health.[64]

Some men still brought infestations. There was an outbreak of 'vermin' – head lice – among trainees in one of the huts at Fermyn Woods in summer 1930.[65] Three Sunderland men were subsequently dismissed: R. Hughes had vermin for two weeks and concealed the fact, admitting later that he had arrived in this state; R. Tench and W. Lamb were reported verminous by other trainees and were also found guilty of concealing the fact. Another forty-three men walked out, refusing to have their hair inspected.[66] All the huts were scrubbed and sprayed twice, and the blankets fumigated, before the camp returned to business as usual following a visit from the Ministry's director of training.[67]

Inside the TICs

Other than the risk of lice, what did young men face when they were drafted into the TICs, and how did they react to the experience? Members of a Lancashire employment committee who visited Presteigne in 1930 reported that the men lived in huts with boarded floors, where each man had 'a wooden trestle bedstead, a mattress and five blankets'. Usually, new arrivals were picked up at the nearest railway station, having received a travel warrant from the Ministry to cover the journey from their home. They were interviewed on arrival in the camp, and then sent to their sleeping quarters, where each man collected a knife, fork, spoon, mug, boots and pair of corduroy trousers; a jacket and shirt were also supplied for 'necessitous cases', who – unsurprisingly given that these men had been out of work for some time – were the majority. In wet weather, the men drew oilskin cloaks from the camp stores. Two coal stoves burnt all night, and there was hot water for washing, as well as hot and cold showers. The men received four meals a day.[68]

In spite of the medical test, the camp managers quickly started reporting that many of the men were too undernourished and unfit to cope with pick-and-shovel work. After a week or two of light work, most of the men were 'given more and harder work to do, being moved from one carefully graded gang to another until the last weeks'. By this stage, they were judged suitable for the 'heavy navvy work' on the land that was the TICs' *raison d'etre*.[69] Trainees spent most of their weekdays working outside, digging ditches, grubbing up roots, shifting stones and building rough forest roads, for seven hours, though they also received some instruction in 'rough carpentry', basic metalwork, and boot and shoe repair.

For leisure, there were sports and games: the Ministry had asked the Sports Fellowship to help it recruit sports instructors.[70] After the early days, there were also occasional lectures, organised by the camp welfare officer, as well as a library with 300 novels, magazines and daily papers, and sets of games in the recreation room. Presteigne, according to the Lancashire visitors, also had its own projector, with weekly shows involving the likes of Charlie Chaplin, Harold Lloyd, and other popular stars.[71] The authorities provided some limited and rather basic adult education, 'both for its own sake and to help solve the problem of keeping the men occupied in wet weather'.[72]

All trainees received a weekly allowance. Those who lived at home were paid their benefit, and an additional 2s. 6d. weekly; single men who stayed in lodgings were given 5 shilling weekly out of their benefit, with the remainder being held back against the costs of their food and accommodation. In the residential TICs, all the men received an allowance of 4 shillings weekly. Married men in the TICs were eligible for an additional allowance for their families, though it was left to the man to decide whether he would send the money home.[73]

Of those who completed the course, the vast majority went on to work, though some – rarely more than a handful on each course – were transferred to a GTC. Often, the men found – or were sent to – jobs on public projects of various kinds, usually as a condition of grant to the project. Even then, a number found that for one reason or another, they could not hold down a job, often some distance from their home. The Ministry supplemented its existing placement role by bilateral agreements with employers, who agreed to take on a batch of men under agreed conditions. In 1930, for example, 994 TIC men were placed with Whipsnade Zoo, London University (preparing playing fields), extending the Piccadilly Line of the Metropolitan Railway, and other public or voluntary sector employers. In these cases, the men were paid by the host employer, but were technically trainees rather than employees. In the view of the Ministry, this scheme was 'very successful'; we have no record of what the men thought.[74]

What we do know is that there were several protests and occasional strikes in the centres (see Chapter 10). Were the protests inspired by outside agitation, as some claimed at the time? Certainly,

Bondfield had plenty of critics on the left. One Communist claimed that she was driving young men 'into slave compounds – so-called "training centres" – under well-nigh incredible living conditions, or into the Army'.[75] Others warned that the government was preparing an army, not of soldiers, but of strike-breakers.[76] Yet the fact that similar strikes and other protests took place in local authority labour colonies (there were three in Belmont alone in 1930–31) suggests that the protests in the TICs were largely triggered by local grievances. Moreover, as Chapter 10 shows, men in the camps continued to protest and occasionally strike after 1932, when the National Government returned to voluntary recruitment. Compulsion almost certainly had some influence, though; managing a group of volunteers was one thing, but maintaining order and work patterns was a challenge when many of the men did not want to be there in the first place. Nevertheless, after 1932, the Ministry of Labour invariably resisted attempts to reintroduce compulsory recruitment, repeatedly making it clear that the camp managers preferred to take volunteers.[77]

Crisis and growth

Unemployment and public spending – the most difficult of the many challenges that MacDonald's government faced – fell particularly hard on the Ministry of Labour. Under such pressure, it is remarkable that the TIC system grew steadily until the middle of 1931. They were, after all, expensive. When the Isle of Man government asked how much the Ministry of Labour would charge it to send men to Brandon and Claydon, they were told that the weekly costs – including a contribution to buildings and equipment – came to 58 shillings a man; even at this price, the Manx government agreed to take up to 40 places.[78] Most of this cost was made up of four items: the initial investment in huts (which could be much reduced by the use of tents, though these were unsuitable for winters), staff salaries, trainee allowances, and food; but the list of additional expenditure – from shovels and boots to first aid kit and film hire – also mounted up.[79]

By early 1930, the Treasury was spotting potential cuts in the Ministry of Labour's training empire. The first and most obvious cuts were on the margins of the system, namely the farming activities associated with the training centres. Apart from Columbie Farm in Carstairs, which was sold, the Treasury insisted that the farming side of the centres was merely temporary, with a view to putting the farms on the market once land prices improved.[80] In Northern Ireland, the Unionist Cabinet had already put an end to training at its overseas centre in Richhill, though it was maintained as a working farm, with a view to resuming training once the economy improved.[81] No one in the British Ministry of Labour much minded whether the training division ran farmland or not, but the overseas training and testing centres – whose rationale was being undermined by falling demand in the Dominions – were quite another matter. Senior officials set out to woo the Ministry of Agriculture as allies against the Treasury.[82] Meanwhile, John Passmore and other senior officers were drafting alternative proposals for longer-term uses of the overseas centres.

Bondfield had already tried to persuade the Cabinet to use the TICs to bring land into cultivation in spring 1930. The farmland at Brandon, she suggested, might allow for an 'experiment'.[83] Shortly afterwards, a core group of officials at the Ministry of Labour debated a proposal for 'alternative uses of Overseas Training Centres'. The group, which included Alan Barlow, the Principal Assistant Secretary, originally dealt with four training centres, including Cranwich. On reflection, the group decided to focus on Brandon, Claydon and Carstairs. Cranwich had been earmarked for lads, and the Ministry reflected that the 'task of keeping a large number of boys contented and out of mischief by means of organised games and amusements over a period of some weeks' would be expensive. Even worse, the Treasury would 'say that such a service is not now a function of Government', or worse still, dismiss it as a 'holiday camp'. It was decided not to mention Cranwich, holding it in reserve as a possible TIC.[84]

John Passmore, the Ministry's director of training, presented the final plan to his minister in mid-April. In a handwritten note for Bondfield, Passmore outlined his thinking on the three main overseas centres:

> Obviously it would be wrong to dismantle them. We can make considerable use of them for Transfer Instruction (for which there is increasing need) and for Handyman Training; so far as they are not used in this way they are to be kept ready for re-opening at short notice if required for any of our purposes … I sh[ould] like to have your early approval of this, if you agree.[85]

Within a week, Bondfield replied: 'I agree this is the best plan: Go ahead.'[86] The proposal went off to the Treasury five days later. In early May, the Treasury replied, approving the bulk of the plans, leaving the Ministry free to carry out 'reconditioning' at Claydon (100 places), Carstairs (50), West Tofts (200), High Lodge (200), and Cranwich (200).[87]

Fresh from its victory over the oversea training farms, the Ministry then pressed forward new plans for the overseas 'testing centres'. Originally opened as short-term centres, where men bound for Canada could be 'tested' through exposure to heavy farm labour, most of the testing centres were also converted into TICs. Plans had been submitted to convert Presteigne into a TIC in 1928; but the site was on a rented farm, and when the lease ran out in 1931 the Ministry decided to focus its efforts in the Anglo-Welsh border area on Shobden.[88] Following a dispute with the landowner about the condition of the site, Presteigne was finally vacated in spring 1932.[89]

Still, the system remained relatively small. There were nine TICs in all when the Labour government fell apart. Carstairs was the sole Scottish camp; apart from Presteigne, which was on the verge of closing, Wales was served by Shobdon TIC in Herefordshire. The remaining centres were clustered in two areas of England. East Anglia had Claydon, Cranwich Heath (which closed in October 1931), High Lodge (also closed in October), Weeting Hall, and West Tofts. Only Bourne was open in Lincolnshire, while nearby Fermyn Woods was shut for disinfection. Non-residential centres at Poole and Blackpool had closed when the work was completed, though around 100 men continued to level land for the National Playing Fields Association at Carshalton.[90] By mid-1931, the impact of budget cuts meant that fewer men were being placed, and one residential and two non-residential TICs were closed.

In August 1931, MacDonald's government collapsed. Always aware of their minority status in Parliament, Ministers, nevertheless, failed to reach a compromise over the level of spending cuts that would be required to win parliamentary support for a budget. The end came when the Cabinet split over proposals to reduce unemployment benefits under the National Assistance Scheme. Bondfield lost her seat in the 1931 election and in 1932 she lost her place on the TUC's General Council. She stood again in the following years, but was repeatedly voted down. This reflected a wider distrust of Bondfield in the unions, rather than specific misgivings about training policy.[91] Of course, she had misled the TUC over her plans for compulsion, particularly in respect of men who refused to attend a GTC course. The TIC programme was closely associated with her and her party, and it might have been expected that the incoming National Government might abandon the scheme altogether. Yet, though her insistence on compulsion was rapidly disowned, the TICs were to survive her political demise. Bondfield herself was not so fortunate; she lost her Wallsend seat in the election, and her political career effectively came to an end.

Of course, the TICs were only a small part of Labour's solution to the corrosive effects of unemployment on working-class bodies. Despite the steady growth of the Labour years, the system remained relatively small in capacity. Yet it is difficult to find many other measures that were aimed at men's bodies, other than Labour's general proposal for attending to the health of the population. And uniquely, it was working men who found that the government's proposal for improving their physique was to send them to the countryside, voluntarily or not, where they would eat well and work hard. They were the first national system of government work camps in Britain, providing a point of entry that would be steadily widened in the following decade.

John Welshman has suggested that a number of inherited ideas about 'the unemployable' lost ground, and even disappeared, in the post-war years.[92] The most obvious reason for this was that, in time of war, many men and women who once had been denounced as incorrigible loafers had found jobs. Welshman also notes the importance of newer approaches to social science, which tended to pinpoint structural economic factors as the main causes of unemployment, treating the responses of the unemployed themselves as the result of material circumstances rather than an innate characteristic of the congenitally workshy. Welshman is wrong to suggest that the debate over physical deterioration disappeared after 1918.[93] On the contrary, as we have seen, and will see again, it was very much alive throughout the 1920s. However, it rested increasingly on medical and epidemiological analyses of nutrition and muscular-skeletal structure, rather than on quasi-Darwinian fears of national degeneration. Reconditioning, through heavy work and a steady diet, was replacing punitive segregation as the remedy for the worst ills of unemployment.

Notes

1 M. Cole (ed.), *Beatrice Webb's Diaries 1924–1932*, Longmans, Green & Co., London, 1956, 194.
2 For example, *The Times*, 4 December 1907.
3 R. Croucher, *We Refuse to Starve in Silence: A history of the National Unemployed Workers' Movement*, Lawrence & Wishart, London, 1987, 95–100.
4 Cole, *Webb's Diaries*, 150–1.
5 R. Lowe, *Adjusting to Democracy: The role of the Ministry of Labour in British politics, 1916–1939*, Clarendon Press, Oxford, 1986, 139.
6 Ibid.
7 R. McKibbin, 'The Economic Policy of the Second Labour Government, 1929–1931', *Past & Present*, 68, 1975, 104–5.
8 *The Times*, 9 December 1929.
9 McKibbin, 'Economic Policy', 112–13.
10 MoL, *Annual Report, 1929*.
11 London County Council (LCC), Public Assistance Committee, General Purposes Sub Committee Report by Chief Officer of PA on the Residential Training Colleges, 23 June 1930, LMA, LCC/CL/WEL/1/1.
12 Sir John Gilmour to Baillie John Mitchell, 18 October 1928, NAS DD10/195; *First Annual Report of the Scottish Department of Health, 1929*, HMSO, Edinburgh, 1930, 177.
13 Transfer of Miners. Memorandum by Minister of Labour, 1 July 1929, NA CAB24/204.
14 Industrial Transference Board, *Report*, 15.
15 See *Parliamentary Debates*, 7 November 1928.
16 Unemployment Insurance Bill. Memorandum by Ministry of Labour (MoL), 19 October 1929, NA CAB/24/206.
17 Unemployment Policy. Memorandum by Lord Privy Seal, 23 October 1929, NA CAB/24/206; Cabinet Conclusions, 25 October 1929, NA CAB/23/62.
18 Trades Union Congress (1929), *Administering Unemployment Insurance*, TUC, London.
19 *Parliamentary Debates*, 27 February 1929.
20 *Parliamentary Debates*, 30 April 1928.
21 *Labour Magazine*, November 1929, 7.
22 S. Webb and B. Webb, *English Poor Law History, Part II: The last hundred years*, Longmans, London, 1929, 694.
23 *Parliamentary Debates*, 14 April 1927.
24 *Parliamentary Debates*, 30 April 1928.
25 *Parliamentary Debates*, 7 May 1929.
26 W. R. Garside, *The Durham Miners, 1919–1960*, Allen & Unwin, London, 1971, 279.

27 *The Times*, 10 December 1928.
28 *The Times*, 7 December 1928.
29 Bowers to A. W. Hurst, Treasury, 12 December 1928, NA T161/902; Lowe, *Adjusting to Democracy*, 58.
30 Labour Emergency Expenditure Committee. Proposal, 21 December 1928, NA T161/902.
31 F. W. Leith Ross to MoL, 28 December 1928, NA T161/902.
32 Turner to Upcott and Hurst, Treasury, 12 December 1928; Bowers to Treasury, 21 December 1928, NA T161/902.
33 Memorandum by the Minister of Labour, 1 November 1928, NA CAB24/198.
34 *The Times*, 12 April 1929.
35 Transfer of Miners. Memorandum by Minister of Labour, 1 July 1929, NA CAB24/204.
36 Passmore to Major Hall & Mr Steward, 20 December 1929, NA LAB2/1384/7.
37 Goldberg to Tribe, 21 February and 11 March 1930, NA LAB2/1384/9.
38 Cabinet Minutes, 21 June 1929, NA CAB/23/61.
39 *The Times*, 4 July 1929.
40 Cabinet Conclusions, 6 November 1929, NA CAB23/62. The previous day, of course, had also seen Guy Fawkes Night.
41 Distressed Areas. Withdrawal of benefit from men refusing to attend a training centre. Memorandum by the Minister of Labour, 3 February 1930, CAB24/209.
42 *Parliamentary Debates*, 14 April 1927.
43 Ibid.
44 MoL, *Annual Report (AR) 1929*, 39.
45 *Royal Commission on Unemployment Insurance (RCUI): First Report, Appendices, Part I*, HMSO, London, 1931, 419.
46 MoL, *AR 1929*, 38.
47 MoL Memorandum, Training or reconditioning of men from distressed areas, 8 January 1930, TUC Archive, MRC 292/131/3/3.
48 Cabinet Conclusions, 23 December 1929, NA CAB23/62.
49 MoL Memorandum, Training or reconditioning of men from distressed areas, 8 January 1930, TUC Mss, Modern Records Centre (MRC), 292/131/3/3.
50 J. L. Smyth to Barlow, 23 January 1930, TUC Mss, MRC 292/131/3/3.
51 Distressed Areas. Withdrawal of benefit from men refusing to attend a training centre. Memorandum by the Minister of Labour, 3 February 1930, CAB24/209.
52 Secretary, Social Insurance Department, to J. A. N. Barlow, 23 January 1930, TUC Archive, MRC 292/131/3/3.
53 Webb and Webb, *English Poor Law, Part II*, 694; *The Government*

Organisation of Unemployed Labour: Report made by a committee to the Fabian Society, George Standring, London, 1886.

54 Webb and Webb, *English Poor Law History, Part II*, 1010–11.

55 *RCUI: First Report, Appendices, Part I*, HMSO, London, 1327.

56 G. D. H. Cole, *The Next Ten Years in British Social and Economic Policy*, Macmillan, London, 1929, 48–55; see also Cole's evidence in *RCUI: First Report, Appendices, Part I*, HMSO, London, 744–9.

57 Note ET 3738/1930, NA LAB2/1278/ET5420.

58 *RCUI Final report*, HMSO, London, 328.

59 MoL, *AR 1930*, 47.

60 Note ET 3738/1930, NA LAB/2/1278/ET5420.

61 *RCUI: First Report, Appendices, Part I*, HMSO, London, 412.

62 MoL, *AR 1930*, 48–9.

63 Calculated from the Ministry's Annual Reports.

64 Confidential Circular, J. F. G. Price to Divisional Controllers and Managers of following Local Offices [including Kettering, Bishop Auckland, Chopwell, Durham, Morpeth. Spennymoor], 6/5/29, NA LAB2/1260/ED15667.

65 Passmore to Reid, 11 September 1930, NA LAB2/1275/ET5990.

66 Manager, Fermyn Woods, to G Wade, Leeds Divisional Office, 1 October 1930, NA LAB2/1275/ET5990.

67 Manager, Fermyn Woods to Director of Training, MoL, 5 September 1930, NA LAB2/1275/ET5990.

68 Farnworth local employment committee, report of sub-committee appointed to visit the Ministry of Labour TIC, Presteigne, October 1930, TUC Archive, Modern Records Centre (MRC) 292/131/3/3; B. Barnes, Ministry of Labour, to L. Cuthbertson, Treasury, 15 November 1935, NA T161/902.

69 MoL, *Annual Report 1929*, 38.

70 *The Times*, 13 May 1929.

71 Farnworth local employment committee, report of sub-committee appointed to visit the MoL TIC, Presteigne, October 1930, TUC Mss, MRC 292/131/3/3.

72 MoL, *AR 1929*, 37–8.

73 Ibid., 41.

74 MoL, *AR 1930*, 37.

75 *DW*, 18 July 1931.

76 *DW*, 2 February 1932, 4 August 1932.

77 *Ministry of Labour. Reports of investigations into the industrial conditions in certain depressed areas*, HMSO, London, 1934, 38; Passmore to Allen, 5 September 1933, NA LAB/2/2037/ET4880.

78 S. J. Baker, Home Office, to Eady, 24 January 1929, NA LAB2/1266/TFM160.

79 Brighton TIC Schedule, no date [1929], NA LAB2/1266/TFM535.

80 Reid to Barlow, 19/6/31, NA LAB2/1271/2/F2255.
81 Col. W. B. Spender, Ministry of Finance, to Blackmore, 16 March 1931, PRONI CAB/9C/20.
82 Reid, MoL, Note on Proposed Alternative Uses of Overseas Training Centres, 16 April 1930, Bindloss to Reid, 25 April 1930, NA LAB2/1271/2/F2255.
83 Training Centres and Agriculture. Memorandum by the Minister of Labour, 7 March 1930, NA CAB/24/210.
84 Note prepared for Margaret Bondfield by Reid, 16 April 1930, NA LAB2/1384/8.
85 Passmore, note to Minister, 17 April 1930, NA LAB2/1384/8.
86 MJB, handwritten note, 23 April [no year], NA LAB2/1384/8.
87 R. Nind Hopkins, Treasury, to MoL, 10 May 1930, NA LAB2/1384/8.
88 Owen, Manager Shobdon, 30 July 1931, NA LAB2/1278/ET5209.
89 Barber, Office of Works, to G Anderson MoL, 31 March 1932, NA LAB2/1278/ET5209.
90 MoL, *Annual Report 1931*, 37.
91 S. Shaw, 'The Attitude of the TUC Towards Unemployment in the Interwar Period', PhD, University of Kent at Canterbury, 1979, 9.
92 J. Welshman, 'The Concept of the Unemployable', *Economic History Review*, 59, 3, 2006, 596–602.
93 Ibid., 596.

7

Incremental growth

Instructional Centres under the National Government

In summer 1934, a Liverpudlian called Anthony Divers talked to the BBC about his life in Fermyn Woods Instructional Centre. After months of looking for a job, Divers heard the Centres described as army-run 'concentration camps', so he and his friends 'swore we wouldn't go to such places'; then, concluding that he 'couldn't do worse', he applied to his local labour exchange. Ten days later he set off by train to Kettering, completing his journey on the camp lorry before signing in and duly collecting his pair of boots and corduroy trousers.[1] Divers did not mind the work, mostly ground clearing and planting saplings, with the occasional morning 'keeping the lawn decent', and he enjoyed basic carpentry and metalwork classes. The 'grub is fine and there's plenty of it', and he was saving most of his weekly allowance. Above all, he now felt part of the community: 'We don't feel set apart no longer.'[2]

Divers may have been untypical, for he was on the radio again shortly after leaving Fermyn Woods.[3] He had, of course, been selected to tell an individual's part in a wider story. By 1932, few policy makers believed that unemployment was only a temporary hiccup. The scale, and duration, of the crisis placed enormous strains on Britain's system of unemployment benefits, based in theory, if no longer in practice, on the insurance principle. Harold Butler, director of the International Labour Organisation, voiced the thoughts of many when he wrote that 'Unemployment insurance was never conceived as being needed to ensure a quarter or a third of the industrial population against destitution'.[4] In his history of the Ministry of Labour, Rodney Lowe describes the years between 1931 and 1934 as the period of the 'final solution', when insured unemployed benefits were complemented by a national scheme of unemployment assistance, and the Poor Law was set aside to deal with vagrants and others who, although able-bodied, were on the margins of the labour market.[5] It was also a period when the Instructional Centre (IC) system expanded steadily, so that while never large, it formed an ever more important part of the wider regime for regulating and managing unemployment.

From TICs to ICs

In 1932, MacDonald appointed a Cabinet Unemployment Committee. Among other proposals, Sir Henry Betterton, the National Government's first Minister of Labour, submitted plans for 'training on a new basis'. Initially, it seemed that the government's transference policy had died with Labour's collapse, as there were now no public works schemes for the unemployed to transfer into, and therefore no need for the TICs. But as with emigration, the Ministry still had the premises and the staff. Betterton proposed lifting compulsory attendance, while expanding capacity from 835 to 3,000 places, training some 10,000–11,000 men a year. He also intended to introduce physical training for young unemployed men.[6] The committee advised the Cabinet to try the scheme for six months, to determine whether the renamed camps – Instructional Centres – had a role.[7] The Cabinet concurred, allowing the Ministry to run the six existing centres as well as reopening five that had been closed as an economy measure.[8]

Success was by no means a given, for other plans were on the table. The Cabinet Unemployment Committee favoured an ambitious scheme of land settlement, using Brandon and Claydon to train unemployed men with no farming experience.[9] Neville Chamberlain at the Treasury had plans for reconfiguring the Poor Law on a national level, leaving the Ministry of Labour fighting to retain overall control of unemployment benefit.[10] An unlikely ally emerged in the form of the Royal Commission on Unemployment Insurance, created by the embattled Labour administration, alarmed by the increasingly debt-ridden unemployment insurance fund. While the Royal Commission's main concern was with those unemployed who were no longer entitled to benefit, it commented favourably on the Ministry's training programme, recommending an increase in the number of TICs.[11] Even the two commissioners who dissented from the majority's other proposals concurred that the training 'sometimes known as re-conditioning' suffered from the fact that 'there are so few openings'.[12]

Still, the Ministry had to absorb some cuts. The Treasury insisted that it should sell its training farms, which were being farmed on a quasi-commercial basis with unemployed labour.[13] Within the Ministry, Passmore started to argue that closure and sale would cost more than maintaining the farms in working order: while Lampits Farm at Carstairs was valued at £6,500, dismantling and re-erecting the huts would cost £9,500. The Treasury reluctantly agreed.[14] In 1933, the Labour Emergency Expenditure Committee drafted proposals for new ICs. The first was at Hamsterley, 'conveniently situated in relation to the districts in County Durham where the need for facilities for reconditioning unemployed men is acute'.[15] The Forestry Commission (FC) thought there was enough work for 200 men for two years (though Hamsterley continued until 1939). Half of the buildings were made by trainees at Wallsend GTC, with the remainder supplied by Nissen, and the total cost of the new IC was estimated at under £3,500.[16] The Ministry then brought in men from Bourne to build a new camp near Allerston, in North Yorkshire, for men from Cleveland, Redcar and Whitby.[17] Two years later, Allerston men in turn were sent to build a new camp at Langdale End.[18] And in what was frankly described as a 'rush job', Glenbranter opened in summer 1933 with men recruited through labour exchanges in Glasgow, Hamilton and Larkhall.[19]

Glenbranter provides a nicely documented case study of a new IC. In 1933, the Ministry agreed to close Carstairs, but it kept going, supplying trainees to help the Prison Department build a new secure unit for high-risk mentally ill prisoners, until it finally found a purchaser for Lampits Farm in 1935.[20] John Sutherland of the FC, hearing of the closure, wrote to Passmore suggesting four new possible sites in Argyllshire.[21] Despite warnings from local officers about the climate, Passmore picked Glenbranter, announcing that the Glasgow unemployed would be 'glad of the opportunity of reconditioning in what is, in the summer time, a very attractive part of Scotland'.[22] The estate had belonged to the popular entertainer Sir Harry Lauder, and as well as land suitable for forest planting, there was also a mansion house. Passmore, after seeing the local rainfall and temperature records, decided that the camp would start with a base in the big house, with the men living in tents for the summer months.[23] His sceptical colleagues predicted that the camp would be cut off for three or four months of the year, and warned Passmore of 'the midge nuisance' during the rest of the year.[24] These were unusually acute challenges for a London-based ministry with a limited regional presence, but Glenbranter, with abundant prospects of heavy work, was duly opened, and the Ministry had twelve functioning ICs by the end of the year.

The Unemployment Assistance Act

By late 1933, the National Government had introduced legislation that would further transform the IC programme. In April, Neville Chamberlain agreed to chair a new Cabinet committee to reform unemployment relief. While the insured unemployed would receive benefit largely as before, the uninsured would come under a new central Unemployment Assistance Board (UAB), so that for the first time, all able-bodied unemployed would come under the Ministry of Labour, leaving poor law bodies to handle the aged, sick and infirm. The proposal included plans for 'the training and reconditioning of persons under the Board', in collaboration with the Ministry.[25] Betterton meanwhile reported to his Cabinet colleagues that, as the emerging recovery was leaving behind a large number of long-term unemployed, it was 'obviously necessary to do as much as possible to maintain the employability of these workpeople, especially the younger ones'.[26]

In fact, Betterton's plans were well under way before Chamberlain started drafting his legislation. In spring 1932, for example, the 820–acre farm at Brandon was being worked on a commercial basis and training had ceased. The Ministry's presence was limited to a single caretaker, yet Passmore told the Ministry's solicitor that he expected shortly to 're-occupy the huts with trainees, not for training for overseas but in connection with a scheme of occupational training at present under consideration'.[27] Passmore's thinking may have been less a formal plan than a gleam in the eye, but it was given added momentum by the Special Areas legislation. While the Special Areas Act was a largely cosmetic exercise,[28] it increased the number of advocates for the Ministry's training schemes. Chaired by Horace Wilson, formerly permanent secretary at the Ministry of Labour, an interdepartmental committee on the special areas recommended that the capacity of the ICs should be doubled over the next eighteen months, producing 'an annual additional out-turn of approximately 16,000 men'. All the new recruits, the committee emphasised, should be volunteers; and for the first time, they should include married as well as single men; it also considered 'reconditioning camps for boys', to be run by local authorities.[29] Worried about the electoral implications of being seen to ignore the special areas, the Cabinet approved the proposals on transference and training.[30]

With the passing of the Unemployment Assistance Act, responsibility for able-bodied applicants for relief duly passed to the UAB. Betterton resigned as Minister of Labour, and left his safe Nottinghamshire seat to take the post of Chairman (and the title of Lord Rushcliffe). Sir Ernest Strohmenger, Under-Secretary at the Treasury, became Vice-Chairman. Miss Violet Markham, the only woman member, was chair of the Central Committee on Women's Training and Employment (CCWTE), and a Liberal activist with a strong interest in adult education, who succeeded Strohmenger in 1937. The other members were Dr Thomas Jones, secretary to the Pilgrim Trust and previously deputy-secretary to the Cabinet, the Professor of Economics at the Armstrong College, Newcastle, and the director of public assistance for Glasgow.[31]

As well as its responsibilities for relief payments to the uninsured unemployed, the Board also had responsibilities for the work test (intended to discover whether applicants were genuinely willing to work), and training. It took these powers seriously, and initially planned to run its own centres in remote areas 'for semi permanent i.e. residential reconditioning centres of the type at present run by the Ministry of Labour'.[32] Wilfred Eady, an experienced Ministry of Labour officer and secretary of the UAB, persuaded his colleagues to study the Borstal system and approach the FC.[33] Another civil servant visited Palacerigg, where he found the men doing 'just the sort of work that we are looking for', but found the 'present Council' – Glasgow was Labour-controlled – impossible.[34] Eady then asked a colleague to prepare a paper on work centres.

After visiting Hollesley Bay, W. C. Osmond came down in favour of modelling the UAB centres on the ICs. In a telling comment, Osmond added that he had 'looked into the problem of making Work Centres less attractive than ICs but it is difficult to suggest what can usefully be cut out from the latter', adding that life in an IC was less comfortable than in Hollesley Bay or even the average workhouse. Eady, always conservative in outlook, replied that: 'There are trimmings that can be cut off: less "pocket money" and a lower diet.'[35] The UAB decided to send suitable applicants to an

IC, initially as a temporary measure; by the year's end, its applicants accounted for four out of every five entrants to ICs.[36]

Falling unemployment levels led the UAB to focus even more closely on the long-term unemployed. In 1936, the Board persuaded the Ministry to broaden its recruitment beyond the Special Areas, encompassing long-term unemployed men across Britain. The Ministry also used UAB officers to identify and approach potential recruits on an individual basis, as they had 'more intimate knowledge' of individuals' circumstances and attitudes than its own staff in the exchanges.[37] By this stage, the idea of separate UAB work centres seems to have disappeared, and the IC system continued to expand with UAB support. Three new camps opened in late 1936, one at Knapdale in Argyllshire, one at Rendlesham in Suffolk and one at Haldon, near Exeter.[38] During the following year, the Ministry opened two new ICs in Wales (at Gwydwr, Caernaervonshire, and Dovey, near Machynlleth), two in Scotland (Glentress, near Peebles, and Ardentinny, on Cowal Peninsula) and one at Culford, Bury St Edmunds.[39] In Northern Ireland, the Ministry of Labour continued to ponder its plans for 'restoring and maintaining physical wellbeing by providing exercise and fresh air' in ICs, though nothing came of these ruminations.[40]

Recruitment: volunteers or conscripts?

Recruitment at first seemed simple. Betterton envisaged that ICs would handle the long-term unemployed, particularly the young. Local labour exchanges therefore had to find applicants among those men who were receiving unemployment insurance benefit or transitional benefit. Each IC had its own catchment area. In 1933, for example, Kielder was expected to recruit from exchanges in Northumberland and south Tyneside, while Hamsterley recruited from Durham, Cleveland and Whitby; Welsh exchanges sent men to Shobdon and Brechfa, and Scots went to Carstairs or Glenbranter.[41] Yet although the camps recruited steadily, they were rarely full, and the Ministry found itself under constant pressure to consider new ways of persuading the unemployed to volunteer for a spell in its camps.

Did the loss of compulsory powers make a difference? In practice, local exchange officials could still threaten loss of benefit, and no doubt some used more pressure than others. Still, it was not difficult to resist, as Donald Kear discovered in 1933. A machinist from the Forest of Dean, Kear was laid off as soon as he qualified for an adult's wage. At the labour exchange he was sent for an interview with an exchange officer, who:

> began reciting the virtues of these camps – the comradeship, the toning-up of muscles, the good plain food, the fresh air, and the fact that it was for six weeks only. Then he dried up. 'What about it?' he asked. 'Well', I said, 'I wouldn't mind if I thought I'd have a worth-while job at the end of it.'

Kear saw others turning down the opportunity on similar grounds.[42] Clearly, the absence of a guaranteed job was a blow to recruitment.

By the mid-1930s, with recovery under way, recruitment was becoming challenging. The writer and former civil servant Sir Ronald C. Davison thought that this was due in part to an improving economy, in part to Communist campaigning.[43] Though the UAB's Welsh director ascribed 'indifference' less to 'organized or open boycott but to the dissemination of prejudice', most local officials blamed the unemployed. The Newcastle District Officer found the men 'undisciplined and physically soft', Sheffield men were said to dislike leaving home, and in Middlesbrough some gave reasons for refusal that were judged 'simply grotesque'.[44] In Liverpool, the District Officer reported that many young men lost any desire to work, and if the family were out of work, no one would 'make an effort to set him on the right track', leaving him prey to the city's 'temptations to social misbehaviour'.[45] In 1933, Beryl Power ascribed unsatisfactory recruitment rates in the north-west of England to 'the old reason so continually adduced by officers of that Division that the clannish cotton workers cannot be induced to leave home'.[46]

In 1934–35, the Ministry made an unexpected saving of £100,000 because of poor recruitment.[47] It opened the ICs to married men, even opening a special non-residential IC for married men at Rheola, near Resolven in South Wales.[48] Many who volunteered were being rejected on physical grounds. All went for medical inspection, with a view to screening out those who might pose a risk, either to themselves or others. A study of 181 rejects in 1933 showed that most had been diagnosed with heart disease or high blood pressure, while seventeen had previously undetected tuber-culosis and thirteen suffered from 'an offensive discharge from the ears'.[49] In 1935, the UAB noted that in six months it had rejected 17,253 men after medical inspections, compared with a mere 6,854 healthy men who agreed to attend an IC course.[50] Men without teeth were 'told to present themselves for re-examination after obtaining dentures'.[51] Dentures and spectacles were unaffordable to most unemployed men, so the Commissioner for the Special Areas, Sir Malcolm Stewart, offered to fund the costs of minor ailments and defects from the Special Areas Fund.[52]

Periodically, the Ministry of Labour heard demands for a tougher recruitment policy. Reporting shortly after compulsion had been abandoned, the Royal Commission on Unemployment Insurance recommended that applicants should generally expect to accept training or occupation as a condition of benefit, urging that 'every effort should be made to translate that general condition into effective reality'.[53] After experiencing compulsion, the training department preferred volunteers. Their views were also echoed by other informed observers, such as the veteran Scottish Conservative J. C. C. Davidson, who noted in his report on Cumberland that although 'the question of compulsion may have to be considered', he supported 'the view which I gather has so far been taken that compulsion is fraught with danger'.[54]

Memories of compulsion were so troubling that some officials used them to pursue quite different arguments. Grumbling that he was not being allowed to pay an extra allowance to tempt men from Bourne to build the Allerston centre, Passmore reflected gloomily that while 'the powers under Section 7(i)(v) are in reserve', it was 'hardly practicable to develop the site or to build a Training Centre with press gangs'.[55] A year earlier, an anonymous official had rejected compulsion for men receiving transitional benefits as likely to undermine the Ministry's attempts to brand its training places as attractive '"prize" vacancies'.[56] The debate over the Unemployment Assistance Bill provided a new opportunity to discuss compulsion, but once again, the Training Department advised against, with Beryl Power arguing that it did more harm than good within the camps, while outside it damaged recruitment.[57]

Inside the Ministry, Wilfred Eady – soon to transfer to the UAB – took an active interest in the merits of compulsion. In the middle of 1935, the Board decided that it had to tackle the 'deficit of candidates'. In the six months between November 1935 and April 1936, local panels recommended 168,384 young men for IC courses;

fewer than one in ten agreed.[58] The Board prepared a proposal after consulting with the Ministry of Labour, involving 'a certain amount of judicious administrative pressure upon suitable young men in the depressed areas'.[59] Ernest Brown, the new minister, quickly rejected this, leading the Board to insist that 'some measure of disciplinary action will have to be taken in the near future' to deal with young men who refused to enter an IC.[60] The Board returned to its plans for 'discreet use of administrative procedure to induce young men to take the steps necessary to make and keep themselves fit for employment', and once more the Ministry discounted the suggestion as 'politically impracticable'.[61] That winter, faced with continuing shortages of willing recruits, Eady reported that his former colleagues had warned of the repercussions of any further allegations about 'slave camps', particularly if such wild accusations were in any way 'supported by the facts'. Instead, it agreed that the Board could extend IC recruitment beyond the Special and Depressed Areas.[62]

A slightly different discussion took place in Northern Ireland, where the Stormont government was responsible for labour matters. The issue was raised informally with Craigavon, the Prime Minister, by Major Samuel Hall-Thompson, Unionist member of Stormont for Belfast Clifton and vice-chairman of the UAB's Belfast area advisory committee. Impressed with the German labour service, Hall-Thompson urged Craigavon to set up 'Labour Camps' where men would 'carry out some service to the Community as a condition of receiving benefit'.[63] Harry Conacher, permanent head of the civil service at the Ministry of Labour, exploded: Hall-Thompson's thinking was 'frankly absurd', as well as provocative, for the 'working classes would react violently from the "Labour" angle', while 'the Nationalists would be up in arms, literally and metaphorically'.[64] Hall-Thompson duly received a polite reply, but the idea was quietly shelved.

There was to be no British version of the *Reichsarbeitsdienst*, and neither Ministry nor UAB exercised their powers of compulsion.[65] There may have been a principle involved, but if so it was well concealed by more practical considerations. Davison, a sympathetic observer, ascribed the Ministry's opposition as arising partly from 'the political odium of using the power', and partly from the pedagogic belief that a 'compulsory trainee' was 'a contradiction in terms'.[66] In short, the Ministry believed that conscription was undesirable because it would not work. Given the challenge of the NUWM, and the obvious practical problem of educating unwilling learners, the Ministry was probably right.

Inside the camps: routine, organisation and work

Describing his arrival at Hamsterley in 1934, one man recalled that:

> The Camp was typical army style, all the huts were new and shining corrugated iron cladding and the Union Jack in the centre of the lawn. We were introduced to the Manager and Staff and shown to our hut which would be home for the next thirteen weeks. Each bed had a locker with a padlock for personal possessions. The novelty of hot water at the taps and showers was luxury for many of us who had the taps and WCs out in the backyard.[67]

In many ways, the experience was a departure from life on the dole, in a community where other young men were also without a job. In its basics, the regime comprised three elements: residential accommodation, a remote rural setting, and heavy manual labour.

Work was at the centre of the daily routine. As one official wrote, the actual tasks themselves, as well as their operational goals, were 'secondary as a mere means to an end', with the ultimate goal being to 'recondition human material'.[68] The reconditioning process started at 6.30 a.m. when the men rose (or 6.00 if they were kitchen orderlies);[69] at Hamsterley, Major Rendle liked to wake the men by playing 'hot jazz' over the loudspeaker.[70] After breakfast, they went to work, with each group supervised by a ganger working for the Ministry. William Heard, a young unemployed man from Ebbw Vale, remembered that at Shobdon,

> It was 'You, you & you fall in line …' Some were allocated to do one particular thing, some another; it was anything to harden yourself. I always came in for the woodcutting. You used to go out marching with this crew, marching off, axe on your shoulder and all this business, whatever tools you had to use.[71]

As in earlier work camp systems, the work was graded, and allocated on the basis of experience.

New trainees started with a gradual process of physical training. A camp manager filmed by the celebrated documentary director Edgar Anstey was shown welcoming new trainees in clipped tones:

Your own experience will have taught you that long spells of unemployment tend to make a man what most people call soft or flabby. It's our job here to help those of you who've become soft to get back to that state of fitness in which you can hold your end up on a job of work alongside other people who've been more fortunate or in the case of those of you who've not yet become flabby then to help to keep you fit.[72]

One young trainee described his first weeks in Shobdon, writing on headed paper supplied by the YMCA: his first week included PT, arithmetic, spelling and English geography; the second week was spent digging, the third washing up in the canteen, the fourth 'ash walloping', and the fifth 'lopping branches off trees'.[73] How, he wondered, could this be described as instructional? But this was precisely the point.

The toil was designed to harden. In an advertisement for centre managers, the training department described the work as consisting of 'hard manual labour, e.g. felling, grubbing roots, clearing scrub land, quarrying and road making'.[74] At Hamsterley, the men were set to building nearly 70 miles of roads and trails.[75] The Allerston trainees built a six-mile road, involving 'a great deal of heavy pick and shovel work, to be followed by the excavation from the hillside of the stone, the breaking of the stone, and ultimately, the making up of the road'; they would also make fire-breaks.[76] Work at Glenbranter work comprised 'roadmaking, hill drainage, clearing river sources of silt and constructing small embankments', as well as making bridges and culverts.[77] At Ardentinny, as well as the usual roads, the men completed a small bridge, dated 1937, which still serves its purpose today.

Heavy work was accompanied by a heavy diet, based mainly on meat and carbohydrates, with limited vegetables and fruit, swilled down with tea. The men ate at trestle tables in a canteen, usually a Nissen hut. One reporter, visiting Brandon in 1935, described the food as

> substantial, varied and, so far as I saw it in preparation, appetizing. For breakfast today there was porridge, sausage and egg, bread and butter, marmalade and tea. The midday meal consisted of meat pie, potatoes, peas, beans, prunes and tea. At 5 o'clock in the afternoon when work for the day was at an end the men were back in the dining room for a menu of ham, jam, bread and butter, cake and tea, and before bedtime those who wished could have buns with tea or cocoa.[78]

Anstey's film showed an image of men lining up at the canteen hatch, plates in hand, with a voiceover provided by the camp steward: 'I have to serve 200 meals of two hot courses in twenty minutes. Today there's meat pie, peas and potatoes, then bread pudding and custard.'[79] Such detailed description suggests that the authors thought their audience would be interested, possibly surprised, by this hearty fare. I explore the men's thoughts later.

Space was equally regulated. The residential ICs were more or less isolated; a journalist who visited Allerston, built on exposed scrub and moorland in North Yorkshire, counted fourteen gates on the remote country roads to camp.[80] Camp layout followed a standard pattern. A sign by the entrance announced the presence of a government IC. The buildings themselves, usually Nissen huts, surrounded an open area with a flagpole, flying the Union Jack – a scene that inevitably evoked the army for many of the trainees.[81] Trainees slept in groups, with each Nissen hut, at 55 feet long and 16 feet wide, holding twenty men. Originally, the Ministry had used rather larger huts, but after experimenting with smaller huts at Glenbranter, decided that twenty formed 'a very convenient unit at which to standardize'.[82] Privacy was at a minimum, and the hut community became the basis of planned group identity, with inter-hut competitions and hut-based sporting teams. Time alone was even more minimal in the summer tented camps, usually in even more remote areas. William Dunseath, an out-of-work spinner from Accrington, recalled Pickworth IC as 'rows of bell tents, six trainees to a tent, straw palliasses, army blankets and a big marquee'.[83]

Each camp, holding up to 200 trainees and a complement of staff, was elaborately laid out. The plan for Hamsterley in 1933 allowed for ten dormitory huts for trainees, an office and stores hut, tool store, oil and lamp store, coal store, urinals, sick bay, servery, eight portable latrines, a petrol store, a recreation hut, dining hut, kitchen block, ablution hut, a staff rest room, a garage, a workshop and a football pitch; the buildings all came from the Nissen company.[84] The staff quarters comprised a large Nissen hut divided into ten single bedrooms, with a double-sized room for the camp manager, and a smaller hut divided into two-man rooms for junior staff.[85]

Camps had sporting facilities, usually open fields where men could play football and cricket (though Allerston, as a contemporary postcard shows, had its own swimming pool).[86] Trainees had access to wooden framed latrines with galvanized iron buckets, which were emptied daily into a pit, as well as indoor conveniences for use at night in each sleeping hut, also emptied daily, and a brick urinal with a pipe to a soakaway pit.[87] A small number of ICs contained more substantial buildings. At Weeting Hall and Glenbranter, staff lived in the old mansion, and the trainees in huts in the grounds.[88] Haldon IC also included a big house with eleven bedrooms, and a cricket pitch on the front lawn.[89] When Ardentinny was converted from summer camp to standing hutted camp, the local newspaper compared it to 'a small town', with its 'hospital', concert hall, 'huge sleeping huts', and canteen, all painted inside to offer 'a light and pleasant effect, mainly cream and oak'.[90] The summer camps, though, were considerably more basic, and usually even more remote than the hutted camps.

Management structures were simple and hierarchical. As with buildings and plant, the managers were initially inherited from the oversea training farms. When it was decided to open the five closed centres in 1932, Passmore recruited two men who had managed non-residential TICs: Bertram Waters, who had managed Poole and Blackpool, and S. A. Kettley from Carshalton.[91] Waters was appointed at Swanton Novers and Kettley got Fermyn Woods; Workman, who took on Cranwich, had previously served under Kettley at Carshalton. Only one came from outside the training system, the camp manager at Weeting, who had previously worked at Scunthorpe exchange.[92] Some ex-trainees told Dave Colledge that the managers were mainly military men, though they included career civil servants who had served during the First World War.[93] Under civil service rules, there was no question of looking outside the Ministry, but the training department clearly preferred insiders.

Yet qualities needed by camp managers were not necessarily those of the permanent civil servants who staffed the employment exchanges and divisional offices. IC managers needed, Passmore wrote, 'very special qualifications, e.g. personality to command respect, a liking for camp life, ability to handle men with sympathy, tact, patience and firmness'.[94] One civil servant thought that, in a camp of 200, the managers would 'know the men individually and make their confidence in a "straight deal" the foundation of discipline'.[95] Hence the preference for a degree of experience and maturity, but enough youth to be able to communicate with unemployed lads: Waters was 36 in 1932, by which time he had managed two centres and was about to take on a third, while Workman was

37, and the others were also in their late 30s.[96] Nationality was another consideration, if only in Scotland. Passmore, the Director of Training for the Ministry, was unusually anxious about Glenbranter. As opening day approached, he worried that he did not have a Scot as manager. He decided to transfer a manager from Bourne, until they found 'a likely candidate from Scotland'.[97] This was less of an issue in Wales, where A. H. O'Neill, an Irishman, served as manager of the non-residential IC at Rheola, and was deemed 'one of our own people'.[98]

Staff salaries were on the civil service scale. At Ardentinney, the manager received £6 weekly, as well as free board and lodging. As well as the budget and administration, he had a complement of fifteen staff to manage, including six gangers, two cooks, a welfare officer, a woodwork instructor and a medical orderly.[99] Gangers were responsible for direct oversight of the trainees out on the land, each one of them responsible for 25 trainees. After the gangers petitioned for a salary rise in 1934, the Ministry found a way round the strict civil service rules, and awarded them an additional 4 shillings as an 'instructional allowance', in recognition of the challenges they faced in supervising young men 'who are of course not in receipt of wages, and many of whom are physically weak and ill-disciplined'.[100]

As we have seen, the Ministry emphasised that its managers and supervisors were expected to lead by example and manage by character. In the absence of any serious penalty short of exclusion, some of the TIC managers introduced fines on the small allowance (between three and four shillings weekly, at different periods) given to the men. Predictably, there was usually a scale of fines, depending on the offence. Bertram Waters, at Swanton Novers IC, had a long list of penalties, from threepence for disobeying orders to sixpence for urinating in various specified places (including against the main entrance to the dining hut) and making 'frivolous complaints regarding food' and 'abusive language to Maintenance Orderly and Slackness on Duties'.[101] Out of eleven men fined at High Lodge TIC, two were penalised for lateness, five for absenteeism, four for disorderly conduct, and one for smoking at work.[102]

From the Ministry's perspective, fines were problematic. The Ministry conducted a review, finding that each camp manager had their own systems. TIC managers at Carstairs and Claydon were using fines to pay the men's dental fees, while Shobdon collected the money for the local hospital and High Lodge simply retained it; future fines, the Ministry ruled, should be put into the hospital box.[103] The Ministry also asked camp managers not to record them on the men's pay sheets, treating them rather as 'voluntary contributions to a Hospital or other charity box'.[104] Yet as the men were technically receiving their insured benefit, and the law made no provision for fines, the whole system was arguably unlawful.[105] A meeting of IC managers in 1933 decided that the rulebooks should make no reference to fines, and in the following year the Ministry discontinued the system altogether, preferring other punishments such as exclusion or a reprimand.[106]

In the worst cases, the men ended up in court. As far as I can tell, this was relatively rare, and mostly seems to have involved fairly trivial crimes. An analysis of cases brought before the Sherriff Court in Dunoon helps identify the extent of crime in the four ICs on the Cowal Peninsula and Crinaan canal. While it is possible that the *Dunoon Herald and Cowal Advertiser* did not report all cases, it seems highly unlikely, as the same local Sheriff Court dealt with all cases at the four ICs, and press reporting appears to have been comprehensive and detailed, reflecting perhaps the otherwise slow pace of Cowal life. Between 1933 and 1939, the court dealt with fourteen cases involving twenty-one IC staff and trainees. The two staff both came from Glenbranter: Alex Kirk, a joiner, was fined for disorderly conduct, while Robert Ogilby, Glenbranter camp deputy, had driven a motorbike without a licence. Nineteen trainees accounted for the remaining twelve cases. This hardly seems excessive given the number who passed through the camps, let alone the circumstances in which they lived. None of the cases involved major crimes. The Sheriff usually heard that the men had been rowdy or aggressive after drinking, mainly on Saturday nights. One man, Andrew Connell from an East Ayrshire textile village, was imprisoned for riotous behaviour and obstructing a constable on the Saturday night bus from Dunoon to Ardentinny.[107] The remaining offences were more trivial; the four ICs were clearly not hotbeds of anti-social behaviour.

Perhaps we can see here the beginnings of a new professional identity. The camp managers and supervisors were men who had experience of training as the main qualification for their post, and came from within the Ministry's training department. They were also sought out for the personal qualities that enabled them to command respect and handle men. A professional identity was also emerging within the UAB, which was effectively the Ministry's arm's-length agency. Despite its clear hierarchy, administered on civil service principles, the British system remained relatively small, and the line from camp manager to Passmore at the Ministry of Labour was a relatively short one. While much had to be delegated to the local managers, the impression is of an increasingly cohesive training department within the Ministry, which became ever more confident in its experience and expertise.

Boredom, freedom and control: the problem of leisure

After working hours, the men were free to spend their time as they wished. Most did what other young men would have done with a similar income. One who entered Kielder in 1934 wrote:

> We had 4/- pocket money and that to me was some collateral allowing me a packet of Woodbines every day at 2d. a packet, two nights at the cinema at 6d. a trip, 2 pint of scrumpy, one Saturday, one Sunday at 4d a pint. Total expenditure for week 2s. 10d., leaving 1s. 2d. for cards and the odd razor-blade.[108]

Even in isolated areas there was usually a pub within walking distance or a bus ride away. William Dunseath remembered enjoying a glass of cider after walking five miles to Stamford.[109] Pubs, though, were not always to the Ministry's liking. When the owner of the Ardentinny Hotel applied for a licence, Greenwood, manager of the summer camp, objected on behalf of the Ministry. According to Greenwood,

> The chief attraction, so far as their scheme was concerned, was that there was no hotel there. If there were, it would be a temptation to the lads and might spoil their chances of getting employment.

Cowal licensing court duly refused a licence, and Ardentinny Hotel continued to trade as a temperance hotel.[110]

Inside each camp was a recreation centre, usually a hut with a few facilities. At High Lodge, the recreation hut was equipped with table tennis, armchairs and a radio; a visiting journalist heard the men listening to *Pagliacci* on a gramophone.[111] By 1935, Weeting Hall offered darts and badminton as well as table tennis, and was used for film shows once a week.[112] In Pickworth, William Heard remembered the camp manager organising a day of races; as a non-smoker, he was much amused by receiving cigarettes as a prize.[113]

Much of the entertainment was home-made. William Heard loved the sing-songs: '300 men singing, it was good, it really was good. "Home on the range", and that sort of business.'[114] The men also organised football, cricket and boxing matches, with keen – sometimes violent – rivalries between men from different regions. Religion was permissive, rather than – as in some labour colonies – compulsory. Mr Hitman, a volunteer missionary, reported to the Presbytery of Dunoon that although the 'great majority' of Glenbranter men were Catholics, forty-five came to his services.[115] There was, though, no question of the Ministry diverting funding to the Kirk, nor of obliging the men to attend.

Inevitably, despite the attractions of darts or a sing-song, the men were often bored. Some found other ways of amusing themselves. William Dunseath was told off by a landowner for swimming in his pond, and risked prosecution for rabbit-hunting; he recalled the Teesside trainees as 'very big gamblers', willing to bet on anything.[116] Although Dunseath remembered nothing apart from some arguments about gambling debts, William Heard described more serious tensions: 'Fighting, all sorts – we had people mad there, men were mad there, absolutely turned mad. Fighting – I was as bad, I dare say.' One night, the men in Shobdon smashed up the recreation room and the staff social room, and: 'We enjoyed that.'[117]

This was not what was originally envisaged. As the Minister of Labour had put it in 1933, 'The residential centres provide the most effective method of improving the employability of the men because the corporate activities of the centre after working hours are not the least important part of the course.'[118] Edgar Anstey's film showed one of the men standing to announce the week's recreation programme:

> Tonight we have boxing, Friday concert with community singing, Monday we have our own cinema including Charlie Chaplin in Easy Street [cheering, and shouts of 'Good old Charlie'], on Tuesday we have a whist drive, general games in the recreation hut every evening from five thirty'.

There were also reduced price tickets for the local cinema.[119] For those who opted to stay in the camp over public holidays like Christmas, the staff organised seasonal entertainment. At Kielder, for example, the programme for Christmas 1937 included a whist drive, a five-a-side football tournament, and an indoor 'sports gymkhana', as well as a performance by Tyneside mummers on Boxing Day. For good measure, the programme added a few lines from Robert Burns:

> Then let us cheerfu' acquiesce;
> Nor make our scanty pleasures less,
> By pining at our state.[120]

Yet if such activities compared well with the leisure life of an unemployed man in a mining village, they probably did little to compensate for the boredom and isolation of life in camp.

Unlike many of their continental European counterparts, the British camps were not closed institutions. Men were given railway warrants and sent home for the major bank holidays.[121] More routinely, by agreement, trainees used the camp lorry when taking part in sports fixtures, religious services, adult education classes and concert parties.[122] Men visited local churches and dated local girls. And, albeit at risk to their benefits, they could simply leave – as many did.

Journalists from the mainstream press were also generally enthusiastic about conditions in the centres. John Macaskie compared the camp regime to that of a public school: 'Not as slaves or soldiers were they treated, but rather as members of a boarding school and even without some of the discipline associated with such institutions … The carefree singing and whistling of those who had already felt the benefit of this new job in a healthy atmosphere was indicative enough.'[123] Christie Tait, who visited Kershopefoot in 1935, reported that

> The discipline is strict but quite informal. There is nothing which suggests military training in the remotest degree. On the contrary, everything is done to avoid the least suspicion of anything military throughout the course. There are no uniforms, there is no marching to and from work, there is no saluting either when the manager speaks to the men or at any other time. There is a large Union Jack to remind the men that they are part of the British nation, and that is all.[124]

One Lanarkshire man who trained at Glenfinart, though, claimed that the camp authorities were serving up special meals whenever visitors were expected.[125]

The impact of instructional training

In late summer 1939, the ICs closed. Some staff members were reservists or territorials, and few of the men were in reserved occupations, so closure plans were prepared well in advance. A minute in the Ministry of Labour war book for February 1939 notes that 'we must have all the trainees out ... if possible before war starts'.[126] In August, the Ministry instructed camp managers to prepare for instant closure.[127] Although several later served as prisoner-of-war camps, or lumberjack camps, only Kershopefoot and Rendlesham continued, with conscientious objectors taking the places of the unemployed.[128] Britain's experiment with civilian work camps was over.

What purpose had they served? It is difficult at this distance to judge the effectiveness of the IC regime; Ministry of Labour files rarely refer to the men's work rate, though FC officials tended to take a close interest. At Knapdale, a few yards south of the Crinaan Canal, one FC inspector described the IC as

> a fine camp, but very disappointing. A feeble manager, only 50 out of 150 men said to be on our work; most of the men hanging about the camp. The new road to Dunans just begun ... 14 men seen working on this, though alleged to be 20.[129]

So there is some evidence that the labour routine could be less than intensive, depending on the quality of management at local level. But many other contemporary witnesses were more positive. Lord Rushcliffe thought that, regardless of whether trainees found jobs, the ICs' merits would be clear to 'anyone who has seen unemployed men go into the centres and has seen the same men again at the end'.[130] Visitor after visitor echoed his view. Davidson wrote enthusiastically about Kershopefoot IC, where he saw men working 'willingly amid beautiful surrounds on health-giving and muscle-building work'.[131] Another visitor described the men as 'fit and well', with 'the golden brown tan of the countryside'.[132]

As ever, the managers set about weighing and measuring the men's bodies. At Kershopefoot, Christie Tait saw a file showing 'cases in which a man had gained as much as two stone after a period of eight weeks in the centre'.[133] Violet Markham often jotted down the weights of men she saw during her regular visits as a member of the UAB. At Cranwich Heath, for example, she described the trainees – mainly from the north-east of England – as a 'Good type of men morally but physically rather poor', with 48 out of 157 weighing under 10 st., five of whom came in at under 8 st.[134] At least some men were also apparently interested in their own bodies; one young trainee from Jarrow told a reporter that he had put on 12 lbs in eight weeks.[135] As a health measure, then, camp life bestowed temporary bodily benefits.

Measured against the public rationale for the camps' existence, though, they must be counted a failure. TICs were originally established to prepare men for employment on public relief works, but once the government cut spending on relief works, placement rates fell sharply.[136] Subsequently, as Sir Arthur Rose noted, the camps usually returned the men, 'splendidly reconditioned, to their former dreary condition of unemployment'.[137] Placement rates remained low throughout the 1930s, not something the Ministry liked to discuss, claiming in one publicity brochure, published in 1938, that 'about one third' of those who completed courses went on to a job or a place in a GTC.[138] This was putting a gloss on a rather dismal picture. The risk was that the ICs simply raised expectations only to dash them, as former trainees recalled with bitterness.[139]

So why did the system continue to grow? We should never ignore politicians' fears of the electorate, which led interwar governments to support the occasional initiative in order to be seen to be taking action. In 1932, for example, the Cabinet Committee on Unemployment warned that 'the Government would be subjected to damaging criticism if, after having stopped relief works and reduced unemployment benefit, it failed to carry on the training and re-conditioning arrangements'.[140] Discussing the reports of the investigators into the depressed areas two years later, MacDonald's Cabinet agreed that some broad action was required 'to satisfy the expectations that had been created in all quarters by the appointment of the Inspectors'.[141]

Yet the ICs were never a large-scale programme, despite the Ministry's success in ensuring their survival and growth, and despite the repeated disappearance of their underlying rationale. That rationale, as Desmond King points out, rested more on a shared 'common sense' about the unemployed than systematic analysis of evidence, and he accordingly interprets the programme as 'pragmatic experiments, implemented with strikingly little knowledge'.[142] While we can understand this partly as a result of the manoeuvring of a small and new department with able leaders, it also reflected the need to be seen to be doing something about long-term unemployment among men. At their peak in 1937, there were no more than thirty ICs, including tented summer camps; in total, some 200,000 passed through the ICs and TICs together. Simple political calculation produced a small and impermanent fig leaf, which developed a life of its own, and survived long after the original rationale had vanished.

Notes

1 *Daily Express*, 27 November 1933.
2 *The Times*, 11 June 1934.
3 'Time to spare', in F. Greene (ed.), *Time to Spare: What unemployment means*, Allen & Unwin, London, 1935, 47–8.
4 *International Labour Conference (ILO), Report of the Director, 1933*, ILO, Geneva, 1934, 18.
5 Lowe, *Adjusting to Democracy*, 154–5.
6 Proposals for Training on a New Basis. Memorandum by MoL, 10 March 1932, NA CAB24/229.
7 Cabinet Employment Committee. First report, 21 April 1932, NA CAB/24/229.
8 Cabinet Conclusions, 4 May 1932, NA CAB23/71.
9 Cabinet Unemployment Committee, Second Report, November 1932, NA CAB24/235.
10 F. M. Miller, 'National Assistance or Unemployment Assistance? The British Cabinet and relief policy1932–33', *Journal of Contemporary History*, 9, 2, 1974, 173–7.
11 *Royal Commission on Unemployment Insurance (RCUI): Final report*, HMSO, London, 1932, 333, 337.
12 *RCUI: Final Report*, 465.
13 Minute to Passmore 29 July 1932, NA LAB2/2034/2F/1572.
14 Passmore to Allen and Barlow, 28 September 1932, Passmore to Barlow, 7 November 1932, NA LAB2/2034/2F/1572, H Cuthbertson to Bowers, 5/11/32, NA LAB2/2034/2F/1572, Minute sheet, Eady to Allen, 20 February 1933, Passmore to Allen, 18 August 1933, NA LAB2/2034/2F/1947.
15 LEEC Proposal to establish residential IC at Hamsterley, 28 September 1933, NA LAB2/2035/1871/Part II.
16 Passmore to Allen 14/3/33, NA LAB2/2035/1871/Part I.
17 Passmore to W. L. Taylor, Assistant Commissioner, Forestry Commission, 7 April 1933, NA LAB2/2037/ET4880.
18 Passmore, Note: Langdale Moor, 28 August 1933; MoL Proposal, 30 May 1935, NA LAB2/2040/ET5609.

19 W. Barker to W. C. Osmond, August 1933, NA LAB2/2037/ET4880; *GH*, 16 August 1933, 18 August 1933.
20 Allen to Passmore, 17 August 1933, NA LAB2/2040/ET6119.
21 John Sutherland to Passmore, 31 October 1932, NA LAB18/31.
22 Passmore to Barlow, 9 November 1932, NA LAB18/31.
23 Passmore to Allen, 3 January 1933, NA LAB18/31.
24 Labour Emergency Expenditure Committee. Proposal, 23 March 1933, NA LAB18/31; G Anderson to Passmore, 23 June 1933, NA LAB18/31.
25 Cabinet Unemployment Insurance Policy Committee, Report, 21 July 1933, NA CAB24/242.
26 Training and Occupation for the Unemployed Next Winter. Memorandum by Minister of Labour, 21 July 1933, NA CAB24/242.
27 Passmore to Solicitor, 28 April 1932, NA LAB2/1279/ET771.
28 A. C. Page, 'State Intervention in the Interwar Period: The Special Areas Acts, 1934–37', *British Journal of Law and Society*, 3, 2, 1976, 194–5.
29 Inter-departmental Committee on Reports of Investigators into Depressed Areas, 4 October 1934, NA CAB 24/250.
30 Cabinet Conclusions, 24 October 1934, NA CAB23/80.
31 *Parliamentary Debates*, 29 June 1934.
32 Ryan, Notes of a discussion with J. J. W. Handford, 25 October 1934, NA AST10/3.
33 J. Mason to C. N. Ryan, 4 August 1934, NA AST10/2 .
34 C. N. Ryan, Notes of discussion with Mr Reynard, Director of Public Assistance, Glasgow, on 11 October 1934; Ryan to J. J. W. Handford, Department of Agriculture for Scotland, 29 October 1934, NA AST10/3.
35 W. C. Osmond to Ryan and Eady, 29 September 1934, NA AST10/2.
36 UAB, *Report for 1935*, 58.
37 UAB, *Report for 1936*, 46–7.
38 MoL, *AR 1936*; D. Madeley, MoL to J. Mason, UAB, 13 July 1936, NA AST10/4.
39 MoL, *AR 1937*.
40 Memorandum by Minister of Labour, 14 June 1938, PRONI LAB/5/2.
41 Instructional Centres. Statement showing recruiting local offices. 1933, NA LAB2/20141ET2851.
42 Quoted in N. Gray, *The Worst of Times: An oral history of the Great Depression in Britain*, Wildwood House, London, 1985, 164.
43 R. C. Davison, *British Unemployment Policy: The modern phase since 1930*, Longmans, London, 1938, 118.
44 UAB, *Report for 1936*, 85.
45 Ibid., 101–2.
46 B. Power, note, 28 March 1933, NA LAB/2/2039/ET204/1.
47 *Parliamentary Debates*, 1 March 1935.
48 Training and Occupation for the Unemployed Next Winter. Memorandum by Minister of Labour, 21 July 1933, NA CAB24/242.

49 Clark to Power, 27 March 1933, NA LAB2/2039/ET204/1.
50 Information for the First Meeting of the Training and Welfare Sub-Committee, UAB, no date [1935], BLPES Markham Papers 5/8.
51 B. Power, note, 28 March 1933, NA LAB2/2039/ET204/1.
52 *Second Report of the Commissioner for the Special Areas (England and Wales)*, HMSO, London, 1936, 71.
53 *RCUI: Final Report*, 312, 320.
54 MoL. *Reports of investigations into the industrial conditions in certain depressed areas*, HMSO, London, 1934, 38.
55 Passmore to Allen, 5 September 1933, NA LAB/2/2037/ET4880.
56 Draft – Area of Recruitment, 20 April 1932, NA LAB/2/1280/ET6379.
57 Power to Allan and Eady, 3 July 1933, NA LAB2/2039/ET204/1.
58 Information for the First Meeting of the Training and Welfare Sub-Committee, UAB, n.d. [1935], BLPES Markham Papers 5/8.
59 UAB: Board Memorandum 86, 22 May 1935, BLPES Markham 7/11.
60 UAB: Board Memorandum 97, 29 October 1935, BLPES Markham 7/11.
61 UAB: Board Memorandum 148, 23 June 1936, BLPES Markham 7/11.
62 Eady to M. A. Reynard, 11 December 1936, BLPES Markham 7/11.
63 S. H. Hall-Thompson to Prime Minister, 24 August 1938, PRONI CAB/9C/13/2.
64 Conacher to Blackmore, 26 August 1938, PRONI CAB/9C/13/2.
65 See also D. King, *In the Name of Liberalism: Illiberal social policy in the USA and Britain*, Oxford University Press, Oxford, 1999, 167–8.
66 Davison, *British Unemployment Policy*, 119.
67 E. Rendle, 'Social and Economic Changes in Forestry in the Inter-war Years', *Scottish Woodland History Discussion Group Notes*, VIII, 2003, 30–1.
68 Bulier [?] to Passmore, 3 September 1934, NA LAB18/61.
69 *Daily Express*, 27 November 1933.
70 E. Rendle, 'Social and Economic Changes', 30.
71 In D. Colledge and J. Field, 'To Recondition Human Material: An account of a British labour camp in the 1930s', *History Workshop Journal*, 15, 1, 1983, 163.
72 E. Anstey, 'On the Way to Work', MoL, 1936, National Film Archive.
73 *Daily Worker*, 14 September 1933.
74 MoL Circular Minute 58/1932, 1 June 1932, NA LAB2/1775/SE774.
75 W. C. Osmond to Allen, 26 July 1933, NA LAB2/2035/1871/Part I.
76 Passmore, Memorandum. Allerston, 18 May 1933, NA LAB/2/2037/ET4880.
77 Labour Emergency Expenditure Committee. Proposal, 23 March 1933, NA LAB/18/31; *Dunoon Herald and Cowal Advertiser*, 21 April 1933, 4 August 1933.
78 *The Times*, 19 July 1935.

79 Anstey, 'On the Way to Work'.
80 *Yorkshire News*, 29 November 1933.
81 *Daily Express*, 27 November 1933; D. Colledge, *Labour Camps: the British experience*, Popular Publishing, Sheffield, 1989, 40; William Dunseath, interview, 30 January 1986.
82 W. Barker to W. C. Osmond, August 1933, NA LAB2/2037/ET4880.
83 Dunseath interview.
84 Osmond to Davis, Office of Works, 1 August 1933, NA LAB2/2035/1871/Part I.
85 Plan, 12/4 [no year given,?1933], NA LAB/2/2035/1871/Part1.
86 Card in author's possession.
87 Copy of report of the District Surveyor 26 July 1933, NA LAB2/2037/ET4880.
88 *Daily Express*, 12 March 1935; *Dunoon Herald and Cowal Advertiser*, 21 April 1933, 4 August 1933.
89 Catalogue, Haldon Estate, no date, Devon Record Office 62/9/2/Box5/55.
90 *Dunoon Herald and Cowal Advertiser*, 13 March 1936.
91 Passmore to Glen, 5 May 1932, NA LAB2/1775/SE774.
92 Timetable of Interviews, 29 June 1932, NA LAB2/1775/SE774.
93 Colledge, *Labour Camps*, 9–10.
94 Passmore to Glen, 5 May 1932, NA LAB2/1775/SE774.
95 Osmond to Ryan and Eady, 29 September 1934, NA AST10/2.
96 W. Wilson, MoL, to H. Biggs, Treasury, 31 October 1932, NA LAB2/1775/SE774.
97 Passmore to R. C. Douglas, 27 May 1933, NA LAB18/31.
98 Balthrop, Divisional Controller Wales, to Osmond, 12 August 1933, NA LAB2/2000/S&E456.
99 Passmore, Statement for Whitley Council, 22 May 1934, NA LAB12/20.
100 Allen, 18 July 1934, NA LAB2/2000/S&E456.
101 B. L. Waters, Manager, Fulmodestone IC, Note, 22 December 1932, NA LAB2/2037/ET5513.
102 J. H. Slade, Manager, High Lodge, to Watts, 27 January 1931, NA LAB2/2037/ET5513.
103 F. C. Watts to Mr Hoare, 7 February 1931, NA LAB2/2037/ET5513.
104 Haycock to Levey, 31 May 1930, NA LAB2/2037/ET5513.
105 I. N. Levey, Minute no. 5, 11 June 1930, NA LAB2/2037/ET5513.
106 Manager, IC, Swanton Novers, 21 January 1933, NA LAB2/2037/ET5513; TC Circular 151 – Passmore to IC Managers, 7 November 1934, NA LAB2/2037/ET5513.
107 *Dunoon Herald and Cowal Advertiser*, 19 August 1938.
108 Cited in Rendle, 'Social and Economic Changes', 31.
109 Dunseath, interview.

110 *Dunoon Herald and Cowal Advertiser*, 2 November 1934.
111 *Daily Express*, 27 November 1933.
112 *Daily Express*, 12 March 1935; Note of 19 December 1933, NA LAB2/2037/ET4905.
113 Dunseath, interview.
114 Colledge and Field, 'Reconditioning', 164.
115 *Dunoon Herald and Cowal Advertiser*, 8 February 1935.
116 Dunseath, interview.
117 Colledge and Field, 'Reconditioning', 164.
118 Training and Occupation for the Unemployed Next Winter. Memorandum by Minister of Labour, 21 July 1933, NA CAB24/242.
119 Anstey, 'On the Way to Work'.
120 I am grateful to Dr Ian Roberts, and Bellingham Heritage Trust, for a copy of the programme.
121 Mears to Passmore, 8 November 1932, NA LAB2/1279/ET166.
122 Assistance Circular (1937) No. 80, NA AST/10/4.
123 *Yorkshire News*, 29 November 1933.
124 D. Christie Tait, 'Unemployment of Young People in Great Britain', *International Labour Review*, 31, 2, 1935, 185.
125 *DW*, 3 November 1937.
126 War Book. MoL. Minute Sheet, 23 February 1939, NA LAB25/31.
127 Letter to managers of ICs, 14 August 1939, NA LAB25/31.
128 Letter to Managers of Kershopefoot and Rendlesham ICs, 14 August 1939.
129 Inspection, Knapdale Forest, 2 and 3 September 1937, NA F/43/371.
130 *Report of the UAB, 1936*, 4.
131 *MoL. Reports of Investigations*, 39.
132 *The Times*, 19 July 1935.
133 D. Christie Tait, 'Unemployment of Young People', 186.
134 Visit to Instructional Centre. Cranwich Heath. December 1 1936, BLPES, Markham 8/11.
135 *Daily Express*, 27 November 1933.
136 Training and Occupation for the Unemployed Next Winter. Memorandum by Minister of Labour, 21 July 1933, NA CAB24/242.
137 *MoL. Reports of Investigations*, 233.
138 *Instructional Centres*, MoL, 1938, BLPES Markham Papers 7/29.
139 Colledge and Field, 'Reconditioning', 165; Dunseath, interview.
140 Cabinet Employment Committee. First report, 21 April 1932, NA CAB24/229.
141 Cabinet Conclusions, 24 October 1934, NA CAB23/80.
142 King, *In the Name*, 178–9.

8

'Light green uniforms, white aprons and caps'

Training unemployed women

On Wednesday 22 February 1928, Nellie Dear walked down the gangplank from the SS *Otranto* at Brisbane, to start a new life as a lady's companion. Along with seven other young women from Britain who landed at Brisbane that day, she had spent two months under training in The Elms, a large stone property in Market Harborough. Miss Dear apparently spoke enthusiastically about the training she had received, and expressed the hope that her parents would follow in due course. After meeting immigration officials, along with representatives of the New Settlers' League and the Country Women's Association, she went to her first situation.[1] After that, Nellie Dear disappears from the records.

Between the wars, thousands of young British women trained for a life of domestic service, some staying in Britain and others emigrating overseas. Emigration, particularly for girls and younger single women, had become a focus of activity for a host of voluntary organisations and poor law agencies during the nineteenth century, actively supported by the Dominions governments (together with large parts of their male populations), as well as by British supporters of imperial loyalty and cohesion. By 1914 there was a wide range of well-established services to promote movement to the Dominions.[2] While some offered a range of different training programmes for women, most were concerned with domestic occupations, preparing their young charges for a life of service and marriage.

As in other fields of social and economic policy, rising unemployment ultimately led to state intervention. Yet while men were viewed as suitable objects of state-provided training in camps, women were rarely involved in camp movements, and much of the state intervention was mediated through voluntary agencies and semi-governmental bodies, such as the Central Committee on Women's Training and Employment (CCWTE). Most training programmes for women were primarily directed at placing women back in the home; and although some women were sent to residential institutions, they lived not in tents or huts in the countryside, but in the upper floors of suburban middle-class homes. And while work camps for men were designed to build muscular bodies and remove them from urban influences, residential training for women was designed to remove any sign of industrial 'roughness' or dirt, and familiarise them with life in a suburban middle-class home. Age, gender and class came together to shape the experiences of unemployed men and women alike, but they did so in rather different ways, and in turn provoked rather different responses.

The domestic ideal

Training had long been seen as a way of increasing the supply of servants and removing women from poverty – or worse. It was estimated in the late 1870s that twenty charities in London alone were training girls as domestic servants.[3] Best known was Urania Cottage, created in 1846 by the wealthy heiress Angela Burdett-Coutts and the novelist Charles Dickens with the aim of 'reclaiming young women, instructing them in all sound domestic knowledge, and sending them out to Australia or elsewhere'.[4] Urania Cottage was following a path well trodden. From the early years of the nineteenth century, Anglicans were prominent in founding penitentiaries to reclaim fallen women, teaching the skills of laundry work and other tasks, with a view to finding the girls employment in a Christian household.[5] Mary, Countess of Meath, supported training for girls in Irish workhouses as domestic servants, while a Glasgow charity promoted 'formation of character' through its Training School and Temporary Home for Girls.[6] In Birmingham, the Ladies Association for the Care and Protection of Young Girls opened a training home to accommodate around twenty young women, and taught basic domestic skills to those who were judged not yet to have fallen into prostitution.[7] Some local government bodies were also active in the field.[8]

Such initiatives were mainly meant to lift young women from prostitution or poverty. Of course, poverty was a relative term; in 1909 the British Women's Emigration Association opened a residential training home at Leaton, Shropshire, charging 10 shillings weekly to train 'genteel' women in colonial housework for three months.[9] Even for the genteel poor, domestic service looked a safe bet: the demand was endless, and not only from the wealthy. The outbreak of war in 1914 came as a shock, for not only were young women needed to make munitions and fill other gaps left by men, but the experience of war also raised their aspirations. The number of servants fell by a quarter during the war, and in 1918 an anxious Ministry of Reconstruction established a domestic service committee to explore ways of improving the supply once peacetime conditions returned.[10] At the same time, the British government was also fearful of post-war unemployment among women industrial workers and ex-servicewomen. An enquiry into the possible emigration of veterans and war widows, though stopping short of recommending anything more radical than encouraging existing agencies, recommended supporting 'female emigration as the essential foundation of all effective Empire Settlement', and noted that much of the demand in the colonies was for domestic servants.[11]

By 1921, well over a million women in Britain were working as domestics, and their number continued to rise in the following decade. The popularity of this job among young women is as controversial among historians as it was at the time.[12] Before 1939, most domestic servants lived in their employers' homes, worked long hours, and usually faced close restrictions on their social lives. Employers generally insisted that servants wore a uniform, and many expected the servant to own at least two sets of suitable clothing. While wages were broadly comparable with factory or shop work, if board and lodging are taken into account, many young women did not like living in their employer's home; and holidays were unregulated, and therefore at the whim of their employer.[13] Turnover was high, few servants staying in the same position for more than two years and most leaving on marriage.[14] Increasingly, family employers had to compete with institutions, as hospitals, factories, hotels and care homes started recruiting greater numbers of cooks, cleaners and waiting staff. As a result, demand remained high throughout the inter-war years, and many reformers saw upskilling as a way of making the role more attractive to young women.[15]

The CCWTE, originally known as Queen Mary's Committee for Women's Employment, was formed in summer 1914 to help women who had lost their jobs as a result of the war. By 1918 it included several able and talented members, such as the Liberal and social worker Violet Markham (later its chair), the trade unionists Mary MacArthur and Margaret Bondfield, the Poplar socialist Susan Lawrence, and the health campaigner Dr Marion Phillips. These women used the CCWTE as a platform, lobbying and pressing government on behalf of women workers, something its creators had never intended. With the Ministry's approval, Markham established a Scottish Committee in 1920, chaired by Ishbel Hamilton-Gordon, Marchioness of Aberdeen and Temair, the long-serving president of the International Council of Women.[16] In addition, the Ministry of Labour asked its local advisory committees to set up women's sub-committees, advising local labour exchanges on issues of women's work.[17] The CCWTE thus sat at the centre of an important web of connections, involving local officials and honorary advisers through to the UK-wide networks of women trade union leaders and socialist feminists, as well as the rather elevated centre-left luminaries associated with Markham. While always working within limits set by the Ministry, this was an influential body, and it is surprising that it has not attracted greater attention from historians.

Immediately after the war, the Committee's early schemes focused on scholarships for courses in professions such as nursing, teaching and clerical work.[18] By 1921, however, its work was increasingly directed towards domestic service. In its 1919 report, the Ministry of Reconstruction's committee on domestic service had expressed surprise over what it called 'the present totally inadequate amount of facilities for training', seeing proficiency and qualifications as central to raising the status of domestic to that of a skilled trade.[19] Funded by the Ministry of Labour, the CCWTE opened a number of training centres, running 'homecraft' courses, mainly for younger women who promised to enter service at the end of their courses, and a smaller number of 'homemaker' courses for unemployed adult women, whom it expected to remain as full-time housewives until they found another job. Most, if not all of its members, had at least some misgivings about the focus on domestic service, but virtually no other form of training was on offer.[20]

Training hostels for the Empire

While CCWTE institutions may have produced servants for the home market, Dominions governments were keen to attract suitable women as immigrants. In 1919, a delegation from the Oversea Settlement Committee (OSC) investigated openings for British women in Canada, which duly reported that there were good opportunities for emigrants, particularly in general domestic service, waitressing and cookery, yet although the delegation was asked to consider training, it confined its observations to what was available after the women were in Canada.[21] Voluntary organisations such as the Salvation Army and the Society for the Overseas Settlement of British Women (SOSBW) continued to support emigration for unemployed women, and some local government initiatives survived, but these tended to be small scale, and designed more to meet the needs of the providers than those of the Dominions.[22] The Dominions governments, in their turn, provided little more than assisted passages.

In mid-February 1927, however, Betterton announced that the Oversea Settlement Department (OSD) was negotiating with CCWTE to open 'an experimental residential centre for training about 40 women at a time for domestic service in Australia'. The running costs were to be shared equally between the Australian and British governments, under the terms of what Betterton tactfully referred to as the 'Oversea Settlement Act'.[23] These discussions had been on-going for some time before Betterton's announcement. Dame Muriel Talbot, of the OSC, was enthusiastic about the idea, expressing much admiration for the servant's lot in Australia and only one reservation: Northern Australia, she warned, was 'tropical, and extremely trying for white women and their families'.[24] While all the Dominions were keen to recruit British women, Australia was, in Hamilton and Higman's words, 'a singularly exclusive seeker' of white female immigrants.[25] In late 1925, Miss Nansen, seconded from the Ministry of Labour to serve CCWTE as its executive officer, heard of a 'tentative suggestion' that there might be special training programmes for overseas emigrants. Ever quick to defend its role against incursions, the Committee resolved that 'if such a request were made, the Committee should undertake this work'.[26]

A year later, Violet Markham reported that as chair, she had received a 'semi-formal letter' from Alan Barlow at the Ministry of Labour, referring to a discussion of possible 'short courses of training in domestic work for women selected for migration to Australia'. After some discussion, Markham proposed that once an official approach had been received, she would be willing to organise 'a social meeting' at her home involving representatives from the British and Australian governments and selected home training centre (HTC) superintendents, to be followed by a visit to an HTC 'in good premises'.[27] Markham had stage-managed things well. The OSC supported CCWTE's claim to lead the new 'Australian Training Centre', and in 1927 the partners created a joint committee comprising two women members of the OSC, two nominees of the Australian government, and two members of CCWTE, with Markham as its chair.[28]

The Australian government was equally keen. Bruce, the Australian Prime Minister, had attended the 1926 Imperial Conference in London, where the Australian delegation agreed to recommend contributing to the cost of a training scheme in Britain. The idea had in part come from Herbert W. Gepp, chairman of the federal Development and Migration Commission, who had also been in London, representing Australia during the conference's discussions of oversea settlement.[29] There was, of course, a strong racial and national dimension to this. One Australian publicity brochure explained to potential migrants that: 'For all practical purposes as well as to the outward eye or ear of the observer, the Australian population is as completely British as the population of Great Britain.'[30] But similar hopes and convictions could be heard across Britain. Florence Harrison Bell, as a suffragette and supporter of the Independent Labour Party (ILP), was hardly a stereotypical Empire loyalist, but she believed that 'the really great opportunity for the women of the country is as wives of the present, and mothers of the future generations, of our kinfolk overseas'.[31]

By the time of Betterton's announcement, CCWTE was looking at premises. By April 1927 it had agreed terms for The Elms, in Market Harborough, which one broadcaster described as a 'charming old Georgian house standing in a large garden'.[32] Initially, it was short of equipment, including – vitally – items to polish and dust, and Miss Nansen appealed to the Committee members to lend 'white elephants', such 'as brass and plated articles, ornaments, etc.'[33] The Committee found a superintendent, Miss P. C. Ball, a qualified domestic science teacher, and the centre – still presented as an 'experiment – opened on 1 September 1927 with an initial intake of five young women.[34] Elizabeth, Duchess of York, duly conducted the formal opening ceremony.[35] In February the Committee heard that 49 young women had completed their training, of whom 48 were sailing for Australia, while seven had left before completing their course.[36]

For the most part, the curriculum at Market Harborough was based on practical work around the house. Trainees attended lectures on Australian life, the history and geography of the Common-wealth, and citizenship, but otherwise spent their days learning housewifery, cookery, laundry, needlework and basic health and hygiene, in what two American observers described as 'conditions approximating as closely as possible those in typical middle class British homes'.[37] Among other things, they learned needlework by making their own uniforms, which they were expected to take to Australia. Some Australian immigration agents apparently thought this curriculum 'too scientific' and not nearly practical enough, given the circumstances of life in rural and small town Australia.[38]

Activity increased as the crisis deepened. By July 1928, 151 trainees from The Elms had sailed for Australia.[39] In the wake of the industrial transference report, the government approved plans for the OSD to fund new training hostels in Newcastle, Paisley, Cardiff, London, and St Albans.[40] Most were run through voluntary bodies, such as the SOSBW's small hostel at St Alban's, or faith groups such as the Church Army hostel in Cardiff and the Dominican Sisters' programme in their Portobello Road convent; in Scotland, the OSD invited the CCWTE's Scottish Committee to manage its new training hostel in a house called Millersneuk at Lenzie, near Paisley.[41] Mean-while, the CCWTE was exploring other possibilities. As well as a new centre in London, the Ministry's Chief Woman Officers put the case for a new residential centre in the English Midlands, and the OSC hoped to establish a further centre in Scotland.[42] After inspecting premises in Kettering and Bourneville, the Committee decided to purchase Newbold Beeches, in Leamington Spa, allowing Market Harborough to specialise in 'the better class of girls'.[43]

In the meantime, the Ministry sent Miss Ball on a tour of Australia. She visited 'old Elms' in towns and cities across the country, and took great interest in the details of Australian home life and conditions. She called on voluntary organisations who were concerned with migrant welfare, from the Catholic Daugh-ters of Australia to the Queensland Countrywomen's Association.[44] She also addressed the New Settlers League on the difficulties of training girls in England for conditions in Australia, welcoming criticisms as helpful.[45] Most Australian employers, she reported, were sympathetic and fair, though she also found a minority overly critical, forever telling British servants how badly they compared with native Australians.[46] The Ministry also sent Miss A. M. Cox, senior women's officer from the Leeds labour exchange, to gather information on the training needs of domestic servants, and visit ex-trainees. She praised Australian housing, judging the girls 'fortunate' to live in a country 'where climatic conditions allowed them to wear such pretty and dainty clothes'.[47]

The end of assisted migration came as a severe shock to the emerging training system. Not only did the CCWTE enjoy financial support from the Australian government; the British contribution, although channelled to the CCWTE through the Ministry of Labour, came from the vote for the Colonial Office.[48] The Australians' decision to stop their grant to Market Harborough threatened the entire system.[49] To make matters worse, labour exchanges were failing to send recruits: Newbold Beeches only had fourteen in training in February 1930, when the Committee decided to invite Margaret Bondfield – a long-standing member, except when serving as Minister of Labour – to perform the official opening.[50] There was little that the Committee could do in the short term, and it postponed its plans for a London centre.[51]

Yet, with Bondfield as Minister of Labour, the CCWTE was in a relatively strong position. Within weeks, it had invented a whole new rationale for its residential training programme. Initially, the proposal came from the Labour Emergency Expenditure Committee, an internal group of senior staff in the Ministry of Labour, who proposed that, while they were not required for oversea migrants, the Ministry should use the training hostels for training unemployed women for domestic employment in Britain. This proposal concerned four centres associated with the OSD: Millersneuk; St Mary's Convent, Portobello Road, London; the Church Army Hostel in Cardiff; and Harden, near Newcastle.[52] While the CCWTE was perfectly willing to expand its residential training system in this way, it indignantly rejected any suggestion that others – particularly the OSD – should interfere. A sub-committee was created to consider the proposal was chaired by Markham, while Marion Phillips was a member. Predictably, given Markham's record and connections, it saw off the OSD, telling the Ministry that the CCWTE was 'the responsible authority for any training for domestic service in Great Britain to which the Ministry contributed and they could not tolerate any other body but themselves as being allowed authority for such training'.[53] Further, there should be no 'division of control for home training even as a temporary measure'.[54]

Rather than handing any authority to the OSD, the CCWTE acquired complete control of Millersneuk, Harden, and Market Harborough, and withdrew the grant from the Portobello Road convent.[55] In 1930, it approved proposals for new centres in Yorkshire and the north-west of England, and renewed its search for suitable premises in London.[56] By 1931, the CCWTE was operating five residential centres, with almost 200 places. The largest was Appleton Hall, in Cheshire, which opened in 1931 with space for 60 trainees; Newbold Beeches and The Elms offered 40 places apiece, while Millersneuk had 33 and Harden 25.[57] In the following year the Committee opened new residential programmes in Warrington, Harrogate and London.[58] This period of expansion stopped in August 1931; MacDonald's National Government was formed around a platform of fiscal economies, and these applied to the Ministry of Labour as much as any other government department. The Committee's initial response was to preserve the residential centres, making savings by reducing staff salaries and trainee responsible.[59]

Describing the closures as 'unfortunate', the Royal Commission on Unemployment Insurance expressed the hope that the programme 'will be resumed as soon as possible', and would not be 'hampered for lack of the necessary funds'.[60] The Committee stuck to its guns, announcing plans to close Harden, where the accommodation was unsatisfactory, while developing new centres in at Lapsewood, Sydenham Hill, London and Aberystwyth in Wales.[61] By summer 1933, the CCWTE was responsible for 26 non-residential and 7 residential centres, and was finding it difficult to fill the places.[62] This did not stop the Committee from exploring its options: in the mid-1930s it considered opening a seasonal residential centre in Scarborough, in North Yorkshire.[63] In summer 1938, after an outbreak of scarlet fever made Millersneuk unusable, the Scottish committee opened a temporary centre in Edinburgh, then extended the lease after Millersneuk had reopened, but it proved impossible to recruit enough young women to fill both centres, and Edinburgh was closed in August 1939.[64]

Experiencing training

Pedagogically, the core training activity comprised intensive domestic labour, closely supervised by experienced instructors. Up to 1935, the women were sent for eight-week courses, though they could extend their stay to ten weeks. The Committee agreed early in1935 to extend the standard course at residential centres to twelve weeks, the shorter period having been introduced for Australian training.[65] Although the trainees were not paid benefit, they received board and lodging, free travel to the centre, pocket money at 2s. 6d. weekly and 'materials for the outfit which they make during training and which becomes their property on taking up domestic employment'.[66]

As well as looking after the house – including cooking, cleaning, laundering and needlework – the girls were required to wait on the staff and each other, taking turns to practise the duties of a parlour maid, housemaid, and dining room maid. Petre Mais, who visited the centres for a series of BBC broadcasts, found them 'bright and comfortable, avoiding as far as possible the institutional atmosphere'.[67] Harden was a 'comfortable homelike house', Appleton Hall a 'very fine mansion' with a 'beautiful garden', Millersneuk a 'fine country house', Waldernheath a 'well-equipped modern house in one of the best residential districts in Harrogate', Lapsewood an 'attractive old-fashioned house', and The Elms a 'charming old Georgian house standing in a large garden'.[68] The training hostels were also well equipped. While the CCWTE was reluctant to invest in its day training centres, many of which were vulnerable to closure and had limited equipment, it was under no such pressures with the residential centres.[69]

Residence was important in preparing young women for domestic service. In the north-west of England, Stanley Warrington of the Ministry of Labour reported that 'sleeping away from home is a very material factor with these girls – it is such a complete change in their habits'.[70] An enthusiastic visitor to a day centre in Cardiff noted that while it was not residential, the girls were required to sleep in for four nights of their twelve-week training, cleaning the staff bedrooms to experience 'the early morning work required in the average household'. According to Miss Blackwell, the centre superintendent, ex-factory girls were accustomed to spending their evenings at home and disliked the residential side of domestic work.[71] This was a common problem in the industrial areas, and the residential centres provided a spatial framework for accustoming young unemployed women to living in a middle-class residence.[72]

Residence also helped build *esprit de corps*. As Miss Andrews, superintendent of Lapsewood HTC, explained to a visiting journalist, 'It is remarkable the affection the girls feel for the centre. Those who have been here a few weeks take a tremendous pride in impressing newcomers with their duties and how they should behave'.[73] And as time went on, recreation was provided on a systematic basis. Afternoons were free between lunch time and tea time, and trainees were free to go out during this period, as well as on their weekly half-day's rest. Recreation rooms were used for games and dancing, as well as for reading or writing. A woman journalist visiting Lapsewood wrote of the homely atmosphere: 'It is excusable for one to expect a Government training centre for out of work girls to be a grim, coldly efficient institution ... I found something altogether different – efficient, indeed, but a thoroughly human institution.'[74] In 1934, fifty young alumni of The Elms who had found work nearby, attended a reunion at Leicester Labour Exchange. It was reportedly a jolly affair: 'The gramophone when it played was hardly heard, until amid much merriment, one of the staff sounded a hefty triangle and the room was prepared for musical chairs.'[75]

In contrast with the men's camps, co-residence did not mean complete loss of privacy. One photograph of The Elms, in Market Harborough, shows that each trainee had her own cubicle, separated from her neighbours by a wooden partition, each with their own chest of drawers in the cubicle, and a washstand with a curtain.[76] Nevertheless, the trainees were exposed to a significant level of inspection and regulation, focusing particularly on cleanliness and appearance. Despite medical inspections before entry, there was 'an outbreak of an infectious skin complaint' among trainees in Harden in early 1932.[77] Skin infections could have damaged the centres' reputation, and the outbreak was dealt with quickly. More routinely, the trainees were required to line up for inspection, with close attention paid to their dress, appearance and personal hygiene.

Recruiting servile bodies?

Recruitment was often a struggle. In 1931, the Ministry circulated local labour exchanges with details of the recruitment procedure that they should follow. Candidates should be British Subjects, aged 16 or over and registered unemployed. On receiving an application and two references, the exchange would arrange for an interview with the local women's sub-committee, who were instructed to select 'only those candidates whose physical fitness and mental alertness fit them to derive full benefit from the training, *and who have a definite intention of entering resident domestic service*'.[78] In 1932, after receiving representations from local women's sub-committees, CCWTE decided to 'experiment' with an entry age of 15.[79] It also considered recruiting older women, for whom it and the Ministry had some sympathy. James Matson, the Ministry's Divisional Controller for Scotland, described older unemployed women as 'war casualties in a sense', as their generation were often left without husbands.[80] But it concluded that the task of converting this group into servants was beyond its powers, after an analysis of day trainees aged over 35 in two northern English industrial cities led one official to conclude that they were 'handicapped by their physical condition'. An appendix listed a number of complaints, including three trainees with rheumatism, one unable to kneel and one with tuberculosis; others were simply described as of a 'rougher' type.[81]

Modern methods of publicity were also exploited. In 1925, the Committee invited six ex-trainees who had attended art school to submit poster designs for a possible promotional campaign; the response was reportedly disappointing.[82] In the same year, Margaret Bondfield offered to broadcast a ten-minute radio talk on the Committee's work.[83] With plans under way for the new residential centre, Violet Markham agreed to draft a magazine article, which the Committee planned to reprint as a leaflet.[84] A government publicity film of Market Harborough was shown in 1928. The Committee made a range of printed publicity materials available to local exchanges, including illustrated leaflets and a picture poster called 'The Happy Maid'.[85] In spring 1936, a Ministry of Labour film did the rounds in exchanges and JICs, as well as 'cinema slides shown at Picture Houses'.[86] The kind of publicity preferred by the CCWTE was typified by a journalist visiting Lapsewood, who wrote of her delight at seeing 35 young women lined up to greet her, 'smart in light green uniforms, white apron and caps'.[87] HTCs instructed and shaped these young bodies in the arts and crafts of cleanliness, tidiness and a strict routine. And they then put them on show.

Despite these efforts, application rates stayed stubbornly below the level needed to keep the centres full. In 1933, the Committee asked the Ministry to encourage its Divisional Controllers in England and Wales to improve recruitment for its residential centres.[88] The greatest difficulties were faced in the North-west of England, where young women, accustomed to expecting the earnings and independence of industrial work, were particularly reluctant to go into service. The Divisional Controller wrote to all labour exchanges in the North-west, asking managers to investigate the reasons behind this reluctance, and to try to overcome it.[89] Similarly problems occurred in Birmingham, where the divisional woman's officer reported on the 'lack of attraction which the occupation has to the Midland young women'.[90] In Scotland, Glaswegians apparently disliked going to Paisley for training, leading the Scottish Committee to propose a second Scottish centre closer to Glasgow.[91] The Principal of Millersneuk told Sir Arthur Rose that families lost income when a daughter attended the centre, as part of their benefit would be diverted to pay for board and lodging.[92] In general, though, the Committee viewed poor recruitment as reflecting popular dislike of domestic service.

Even among those who were willing, rejection rates were relatively high. In 1930, the Ministry reported that at Leamington nearly 50 per cent of women examined failed to reach the Centre, 6 per cent being rejections by the medical officers, 'and the rest wastage'.[93] A few months later, recruitment was so poor that the Committee considered closing Market Harborough and Appleton Hall.[94] Fitness and health were crucial for young women who were to enter middle-class homes as servants. In 1930, the Wales Divisional Office listed nine applicants rejected by the selection committee. Among them were May Samuel, 19, of Llanelli, described as 'Rather heavy looking. Doubtful if she would go away after training', and Anita John, 26, also from Llanelli, dismissed as 'Factory type, very dull'.[95] These women were rejected even before the compulsory medical examination, carried out on every approved applicant in England and Wales by Regional Medical Officers of the

Ministry of Health, and in Scotland by the Department of Health for Scotland, following the same process as the Ministry of Labour, the CCWTE having substituted the phrase 'domestic worker' for 'manual worker' in the otherwise unaltered forms.[96] The results were discouraging: in 1937, Violet Markham wrote to her sister complaining of the difficulties, and noting that particularly among older women, 'the bad health ... is incredible. I sometimes wonder how the country carries on at all with such a dead load at its base.'[97]

In December 1935, the Committee considered the rather sensitive question of head lice. The subject was touchy: officers in the North-east of England reported that any mention of head lice caused great 'indignation', which was 'very difficult to overcome even with the greatest of tact'.[98] One CCWTE member raised her concern over 'the large number of Cleveland women applicants rejected for dirty heads', and asked whether infected women could be treated after admission, a proposal that the Committee rejected. Officials from Cleveland reported that of the 47 women recruited in the current year, 19 were rejected on medical reasons, 14 of whom were suffering from pediculosis.[99] The Committee concluded, rather unconvincingly, 'that the trouble is almost entirely confined to the North Eastern area'.[100] In fact, this was not a new problem, nor was it confined to the North-east, as 'personal cleanliness' had preoccupied the Committee since the mid-20s.[101]

Recruitment continued to be so poor that, as for men, there was occasional talk of compulsion. Early in 1931, the Church of Scotland discovered that local exchange officials were able to insist on attending a day training centre as a condition of benefit, but had no powers to send girls to a residential centre. Dr David Watson, convener of the Kirk's social work committee, thought this 'an obvious weakness in the system, for there were many very sorely in need of training who were refusing it', and offered to provide evidence on the matter to the Royal Commission on Unemployment Insurance (RCUI).[102] Although the Commission favoured training on a voluntary basis, it likely that local officials were free to use at least some pressure to persuade young women to enter HTCs.[103] Violet Markham favoured a robust approach, going so far as to interview some women in person. She accused one, a 32-year-old Liverpudlian called Alice Caddick, of playing along in interviews then going home to live on her allowance; the UAB reduced Caddick's weekly benefit from 12 shilling to 10 shillings.[104]

Above all, the challenge was to recruit the right 'type of girl'. When the Scottish committee opened a temporary centre in Edinburgh, after an outbreak of scarlet fever at Millersneuk, it was impressed by the results: 'the Edinburgh Centre had attracted a nice type of girl', many of them coming down from the north of Scotland.[105] As the upturn in the economy provided alternative occupations for young women, the Elms started to specialise in domestic science training, offering a more substantial – and certificated – form of vocational training in the hope of attracting 'girls of good education' into careers in large organisations such as companies, hospitals or schools.[106] The Committee also turned to young Jewish refugees. With the arrival of the first *Kindertransporte*, the Scottish committee proposed that CCWTE should admit 'a percentage of juvenile refugees to existing Centres at an appropriate charge, always provided that knowledge of English has been acquired and preferably one or more years spent in a British school'.[107] The 'appropriate charge', incidentally, was most likely to fall on those individual citizens who had sponsored the young refugees.

If recruitment was a struggle, placement was not. At Millersneuk, trainees were placed through the Private Domestic Clearing Section of Glasgow South Side Exchange.[108] Market Harborough trainees were placed through the Leicester Exchange; as might be expected, demand was high, and in the early 1930s two out of five Market Harborough trainees found places in or near Leicester.[109] With a buoyant market for domestic servants, and growing demand for cooks and the like in institutions, there was never any difficulty in finding posts. As Miss M. E. Andrews, superintendent of Lapsewood HTC, told one reporter: 'We have so many applications for these girls, we do not know how to cope with them.'[110]

In the end, it was the availability of jobs that overcame feminist doubts about the value of training young women for careers as domestics. This was the subject of occasional debate even within the Committee. Dr Marion Phillips, a long-standing member, raised the issue on a number of occasions.[111] There were also outside critics, including the National Union of Societies for Equal Citizenship, which wrote to Bondfield in 1931, calling for women to have access to as broad a range of training as that available to men.[112] Bondfield claimed to share these doubts, at any rate while in opposition, expressing the fear that the CCWTE might 'drive unsuitable women into occupations which were distasteful to them, and for which they were not well equipped', though she loyally praised its success in finding young women jobs, and urged ministers to raise its budget.[113] And her pragmatic approach found support across the mainstream political spectrum. Susan Lawrence, Labour MP and former Poplar rebel, sympathised with those women who refused to enter service, but accepted that 'there are a great many women who are happy in domestic service, and for them it is a perfectly good way to make a living'.[114] Violet Markham, a Liberal who had opposed the women's suffrage movement, also shared this view, telling young trainees in Glasgow that they need never fear becoming unemployed again, adding that 'with their domestic training, they made better wives when they got married'.[115]

In fact, domestic service formed a common ground that brought together women from a variety of political backgrounds. Bondfield and Susan Lawrence were Labour politicians and strong supporters of suffrage extension. They shared a long track record of concern for women workers in general, and unemployed women workers in particular. Both argued the CCWTE's case in Parliament, and in opposition they defended it against budget cuts.[116] As a government minister, Bondfield continued to support the CCWTE's work, though she withdrew as a member while holding office. Marion Phillips was also a Labour MP, albeit briefly; she had worked for Beatrice and Sidney Webb in their studies of the poor law, and again had a long record of concern over women's employment. And though Markham was a Liberal, she came from the wing which had considerable sympathy for the working class, and was patron of both the settlement movement and adult education movement in Chesterfield. Dr Elizabeth Garrett Anderson also served as a member, but for a relatively brief period, resigning early in 1925 for reasons that are unclear.[117]

The Committee also enjoyed the support of other influential women. More precisely, it found support among women (and men) interested in the supply and conditions of domestic servants. This included Her Majesty the Queen, who let it be known that she wished to visit the London HTC, albeit with a minimum of fuss; a private visit was duly arranged in summer 1932.[118] The Duchess of York, better known to later generations as Queen Elizabeth, the Queen Mother, performed a number of opening ceremonies. At Lenzie, she 'chatted with some of the girls in training, and wished them luck in Canada', before visiting the Duke of Montrose at Buchanan Castle .[119] As a London-based centre, Lapsewood was particularly popular, and its long list of distinguished guests included the Queen and Ernest Brown, Minister of Labour.[120] Frau Gertrud Scholtz-Klink, leader of the *National-sozialistische Frauenschaft* and head of the Women's Bureau in the *Deutscher Arbeitsfront*, was invited to lunch at Lapsewood when she visited London in March 1939.[121]

A strong body of committed members, and an ability to attract powerful allies, helped counter the Committee's dependence on the Ministry of Labour. Throughout the period, the annual grant from the Ministry was the Committee's main source of income. The level of the grant fluctuated, with a high point of £150,000 for 1920–21 and a low of £63,000 for 1925–26; in 1928, as an economy measure, it was cut to £45,000, but Bondfield immediately raised it to over £100,000. It was reduced again after 1931, recovering to £80–90,000 in the later 1930s.[122]

The Ministry paid the piper, and called the tune; but this did not prevent the Committee from exercising considerable influence over the agenda that it pursued, including its decision to continue residential training at the expense of day training during the crisis of the early 1930s. And if the CCWTE programmes could be criticised for channelling young women into domestic service, pragmatic socialists believed that they were a sight better than no training programmes at all. Others would have preferred the state to stay away from training altogether. Sir Joseph Nall, a Conservative MP and deep-dyed imperialist, thought there was 'no need to squander public funds for such a purpose', given the abundance of middle-class families willing to train their own servants.[123]

It is usually easy to find out what Conservative MPs think on any given topic, and much harder to discover what young unemployed women thought of the centres. One group from The Elms offered a very forthright response, seeing off an Australian journalist who suggested that what they really wanted was not to work but to marry, with the retort: 'We are out to get on, not to get off.'[124] There is no point in debating how typical this view was, in the absence of direct evidence, but the instant response suggests that for some young working-class women, domestic service was not servile at all but rather an active means of achieving independence, at least of a kind. As Selina Todd emphasises, in the end, domestic servants were working class.[125] Like the unemployed men, they had to live by their labour; and like the men, they laboured with their bodies. Unlike the men, their bodies were judged not by muscularity and weight; they had to appear clean, uniformed and smart – above all, they had to act like 'nice girls'.

Notes

1 *Brisbane Courier*, 23 February 1928.
2 B. L. Blakeley, 'The Society for the Oversea Settlement of Women and the Problems of Empire settlement, 1917–1936', *Albion*, 20, 3, 1988, 421–44; J. Bush, 'The Right Sort of Woman: Female emigrators and emigration to the British Empire, 1890–1910', *Women's History Review*, 3, 3, 1994, 385–409; L. Chilton, *Agents of Empire: British female migration to Canada and Australia, 1860–1930*, University of Toronto Press, Toronto, 2007; M. Harper, *Emigration from North-East Scotland, Vol 2*, Aberdeen University Press, Aberdeen, 1988, 232–40; M. Langfield, 'Voluntarism, Salvation and Rescue: British juvenile migration to Australia and Canada, 1890–1939', *Journal of Imperial and Commonwealth History*, 32, 2, 2010, 86–114.
3 P. Horn, *The Rise and Fall of the Victorian Servant*, Gill & Macmillan, Dublin, 1975, 35.
4 Quoted in G. Moore (2004), *Dickens and Empire: Discourses of class, race and colonialism in the works of Charles Dickens*, Ashgate, Aldershot, 8.
5 S. Mumm, '"Not Worse than other Girls": The convent-based rehabilitation of fallen women in Victorian Britain', *Journal of Social History*, 29, 3, 1996, 536–7.
6 *The Diaries of Mary, Countess of Meath*, Hutchinson & Co., London, no date [?1922?], 268; *Glasgow Herald*, 18 January 1898.
7 P. Bartley, 'Preventing Prostitution: The Ladies' Association for the Care and Protection of Young Girls in Birmingham, 1887–1914', *Women's History Review*, 7, 1, 1988, 49–51.
8 Horn, *Rise and Fall*, 35.
9 Harper, *Emigration*, 236.
10 Horn, *Rise and Fall*, 166.
11 *Report of the Committee appointed to consider settling within the empire ex-servicemen who may desire to emigrate after the war*, HMSO, London, 1917, 17.
12 See Horn, *Rise and Fall*; L. Davidoff, 'Mastered for Life: Servant and wife in Victorian and Edwardian England', *Journal of Social History*, 7, 4, 1974, 406–28; S. Todd, 'Domestic service and class relations in Britain, 1900–1950', *Past & Present*, 103, 2009, 181–204.

13 P. Taylor, 'Daughters and Mothers – Maids and Mistresses: Domestic service between the Wars', in J. Clarke, C. Critcher and R. Johnson (eds), *Working Class Culture: Studies in history and theory*, Hutchinson, London, 1979, 125–32.

14 D. Gittings, *Fair Sex: Family size and structure, 1900–1939*, Hutchinson, London, 1982, 78–9.

15 P. Horn, 'Ministry of Labour Female Training Programmes between the Wars: 1919–1939', *History of Education*, 31, 1, 2002, 71–2.

16 Alice Younger, MoL Employment Department, Edinburgh, to Miss Durham, MoL, London, 6 Sept 1920, NA LAB2/769/ED450.

17 K. Laybourn, '"Waking Up to the Fact that there are any Unemployed": Women, unemployment and the domestic solution in Britain, 1918–1939', *History*, 88, 292, 615–16.

18 For example, CCWTE Minutes, 13 January 1921, BLPES Markham 3/2.

19 Ministry of Reconstruction, *Report on the Domestic Service Problem*, HMSO, 1919, 2.

20 Horn, 'Ministry of Labour', 73–7.

21 *Report to the President of the Oversea Settlement Committee of the Delegates Appointed to Enquire as to Openings in Canada for Women from the United Kingdom*, HMSO, 1919.

22 Blakeley, 'The Society', 436–8; Harper, *Emigration*, 237–8.

23 *Parliamentary Debates*, 15 February 1927.

24 M. Talbot, 'Migration for Women', in E. M. Gates (ed.), *The Woman's Yearbook, 1923–1924*, Women Publishers, London, 1924, 371.

25 P. Hamilton and B. W. Higman, 'Servants of Empire: The British training of domestics for Australia, 1926–31', *Social History*, 28, 1, 2003, 68.

26 CCWTE Minutes, 10 December 1925, BLPES Markham 3/4.

27 CCWTE Minutes, 9 December 1926, BLPES Markham 3/4.

28 CCWTE Minutes, 24 February 1927, BLPES Markham 3/4.

29 Hamilton and Higman, 'Servants of Empire', 73; Imperial Conference 1926. *Appendices to the summary of proceedings*, HMSO, London, 1927, 280–1.

30 *Australia Invites the British Domestic Girl*, Development and Migration Commission, Melbourne, 1929, 5.

31 F. Harrison Bell, 'Women and Migration', *Labour Magazine*, 3, 1924, 114.

32 CCWTE Minutes, 7 April 1927, BLPES Markham 3/4; S P B Mais, *SOS Talks on Unemployment*, Putnam, London, 330.

33 CCWTE Minutes, 21 July 1927, BLPES Markham 3/4.

34 Hamilton and Higman, 'Servants of Empire', 74.

35 *Annual Report of the OSC*, 1927, 21.

36 CCWTE Minutes, 9 February 1928, BLPES Markham 3/4.
37 A. C. C. Hill and I. Lubin, *The British Attack on Unemployment*, Brookings Institution, Washington, 1934, 103.
38 Hamilton and Higman, 'Servants of Empire', 75.
39 CCWTE Minutes, 12 July 1928, BLPES Markham 3/4.
40 L. S. Amery, Oversea Settlement – Recent Developments, 6 November 1928, NA CAB24/198.
41 *Annual Report of the OSC* 1929, 23; E M Tomlinson to Valentine 17 October 1930, NA LAB2/1435/ET1561.
42 CCWTE Minutes, 11 October 1928 and 13 December 1928, BLPES Markham 3/4.
43 CCWTE Minutes, 14 February 1929 and 13 June 1929, BLPES Markham 2/4; Foster to Miss K. Propert, MoI Divisional Office, Birmingham, 19 February 1931, NA LAB2/2079/ET3845.
44 *Brisbane Courier*, 31 October 1929.
45 Ibid., 30 October 1929.
46 Hamilton and Higman, 'Servants of Empire', 79.
47 *Sydney Morning Herald*, 24 November 1928.
48 *Parliamentary Debates*, 14 April 1927.
49 CCWTE Minutes, 21 November 1929 and 13 February 1930, BLPES Markham 3/4.
50 CCWTE Minutes, 13 February and 27 February 1930, BLPES Markham 3/4.
51 CCWTE Minutes, 12 December 1929, BLPES Markham 3/4.
52 Labour Emergency Expenditure Committee Proposal, 3 December 1930, NA LAB2/770/ED6002.
53 Minute of Meeting of Sub-Committee, 18 December 1930, NA LAB2/770/ED6002.
54 Miss E. M. Tomlinson to Reid, 19 December 1930, NA LAB2/770/ED6002.
55 Tomlinson to G. T. Reid MoL, 24 February 1931, NA LAB2/770/ED6002; CCWTE, Sub-Committee to consider Oversea Hostels, 18 December 1930, BLPES Markham 3/5.
56 CCWTE Minutes, 16 October 1930, 11 December 1930, BLPES Markham 3/5.
57 MoL Circular 43/38 (1931), NA LAB2/2037/ET4067.
58 CCWTE Minutes, 16 April 1931, BLPES Markham 3/5; E M Tomlinson to G. T. Reid, 24 February 31, National Archives, LAB2/770/ED6002.
59 CCWTE Minutes, 8 October 1931, BLPES Markham 3/5.
60 *RCUI: Final Report*, 333–4.
61 CCWTE Minutes, 8 December 1932, 9 February 1933, 9 November 1933 and 14 November 1933, BLPES Markham 3/5; Tomlinson to Miss Foster, 9 December 1932, NA LAB2/2079/ET3845.

62 Training and Occupation for the Unemployed Next Winter. Memorandum by the Minister of Labour, 21 July 1933, NA CAB24/242.

63 CCWTE Minutes, 17 December 1935 and 13 February 1936, BLPES Markham 3/6.

64 CCWTE Minutes, 4 October 1938, 11 May 1939 and 13 July 1939, BLPES Markham 3/7.

65 CCWTE Minutes, 14 February 1935, BLPES Markham 3/5.

66 MoL Circular 43/38 (1931), NA LAB2/2037/ET4067.

67 Mais, *SOS Talks*, 330.

68 Ibid., 332–3; see also *Daily Express*, 11 May 1934.

69 Horn, 'Ministry of Labour', 80.

70 *RCUI: First Report, Appendices, Part I*, 243.

71 *Western Mail and South Wales News*, 12 March 1932.

72 Horn, 'Ministry of Labour', 78; see also Todd, 'Domestic Service'.

73 *Daily Mail*, 14 April 1932.

74 Ibid.

75 *Leicester Mercury*, 8 March 1934.

76 Tomlinson to Miss Foster, 13 May 1931, NA LAB2/2079/3845.

77 CCWTE Minutes, 11 February 1932, BLPES Markham 3/5.

78 MoL Circular 43/38 (1931), LAB/2/2037/ET4067. Emphasis in original.

79 CCWTE Minutes, 12 May 1932, NA LAB/2/2031/ET3269.

80 *Scotsman*, 4 September 1934.

81 E. M. Foster to Valentine, 19/12/30, NA LAB/2/563/5434/3.

82 CCWTE Minutes, 12 March 1925, BLPES Markham 3/3.

83 CCWTE Minutes, 14 May 1925, BLPES Markham 3/4.

84 CCWTE Minutes, 24 February 1927, BLPES Markham 3/4.

85 Draft Circular, 1935, NA LAB2/2013/ET4121.

86 Scottish Committee Minutes, 8 May 1936, BLPES Markham 3/6.

87 *Daily Express*, 11 May 1934.

88 [Illegible] to Miss Tomlinson, 24 June 1933, NA LAB2/2031/ET3269.

89 Divisional Controller, North Western Division, to Managers, Employment Exchanges. "Confidential". 15 June 1933, LAB2/2031/ET3269; J. and S. Jewkes, *The Juvenile Labour Market*, Victor Gollancz, London, 1938, 77.

90 Miss K. Propert to Miss Foster, 24 February 1931, NA LAB/2/2079/3845.

91 CCWTE Minutes, 1 February 1933, BLPES Markham 3/5.

92 *MoL. Reports of investigations into the industrial conditions in certain depressed areas*, HMSO, London, 1934, 228.

93 Note ET 3738/1930, NA LAB/2/1278/ET5420.

94 CCWTE Minutes, 11 March 1937, BLPES Markham 3/6.

95 E. Owen, Wales Divisional Office, 18.1.30, NA LAB2/2031/ET326.

96 Foster to Miss Tomlinson, 14 June 1930, NA LAB2/1278/ET5420.

97 Horn, 'Ministry of Labour', 82.

98 CCWTE Minutes, 17 December 1935, BLPES Markham 3/6.
99 Ibid.
100 CCWTE Minutes, 14 May 1936, BLPES Markham 3/6.
101 CCWTE Minutes, 12 February 1925, BLPES Markham 3/3.
102 *Glasgow Herald*, 26 March 1931.
103 *RCUI: Final report*, 334.
104 V. Markham, 15 June 1938, BLPES Markham 8/28.
105 Scottish Committee Minutes, 4 October 1938 and 25 April 1939, BLPES Markham 3/7.
106 Report on Market Harborough Training Centre, November 1937– June 1939, BLPES Markham 3/7.
107 Scottish Committee Minutes, 25 April 1939, BLPES Markham 3/7.
108 J. M. Cramond, MoL, Edinburgh, Confidential, to Exchanges February 1931, NA LAB2/2013/ET4121.
109 *Leicester Mercury*, 8 March 1934.
110 *Daily Express*, 11 May 1934.
111 CCWTE Minutes, 8 March 1923, BLPES Markham 3/3.
112 CCWTE Minutes, 11 June 1931, BLPES Markham 3/5.
113 *Parliamentary Debates*, 14 April 1927, 30 April 1928, 27 February 1929.
114 *Parliamentary Debates*, 14 April 1927.
115 *Scotsman*, 4 September 1934.
116 *Parliamentary Debates*, 14 March 1927, 14 April 1927.
117 CCWTE Minutes, 12 February 1925, BLPES Markham 3/3.
118 CCWTE Minutes, 12 May 1932 and 14 July 1932, BLPES Markham 3/5.
119 *The Times*, 7 October 1929.
120 *The Times*, 20 February 1937.
121 CCWTE Minutes, 9 March 1939, BLPES Markham 3/7.
122 Laybourn, 'Waking Up', 618–19.
123 *Parliamentary Debates*, 14 April 1927.
124 *Brisbane Courier*, 6 February 1928.
125 Todd, 'Domestic Service', 188–90.

9

Camps as social service
and social movement

An extraordinary variety of private and voluntary work camp movements flourished in the interwar years. Many young men and women from the middle and upper classes left their comfortable homes to live among the poor, labouring through their long vacations to build playgrounds, swimming pools and libraries.[1] Others created or joined work camps to prepare for a new life, whether as Jewish settlers, Nordic patriots or English communitarians. Some had more self-serving motives: in Sussex, a Commander Lacy helped to found an Agricultural Camps Committee, providing 'flying squads of unemployed' to help farmers bring in the harvest.[2] In County Down, the Marquess of Dufferin and Ava opened a lumber camp for unemployed men on his family estate at Clandeboye.[3] But this chapter focuses on work camps with a social purpose.

Many voluntary work camp systems were inspired by the belief that in some way, the work camp represented a community, however temporary, that showed how life could be lived differently, and prepared men – and sometimes women – to live otherwise. It is conventional to divide social movements into those that provide social service but uphold the status quo and those that seek to challenge and change the social order.[4] This division echoes the contemporary critique of the social service movement as offering at best a palliative, as the TUC claimed, at worst a training ground for 'blackleg labour', to quote the Middlesbrough Communists who heckled Prince George while he opened a social service club.[5] Matters were more complex; while the social service camps were concerned with relieving immediate problems, their members believed in social change as well as relief; and while the social movement camps were trying to build a new life, they also had to get along with circumstances as they existed.

Work camps as social service

John Mangan argues that, after the First World War, public and imperial justifications for sport were replaced by individualistic ideas that put competitive success before service, freedom of choice before loyalty and courage.[6] Ideas of labour, community and service, however, continued to play an important role in the interwar social service movement, which continued alongside, and often in partnership with, the state.[7] Work camps, as one of the more physically demanding and personally testing forms of social service, remained very much a minority within the social service movement. Yet, for some, these rigorous challenges were precisely what gave the work camp its appeal, as a way of subordinating the individual and their comfort to the extraordinary circumstances of mass unemployment.

Jack Hoyland, a lecturer at a Quaker adult college in Birmingham, summarised the International Voluntary Service (IVS) work camp movement as 'Franciscan service with and for the unemployed'.[8] Led by the Swiss Quaker, engineer and conscientious objector Pierre Cérésole, IVS – the British branch of *Service Civil International* – initially recruited young men and women immediately after the Great War, to help repair war damage around Verdun, and a series of summer projects followed. By 1930, these included a camp in the French village of Lagarde, where 178 young men and 20 young women – including 20 Britons (17 university students, 2 teachers and one clerk) – helped villagers tackle flood damage.[9] In the following year, several young men and women from the Lagarde camp took part in the Brynmawr camp, along with Hoyland, helping to build gardens and a swimming pool, turning 'an old rubbish tip into a thing of beauty'.[10] Other IVS camps helped to level spoil heaps, as at Oakengates in Shropshire; restored the stables at Whitby Abbey, for use by the Youth Hostelling Association; and laid out rugby fields at Blaenavon.

Work, for the IVS, was not simply a means of getting things done. While pick and shovel were directly valuable for a group whose founding purpose was to remedy the destruction of war, Cérésole's long-term aim for the IVS was as 'war's moral equivalent in hard work and discipline', as well as in 'costly service and sacrifice'.[11] The IVS referred to its activities as camps in English, and as *services* in French. Sometimes, the volunteers lived communally, sleeping on straw palliasses in halls, huts or, on one occasion, in a disused brewery, bringing their own work clothes, boots and cutlery, and 'a pillow, if required'.[12] Otherwise, the volunteers paid for local lodgings, among the people that they were helping.[13] The more 'community-minded' in the IVS preferred this as a way of integrating the volunteers with the unemployed, while the more 'internationally-minded' wished to bind the volunteers across national boundaries.[14]

The IVS was attractive to students because its work camps took place during the long vacation. As John Barnes recalled, with costs met by charitable sources, they were also a 'source of free accommodation', enabling scholarship boys like him to pass the summer without cost to his parents.[15] The Universities Council for Unemployed Camps (UCUC), though sponsored by powerful patrons, was organised solely by students. In summer 1933, Michael Sims-Williams led a party from Westcott House, Cambridge, to run a camp for unemployed men on Lord Somer's estate at Eastnor Park, Herefordshire. Over six weeks, supported financially by the National Council for Social Services (NCSS) and Industrial Christian Fellowship, they took groups of men from Bristol and South Wales, spending their mornings making a bathing pool, and playing games in the afternoons, followed by hobbies in the evenings, and ending with a singsong around the camp fire.[16] Encouraged by this first experience, Sims-Williams helped form the UCUC in the following autumn, writing its manual on camp organisation. While mainly recruited from Cambridge, the Council was also joined by groups at Oxford, King's College London, Southampton, Glasgow, Liverpool, Leeds and St Andrews.[17] In 1935, the Cambridge Committee recruited 731 men to its seven camps, each of which ran for four weeks; in 1936, it recruited 801. The Cambridge Committee ran seven camps through to the summer of 1939,[18] and was still planning to hold camps in summer 1940, though once the war took hold, its attention shifted from the unemployed to disadvantaged lads.[19]

Unlike more permanent work camps, summer camps were inexpensive. Students and unemployed alike paid a small subscription. In 1936, for instance, the average subscription from men at Chillingham was 1s. 6d., while those at Eastnor paid 5s. 8½d.[20] UCUC sought out sympathetic landowners, where in exchange for pitching their tents for four weeks they offered to undertake heavy labour. In summer 1934, nearly a hundred men from Sheffield and the Potteries worked under 24 Cambridge students on the Marquess of Northampton's estate at Castle Ashby, enlarging a village pond, clearing rough land for afforestation, and repairing a road. Ninety men from London and the South East camped on the Right Honourable Harold Tennant's estate at Rolvenden, in Kent, where Cambridge men supervised the restoration of Rolvenden Mill, as well as helping to clear a lake for bathing.[21] Some of the work had a more public purpose. Men at King's College camps helped Dr Tancred Borenius excavate the remains of Clarendon Palace, while a Liverpool student-led camp spent a fortnight excavating the hill settlement of Maiden Castle, in Cheshire.[22] In Britain archaeology was reported in a matter-of-fact academic way with none of the *völkisch* overtones that accompanied similar work in the *Arbeitsdienst*.[23]

Fellowship was built partly through work and partly through play. Leisure activities could be quite elaborate, as at the Oxford camp at Eynsham. Nevill Coghill, later to become Merton Professor at Oxford and translator of the Penguin Chaucer, directed Noah's Flood, a medieval miracle play, which the campers performed for villagers and other guests, setting up a stage against the lock-keeper's cottage, and constructing stage lighting from a set of car headlamps. Owen Pritchard, a Welshman, played Noah, while Arthur Cook took the part of his wife; Ronald Bendall, an Englishman, played God; all three were unemployed. Coghill himself performed the Londonderry Air on the violin, while Tent Nine performed a version of the Maori Haka, trained by James Bertram, a Marxist rugby-playing student from New Zealand.[24]

Competitive sports were particularly important. Men from Chillingham Castle camp competed in the village sports, while at Harome Harry Rée organised a sports day against an Oxford UCUC camp four miles away, with football match and boat race (both won by Oxford).[25] Harome UCUC teams played the local village sides at football and cricket, as well as taking on a team from Gilling IC, borrowing a pitch from nearby Ampleforth College.[26] Adult education was rare. At Bredon, one lecturer reportedly found himself alone, while the best attendance was for an impromptu talk on the philosophy of socialism, held during a storm.[27] Although a photograph of Bredon shows the men grouped around a flagpole with the Union Jack, in general the organisers 'carefully avoided' any suspicion of militarism.[28]

Usually, the unemployed men were recruited through the Ministry of Labour, coming largely from the cities and the coalfields. Unlike the NCSS camps, the Ministry was satisfied that the UCUC camps offered not a holiday but 'a genuine contribution to reconditioning', and was happy to cooperate with them.[29] As for the students, records show that a number had a background in social service. Some had been Rover Scouts, other were involved in Toc H, who elected two of the Cambridge UCUC committee.[30] There was also a link with the Student Christian Movement, and although attendance at prayers was voluntary, the UCUC camps had 'a definitely religious basis'.[31]

As with the settlement movement, social service through camps was designed to promote 'friendship and trust' between the classes. Sheffield students reported that they and the unemployed 'eat from the same table, intermingle in sport', and were 'together the whole time except when sleeping'.[32] Personal knowledge and contacts were cultivated; the Cambridge students encouraged their camp chiefs to visit the towns from which they recruited, and if possible arrange to meet the managers of the local labour exchanges.[33] Subsequently, shared experiences of work and communal living built true friendship. UCUC claimed that its camps were 'fostering friendship and understanding between these undergraduates – many of whom may later become employers or directors of labour – and the unemployed', a product of voluntarism which could never be reproduced in state institutions such as ICs.[34] Clothing too was selected to emphasise common bonds: Sims-Williams advised the students to 'avoid blazers and sweaters with club colours', prescribing 'only one dress for camp – shorts and gym shoes'.[35]

UCUC's mention of the future careers of its student members raises the question of whether learning through service was also a preparation for a comfortable place in the bourgeoisie. Sims-Williams was adamant that camp life required a particular style of leadership. The man

> who enjoys 'bossing' people about is perfectly useless. The man who will work alongside his men, take his meals with them, and without burdening himself upon them, generally interest himself in their activities is the man who makes a successful leader.[36]

He believed that the 'tent leader can have no authority to urge men to work, if he is not prepared to strip to the waist himself and get down to it alongside them'.[37] The British, Hoyland claimed, prefer 'the leadership of an educated man, always provided that he has the right spirit'.[38]

What camp work taught was precisely that 'right spirit'. Annually, UCUC appointed a chief for each camp, who appointed a student to each tent as tent-leader, while the men were to elect a tent-mate. Together with the chief, the leaders and mates formed the 'camp moot', which considered everyday camp matters and provided a forum for men to air grievances. A sympathetic reporter noted in *The Times* that the 'real measure of self-government' was confined to 'matters of detail'.[39] Nevertheless, given that they had few powers short of expelling unruly men (or sending for the local police in the event of crime), the students had to develop more or less democratic leadership skills – something that reportedly 'came as a revelation to many of them'.[40]

Women and the social service camps

Women's involvement in camping movements differed from men's. Some women helped run social service camps, but these were not usually work camps. The 'sisters' who lived alongside the men in IVS work camps were exceptions; yet while the IVS expected its male members to wield pick and spare, it believed that the sisters' role was 'to cook them a meal after their hard work'.[41] Only in egalitarian Norway do the 'sisters' seem to have worked alongside the men.[42] In Britain, the young Zionist women at the David Eder farm were unusual in sharing the everyday tasks with their male counterparts.

Almost invariably, camps for women and families were designed to provide respite, above all for exhausted mothers. The Girton College student camps fell very much into this category. Sheila Nevell, one of the Girton organisers, recalled that another Girton student had a brother at Cambridge who was involved in the men's camps:

> We had a Social Services Club at Girton and would have liked to help but knew it was not appropriate for women to live in a camp with men ... anyway we reckoned the miners' wives needed a break more than the miners.[43]

In 1937, Miss Mary Duff, Nevell's moral tutor and a fellow Guide, approached Durham Community Service Council (CSC), offering to organise a camp to give the wives of unemployed men a break from the anxiety and drudgery of their everyday lives. Durham CSC was happy to accept this proposal, and invited the Girton women to use Marsden Bay, on the coast of County Durham, along with the services of a site manager, cooks and a nurse.[44] Marsden Bay, with its huts and kitchens, was not to the taste of Miss Duff, who strongly favoured a 'canvas camp', as in 'a real camp everything is new and rather exciting'.[45]

Recruitment was largely organised through the CSC. In May 1937, the CSC circulated a message to its member clubs and associations, asking them to give first preference to nominating unemployed women, wives and daughters of unemployed men, and widows, with others filling any remaining places.[46] The local organisations also arranged for the women's journey to South Shields, where they were picked up by bus.[47] Of the 733 who attended in 1938, 241 were themselves in jobs, but such were conditions in the coalfield that only 41 had not been unemployed at some stage.[48] Inevitably, most were not young: the 1937 campers ranged from an 18-year-old to a lady of 77, but most were between 30 and 50.[49] The women had to find a 5s. weekly fee, though in many cases this was met by local charities, while the CSC provided transport and NCSS provided accommodation, and the camp organisers sought grants to cover other costs.[50]

Like their male counterparts, the university women were volunteers. They similarly paid a small fee – 8s. 6d. in 1938 – to attend, and had to find their own way to South Shields. The two 1937 camps were staffed mainly by the Cambridge students, often Guides, while the 1938 camp leaders included seven volunteers from Edinburgh who became involved through the Girls' Diocesan Association.[51] Most came from Girton, though there were two Newhamites in 1937, including Peggie Sheppard, daughter of Dick Sheppard, clergyman and founder of the Peace Pledge Union, who as an undergraduate had himself served in the High Anglican Oxford House Settlement in Bethnal Green.[52]

Unlike the men's camps, it was not intended that the women's should focus on work. As the organisers put it, 'the women needed rest and freedom from worry more than anything else'.[53] This is not to say that camp life was easy: the women were woken at 5 00 a.m; at 7 00 the 'brave spirits' went for a swim; breakfast, at 8 00, was followed by an hour of camp jobs. After listening to a religious service on the BBC, the women chose between handicrafts, keep fit, the library, or learning to swim. Between 2.15 and 4.00 pm there were games and folk dancing. In 1939, the sports afternoon involved a knitting race, hoop race, 'hobble-poodle' and 'blindfold driving'.[54] But the main bodily exercise was swimming. Many of the Durham women had never swum before, but the camp site – now washed away by the sea – gave direct access to the beach. In the first year, 'Cold and rather foggy weather solved the problem of sharing forty bathing suits among more than two hundred women', while some women were keener to be photographed in swimwear than enter the North Sea.[55] As elsewhere in Britain, this enthusiasm for the modern body divided the generations, with older women disapproving of such immodest exposure.[56]

In the evenings and late afternoons there was a programme of leisure activities. In 1937, this included several slide shows supplied by German Railways Information Bureau covering German Costumes, German Industry, and the Oberammergau Passion Play (in colour). There were film shows, ranging from Harold Lloyd comedies to documentaries from the GPO Film Unit. The students and Durham women came together in performances, with community singing, comedy, and sketches. In 1938, one sketch featured a beauty contest judged by Sheila Nevell, dressed in army uniform and painted moustache as Adolf Hitler.[57] When 'Hitler' offered to organise Keep Fit classes, a group of women ran onstage, accusing him of wearing corsets, then chasing him away to cries of 'Adolf don't worry me'.[58] The final week included a dance, permitting the Durham women to instruct the students in routines such as the Palais Glide, a vigorous and popular line dance.[59]

While education was largely a wet weather pastime in men's camps, the Girton organisers took a more systematic approach. And although the Girton approach did use occasional lectures, their pedagogic practice was modelled on the organised debates of the adult school movement, requiring participants to engage in dialogue rather than passively listening. In 1937, Mr Bristow spoke briefly on 'How the individual can help the State to maintain the health of the nation', followed by 'an instructive and sometimes heated argument', in which all believed that the state should arrange regular examinations of all schoolchildren, but disagreed over the principle of state payment of doctors.[60] Bristow returned in 1938 to lead a discussion on public housing, and in 1939 the campers debated democracy.[61] There was also a camp library, with a book box and magazines.[62]

As for the men, camp life could be presented as forming friendships across the class divide. Blanche Griffiths, Durham CSC's women's organiser, did not doubt that the main achievement was the 'spontaneous enjoyment and friendliness that existed throughout the camp, the new friendships made and old ones strengthened'.[63] The students worried lest Griffiths' role as camp commander created 'an unnecessary, artificial class division between ourselves and the women'.[64] Student volunteers served the food, with four meals a day, which 'always included fruit and meat at least once a day, porridge with milk or eggs for breakfast, and tea at every meal'.[65] However, the students slept separately, in cubicles at the end of each hut.[66]

In 1930s Britain, the Marsden camps offered liberation to the students as well as the Durham women. Women comprised around one quarter of all university students between the wars, but at Oxbridge the proportion of women was much lower. At Cambridge, women were confined to the two all-female colleges, and the University refused to allow them full membership, which included eligibility for receiving a degree, until 1948.[67] Nor was everyday life in middle- and upper-class homes particularly exciting for young women with independent minds and intellectual ability. Sheila Nevell thought that most of her fellow students rather envied her for 'not having to spend the "vac" with families on more orthodox holidays', and dismissed those who told her she was mad as 'upper class' and 'snobby'.[68] And again, camp life proved to be a training ground. Problem solving, inter-cultural communication, and a hearty, cheerful and generally non-authoritarian approach to leadership were the hallmarks of the women's camps as least as much as the men's.[69]

Social change: camps and a new world

If some saw work camps as a form of service, others viewed them as tools for building a new world. Radical utopian thinking flourished in the interwar years, fed by disenchantment with a failing industrial capitalism and a desire for a more vital, authentic human society.[70] Camping lent itself to utopian experiment; whether temporary or permanent, a camp formed a pedagogic working community that bound its members together under demanding conditions, allowing them to test a way of living differently within existing reality, and at the same time to pioneer an imagined alternative.

This section explores three approaches to work camps as utopian social movements. Rolf Gardiner, a young English nationalist who admired the *völkisch* voluntary labour service of late Weimar Germany, organised a number of work camps, in the hope of training leaders for a new England. The Grith Fyrd (GF) movement offered a more communitarian form of English nationalism. An offshoot of the Woodcraft movement, GF (Anglo-Saxon for 'peace army') recruited a mixture of young, idealistic volunteers and unemployed men, who more or less shared its ideals of a post-industrial, post-urban England in which man and nature could live in harmony. Third were the Zionist pioneers of Habonim, who took over a farm in Kent to ready themselves for the cultural, agricultural and political challenges of founding – or re-founding – the land of Israel. All three treated camps as a pedagogic device, teaching people to live in a new way, while foreshadowing the new life to come.

Folklorist, farmer, forester, nudist, poet and visionary, Gardiner was and remains a controversial figure. He once described his task as one of 'national education',[71] and believed that Britain's political future lay in a Germanic European union stretching from Scandinavia to the Netherlands. Of many ties with Germany, Gardiner treasured the *Deutsche Freischar* youth movement as a natural parallel to his beloved scouts. He joined his first camp – the *Freischar*'s second – in 1927, when he organised a naked sun dance to follow reveille at 5.45 am.[72] That winter, Gardiner organised his own camp at his uncle's farm in Dorset. He had overlooked the realities of a British winter, and his attempts to enthuse British students with work camps fizzled out until in 1930 he persuaded the Imperial College Gliding Club to combine a summer work camp with practical gliding.[73] The club was initially enthusiastic about these arrangements, and its officers set about drafting the camp regulations, forbidding firearms and alcohol from the site, and setting out basic rules of conduct. Gardiner no doubt liked Regulation 7, which reminded members that they should follow 'a plain, healthy diet', avoid smoking, and take plenty of exercise.[74] As well as levelling a yard and bringing in the harvest, they held a rat-hunt, recording their enjoyment in the camp report. The students did their own cooking and housework, managing to kill a pig after feeding it leftovers from one of their evening meals.[75] They also built their own glider, which unfortunately crashed on its first flight.[76]

Gardiner encouraged the Imperial students to learn folk song and dance, but otherwise left them to his uncle's farm manager, while he visited the IVS at Brynmawr. Two summers of folk dance and farm labour were enough for the Imperial students, who moved on in 1932. By this time, Gardiner too had developed. While researching sword dancing in Cleveland, he formed a relationship with Major Jim Pennyman, of Ormesby Hall near Middlesbrough, a conservative and paternalist landowner who was encouraging local ironstone miners to combine short-time working in the mine with small-scale farming.[77] In 1929, Gardiner urged Pennyman 'to kindle the life-quality' in Cleveland through 'some form of rural activity', along with 'games, music, dancing, play-acting, tramping, camping, what you will'.[78] By 1932, the pair were organising the 'First Cleveland Work Camp'. Known locally as Heartbreak Hill, this involved unemployed miners and students recruited by Gardiner from England, Germany and Denmark, working together to break rough moorland down for cultivation.

Student recruits, who lived in tents, followed a strict daily routine, starting with reveille at 6.45, followed by breakfast and then work with the unemployed miners from 8.00 to 1.00 p.m. After lunch, the students had a couple of hours to themselves, with two hours of group activities before the evening meal. Evenings were devoted to lectures and discussions, with bed time at 9.30 and lights out at 10.00. For the most part, the mornings were spent breaking up waste land, so that the miners could use it for market gardening, beekeeping and poultry-rearing.[79] For leisure, the students played football against local village teams, sang hearty folk songs, or watched the Lingfield miners performing North Yorkshire sword dances. At one camp, the whole group spent three days hiking, with a 'flag-raiding contest' between Scots and English as the grand finale.[80] In 1932, David Ayerst, a friend of W. H. Auden at Oxford in the 1920s, recruited the youthful Michael Tippett to join the camp. The Communist composer stayed on in the area, living over a shop in Boosbeck, and working on a new opera about Robin Hood, which was duly performed by the miners in a church hall during the following camp.[81]

Once more, though, Gardiner became restless. In 1933, Pennyman proudly showed Prince George, Duke of Kent, around Heartbreak Hill. The Prince, towering over all the locals including Pennyman, inspected the allotments and hen runs and met Rebecca the pig,

Daisy the goat, and a miners' union leader.[82] This was a proud moment for Jim Pennyman, but he no longer trusted Gardiner's politics. After visiting Germany in summer 1933, including a tour of two work camps, Pennyman criticised Hitler's treatment of the Jews and political opponents, making it plain that he wanted no British Hitlerism.[83] Gardiner had meanwhile acquired Springhead Farm in Dorset, and focused his efforts there, hosting regular summer camps, where men worked on the harvest and women worked as cooks. Men slept in white bell tents, in a circle around the camp flag; women slept in the farmhouse.[84] Everybody at Springhead undertook five hours of manual work in the morning, followed by talks on 'various aspects of rural organisation and land settlement' in the afternoon, and cultural activities in the evening.[85]

Gardiner, we now know, was admired by the Nazis. Otto Bene, the Nazi Party's *Landesgruppenleiter* for Britain and Ireland judged the 1934 camp, while amateur by German standards, sufficiently 'above the average English one' for the Nazi *Auslandsorganisation* to give Gardiner their support.[86] In turn, Gardiner shared the Nazis' anti-Semitism, as well as their organicist views of blood and soil (though he also rather unrealistically expected Hitler to promote and strengthen the voluntary labour service movement).[87] His *völkisch* tastes in music and dance were combined with the invention of traditions that owed something to the mysticism of Kibbo Kift, a pacifist youth movement that had broken away from the Scouts. Springhead work campers awoke to the rhythmic beating of a ceremonial gong, and paraded before the flagstaff before breakfast. In the evenings, they linked arms in a circle, lit by single torch, and singing:

> The earth has turned us from the sun,
> And let us close our circle now to light,
> But open it to darkness, and each one
> Warm with this circle's warming,
> Go in good darkness to good sleep,
> Good night.[88]

Gardiner also greatly admired Nordic traditions, praising Nikolaj Grundtvig, founder of the Danish folk high schools. Springhead camps always included plenty of adult education. Lectures in 1934 included Captain George Pitt-Rivers, anthropologist and eugenicist, on 'Race and Leadership', and a series of talks on Alfred the Great as the prototype of a great English leader.[89] In 1939, the campers heard the forestry specialist Richard St Barbe Baker talk about Roosevelt's Civilian Conservation Corps, and discussed Gardiner's ideas about land service camps.[90] Such debates served to integrate and develop notions of nation, leadership, community, work and land.

Work, for Gardiner, had mystical value. Any true work camp, he wrote, 'is religious in the direct sense of the term', involving all in 'physical, intellectual and emotional exercise'.[91] In general, he told conference on student voluntary service, the work camp was 'an answer of the European spirit' to the negative influences of mechanisation, standardisation and international finance, aiming to 'root labour once again in the soil, to restore to work its lost homeland'.[92] Hard work was also a way of building on shared masculine identities: 'A virile form is an absolute necessity for young men. Only by pitching together against difficulties or hardship does comradeship grow'.[93] By bringing unemployed and students together, 'mixed work camps create an experimental form of social university and may, indeed, prove to be the next step forward in national education'.[94] But his commitment to fellowship was a racial one, reaching beyond national borders. The small journal that he edited, and largely wrote, for a small group of like-minded sympathisers and friends, was tellingly called *North Sea and Baltic*. He spoke admiringly of Cleveland as 'populated by a people of robust Scandinavian stock', while the miners came from 'good agricultural stock, and have not been separated from the soil for more than a generation'.[95]

In 1939, Gardiner was fortunate to avoid internment. He was closely scrutinised by the security services, who opened his post and investigated a rumour that he had planted a cluster of trees in the shape of a swastika.[96] But he viewed the Nazis through the prism of the youth movement, describing his Springhead camps as translating 'the original idea of the *Deutsche Freischar* into English terms'.[97] Gardiner also showed considerable interest in Nordic youth groups. Yet although he was certainly interested in the racial roots of Danish culture, he also admired their adult education movement, seeing the Danish Folk High Schools as potentially turning the unemployed into 'the potential bearer of a new order of society'.[98] What that society would involve was not altogether clear, but it was to be based on the land, governed on a regional basis, inspired by strong leaders, and utterly English.[99] It sounds an idealised rural English vision of Nazism – more Midsomer than

Majdanek – and in the end, the British security forces agreed that he was probably no more than a crank.[100]

Gardiner's connections with other youth movements were widespread, particularly with those who, like Grith Fyrd (GF), shared some of his critique of modernity and belief in a more organic and challenging life. GF owed its existence to the Woodcraft movement which in turn drew on the scouting tradition, with its jumble of ideas borrowed loosely from Native American religions, ruralism, and patriotism. Many of its meetings were held on land belonging to the Aubrey Westlake, son of the founder of the Order of Woodcraft Chivalry (OWC) family, at Sandy Balls, in the New Forest. In 1931, Westlake called the OWC to a summer camp and conference to consider a massive project of land settlement and communal living. He originally called this scheme Ephebe, a classical Greek ritualised process of training young men for citizenship and military service. Westlake's plans involved three years of physical training in athletics, sports, nudism, 'military training to the extent of teaching everyone to shoot', camping, trekking', and a period of voluntary community work.[101] In words echoing Cérésole's aims for IVS, Westlake spoke of Ephebe as 'a true and real alternative to militarism, possessing all the positive military virtues', and giving 'scope for hardihood and heroism', along with 'loyalty and patriotism ... as well as a sympathetic understanding of other nations'. Westlake also shared the wider gender assumptions of most work camp movements, hoping that women would join the scheme as 'hostesses to the men'.[102]

In 1931, the OWC folkmoot approved the scheme. Norman Glaister, a war veteran turned pacifist and a radical psychiatrist, proposed a series of camps around the country, each with sixty men who would produce their own food, clothing and other requirements, trading under a barter system.[103] The Order chose what it thought a more accessible name: Grith Fyrd, usually translated from the Anglo-Saxon as 'Peace Army', was undeniably, even exaggeratedly, English. On 8 March 1932, six young unemployed men set about building a bunkhouse for twelve at Sandy Balls. All unemployed, they came from a variety of social backgrounds: an ex-accountant, a cabinetmaker, two laboratory assistants, a Morris dance instructor and an engineer.[104] Chopping down thirty pine trees, this motley community achieved its task in a week; joined by twenty more young men, they built a second bunkhouse, hessian-sided and roofed with tarpaulin like the first, and added an eating house, roofed and clad in reeds cut from the nearby river bank, with a clay oven, and a lorry road from oak and larch.[105] By September, 25 young men were living in wooden huts, preparing for the winter.

When the journalist Petre Mais visited Godshill in 1933, he found 'a sort of Robinson Crusoe life'.[106] The novelist, pacifist and critic of mass society Aldous Huxley also visited Godshill, comparing it to 'an American backwoods settlement of a century ago'.[107] Huxley's image was telling: life in Sandy Balls was the polar opposite of the flamboyant consumer life styles of the 'roaring twenties'. The men rose at 7.00 a.m. to the ringing of a bell, followed by a 'plunge in the river'.[108] Work lasted until one o'clock. As well as building the camp, the work included weaving, woodwork, gardening and caring for livestock; when Mais arrived, he found the men building a goat shed with sticks and heather – an odd choice given the diet of the average goat.[109] They lunched on salad and fruit, then relaxed until 2.30 p.m., when the men gathered for football or wrestling followed by craft activities. Dinner at 6.00 usually consisted of vegetable soup, followed by organised evening activities including Morris dancing, debates and singing.[110] A bread and cheese supper was served at 9.00 p.m., with lights out at 10.30. On Sundays, the men cooked roast beef and Yorkshire puddings in their clay oven, but otherwise meat was too expensive.[111] As well as civic education, and constant debate, there was a twice-weekly camp council, for 'free discussion of camp subjects and routines'.[112] Discipline was reportedly consensual; as one camp leader put it, 'we can't compel a man to do anything here'.[113]

GF promoted simplicity, pioneering and adventure as forms of male community development. Godshill, according to one member, was 'a colony that finds adventure in simple living'.[114] Even in a paper for the Treasury, the movement could not resist applauding its own 'spirit of adventure' which, it claimed, 'sustains pioneers in the pressing ordeals of primitive conditions' and 'cultivates the endurance needed for any kind of successful economic settlement'.[115] The 'main problem of organized camp life' was thus to achieve 'a proper balance between the spirit of adventure and the necessity of routine'. In this way, its camps combined 'a *method* and a *technique* whereby men and women can adapt themselves to a full rural life which is based on a spirit of pioneering and presses on towards self-support'.[116]

If its aims were utopian, and its origins obscure, the movement was by no means isolated. This was partly due to Guy Keeling, its organiser, previously the highly regarded secretary of the Library Association.[117] Keeling, though not a member of the OWC and reportedly finding their internal debates rather childish, was energetic and well connected.[118] As well as pestering unions, the press and government, Keeling appealed to eugenicists, arguing that GF helped maintain a 'healthy stock' by giving men from the depressed areas 'an opportunity of a healthy and natural mode of life'.[119] He attracted such patrons as Margaret Bondfield, the philanthropist Arnold Rowntree, and the author and former civil servant Sir Ronald Davison to sign appeals on Grith Fyrd's behalf.[120] In 1933, Keeling persuaded British Pathé to produce *Army of Peace*, a film report on Godshill, showing footage of bare-chested young men hewing timber, swimming in the river, weaving cloth for their own clothing, and running briskly to the dinner table. GF officials, clearly happy with the results, then used the film for publicity purposes, arranging screenings for invited audiences.[121] The movement had its offices in Toynbee Hall university settlement, whose warden was Jimmy Mallon, described by one sympathetic observer as 'a veritable Pooh-Bah in the world of social service', and Treasurer of the Workers Educational Association.[122] Between 1933 and 1937, GF organisers arranged for the Workers' Educational Association to provide courses in the camp on such topics as 'How the Mind Works', 'Geology of Hampshire', 'The British Commonwealth of Nations' and 'Europe Today'.[123] This connection was of a piece with GF's aim of 'civic brotherhood'.[124]

Yet for all the networking, GF remained small and esoteric. The very name was enough to ensure that it had no broad appeal. A civil servant attending one of its London public meetings described the audience of forty as 'young friends' – that is, Quakers – and 'highbrows'.[125] Major Arthur Ross Ford, one of the Godshill pioneers, was perhaps as typical as any: an engineer from London and war veteran, Ford was described rather confusingly after his death as a Buddhist who worshipped at Woking mosque.[126] Although the movement purchased 100 acres at Shining Cliff Woods in Derbyshire, where it briefly opened a second camp, and then acquiring an estate of 35 acres at Brede, in Sussex, in the hope of settling some of the men on a self-sufficient cooperative settlement, the newly renamed Grith Pioneers were already struggling to recruit.[127] Recruitment was hit both by declining unemployment, and the extreme demands that GF made of its members. Shining Cliff was closed by May 1937, and only six men were left at Godshill.[128] There were also constant divisions within the OWC. An emergency conference at Sandy Balls on 1 April 1934 debated the question 'Whither Grith Fyrd?' No minutes have survived of this meeting, but in June Aubrey Westlake resigned as chair of OWC's GF sub-committee, and the Folkmoot suspended the constitution for a year, setting up a temporary advisory council chaired by Glynn Faithfull, father of the singer Marianne.[129] In 1937 Westlake evicted GF, converting their huts into holiday chalets.[130] The movement was virtually moribund by the time war broke out in 1939, though it did have an afterlife in the form of the Q camp (as ever, the name was symbolic, representing a quest), a form of outward bound education for young offenders.[131]

Eretz Israel

One Friday in 1933, a small group of young British Jews met in London to debate the best form of preparation for living on a kibbutz in Palestine. In the following year, after appealing to the British Zionist Federation for support, and seeking advice from the Hechalutz (preparation) movement in Poland, they opened two small camps in Sussex and Manchester. In April 1935, the newly formed English Hechalutz launched a more permanent training centre on a farm at Ringlestone in Kent. One member later recalled that they were remarkably ill-prepared for their new role as agriculturalists: 'there was no tradition, no routine, no practical knowledge, in fact none of those things which today are taken for granted. But there was spirit and tenacity'.[132]

They had their work cut out. Young Zionists elsewhere, particularly in central Europe, had opened seasonal training farms shortly after the Balfour Declaration, which led them to believe that the British government would support the formation of an Israeli state.[133] Older and more moderate heads, whatever they thought of Balfour, doubted that kibbutzim would thrive in Palestinian conditions, where settlers would have to contend both with a hostile Arab population and an almost complete lack of infrastructure. Nevertheless, the movement persisted; by the end of the 1920s it was in a position to open the first permanent training farm, in Poland.[134] Hechalutz B'Anglia, or the Pioneers of England, opened the David

Eder farm in April 1935 on 85 acres of land, equipped with modern machinery, and stocked with sheep, cattle and poultry. Eder, a leading psychiatrist, had campaigned with the unemployed in the 1880s, and indeed was wounded in the fighting on Bloody Sunday. An admirer of Kropotkin and a regular contributor to Orage's *New Age*, he was also a pioneer of Freudian methods in the treatment of shell-shock, and was a prominent member of the campaign to establish a Jewish homeland in Palestine.[135] His socialism as much as his secular Zionism appealed to the young men and women of Hechalutz B'Anglia. Dr Samson Wright, a leading figure in the farm's creation, was an eminent physiologist at Middlesex Hospital Medical School and an ardent Zionist who knew Eder well.[136]

Samson Wright described the farm's goal as being 'to train English Chalutzim (pioneers) in agriculture so that they will be able, ultimately, to go out to Palestine'.[137] Rather than cutting ties with England, he hoped to see them settling a distinctively English kibbutz. The farm manager, a Mr Chater, shared his dual patriotism, predicting that 'English Chalutzim' would go to Palestine 'nurtured among the Yeomen of England'.[138] Solly Banks became one such yeoman, coming from a family of Latvian Jews who had moved to London at the time of the 1905 pogroms. Born and brought up in London, Solly trained as a cabinet maker before joining Hechalutz, moving on to the Eder farm at the age of 21 in 1938.[139] But Zionist or not, most English Jews did not seem obvious candidates for a life on the land. Many leading Zionists were frankly sceptical at the idea of British Jews ever settling to the land, or indeed engaging in sustained communal living, while ordinary English Jews had more practical doubts. Even Samson Wright acknowledged that: 'The students all come from town and have no experience of country life, and have to be built up physically to be able to withstand the hard work which faces them.'[140] A writes in the *Jewish Chronicle* commented wryly that: 'A Jewish farmer is a rare creature in England.'[141] Banks' father put it more succinctly, demanding: 'What are Jewish boys doing getting their hands dirty for?'[142]

The trainees undertook a one-year programme, with the work divided by gender, women undertaking housekeeping tasks and looking after the animals while men performed other tasks around the farm and buildings.[143] The farm was overcrowded and unsanitary until purpose-built kitchens and laundry and a single-storey dormitory block could be added. As well as farming techniques, it also offered courses in Hebrew, instruction in the strict dietary laws of a kibbutz, and an introduction to the history, geography and politics of Palestine. Leisure activities included folk dance and theatre.[144] Money was short, and even a trip to the local cinema in Harrietsham involved a certain ingenuity in raising the funds. Solly Banks recalled the Sabbath as a particularly lively day for debate, argument, walks and lectures – though it was not marked by any particular religious observance. Those who could speak Hebrew taught their comrades, and some meetings were held in Hebrew only (though the Londoner Shalom Bordoley wrote home from Palestine, complaining that his Hebrew was useless for all but the simplest conversations). By spring 1936, there were 24 trainees (8 were women) living on the farm.[145] Most were young adults, the majority drawn from the 'professional classes', and had no experience of manual work.[146] Nine emigrated at the end of the first year – including the Hungarian Zionist Teddy Kollek, later to become mayor of Jerusalem – heading for a further year of training, periodic illness and regular conflict with local Arabs before moving to kibbutzim as settlers.[147]

By 1939, with recruitment boosted by European refugees like Kollek, eighty young people were ready to leave for Palestine; over half were refugees, a need that was growing so fast that a new training farm was planned at Tingrith, near Bedford.[148] Although the Eder Farm was still training young people in a new way of life, its function had changed, with refugees like Kollek in the majority. For Solly Banks, as for so many young English Jews, events intervened. He was called up in 1939, serving with distinction in the Royal Engineers before returning to London. He never did make *aliyah*, but recalled his time in Ringlestone with enthusiasm as 'wonderful experience, a unique experience', almost 'a topsy turvy life'.[149]

Camping and a new life

Overturning conventional life and its values was clearly important to the voluntary work camps, however much they differed in other ways. In a profoundly unequal society, the shared challenges of work and collaboration tended to equalise relationships, however briefly, and to form a community, however transient. The discovery of shared bonds could be electrifying: Nicholas Gillett wrote that the IVS camps showed that joining in 'hard manual work' with the 'dispossessed' led privileged young students 'to begin to learn that existing society required a radical change'.[150] Gardiner's camps, as well as the David Eder farm, were designed to forge unity through common living and labour, reinforced by free time activities that taught the values, rituals and language of a new national identity. Social divisions also preoccupied the student organisers of the UCUC camps. 'As a nation', reflected the Camp Chief at Bredon, 'we tend to lead unhealthy lives, either because we follow sedentary occupations, or because we live in unhealthy surroundings; then we are as a rule unable or unwilling to think and act outside one's surroundings with open minds; worst of all, our national community is divided; one section does not know what the others are doing'.[151]

Work, and presumably therefore the comradeship and bodily strength that flowed from it, was largely confined to the men. The Durham women were expected to do a minimum of domestic labour. Even in mixed camps, the genders were segregated. At Pangbourne, Diana Hewitt recalled, the Oxford students slept in separate bell tents, so she and her husband went to bed 'under our sleeping bag on the cold, cold grass after the nightly camp fire'.[152] The work was equally segregated. IVS, while worshipping 'pick and shovel' work, limited its 'sisters' to such activities as cooking, washing and mending for the camp, colour washing of houses, and during August, organising games and rambles for children.[153] Within the men's camps, the Anglican Sims-Williams sought to desexualise the body. Discovering at Eastnor that that young working-class men quickly fell to talking about women, Sims-Williams advised the students to encourage the men to discuss masturbation without exaggerating the dangers, suggesting 'remedies ... as you would suggest a cure for a cold or a nervous headache'.[154]

Work promoted unity and exemplified service. The most elaborate formulation of this belief was expressed by the IVS, whose volunteers wore a badge shaped like a shovel, bearing the word PAX against the background of a broken sword. Marked as its founders were by the profound scars of the Great War, IVS represented a beacon of hope, 'war's moral equivalent in hard work and discipline'.[155] Work's bodily effects were also measured in more concrete ways. Most of the work camp movements weighed people. In 1932, one camp leader claimed that 'Grith Fyrders gain on an average eight pounds the first six weeks. No useless fat to that either.'[156] Even the Durham women were weighed, and took pride in it.[157]

Such measuring may seem like a crude Foucauldian instrument of surveillance, exercised upon docile bodies as a subtle technology of control. It was certainly clear who did the measuring and who was measured, but remember the context: unemployment, along with the struggle to live on a miserable dole, caused bodily damage. Some contemporaries blamed the unemployed for this, while others thought it a necessary corrective to an uncompetitive labour market. Work, sports and a hearty diet were, in these circumstances, not the worst solution on offer. But if the unemployed possibly gained some benefits, if only relief from the monotony of home and the dole, I suspect that many of the volunteers gained far more. As with many gap-year volunteer projects today, the social movement camps were organised for the unemployed by others, pursuing agendas in which the unemployed were the objects of others.

Notes

1 J. Hoyland, *Digging for a New England: The co-operative farm for unemployed men*, Jonathan Cape, London, 1936; UAB for Northern Ireland. Memorandum by the Chairman on Training, 1 January 1935, PRONI LAB/5/2.

2 *Children's Newspaper (CN)*, 27 May 1933.

3 *CN*, 7 July 1934.

4 N. Parton (ed.), *Social Theory, Social Change and Social Work: The state of welfare*, Routledge, London, 1996; T. Lovett (ed.), *Radical Approaches to Adult Education: A reader*, Routledge, London, 1988.

5 *Daily Worker (DW)*, 17 February 1933.

6 J. Mangan, 'Athleticism: A case study of the evolution of an educational ideology', in B. Simon and I. Bradley (eds), *The Victorian Public School: Studies in the development of an educational institution*, Gill & Macmillan, Dublin, 1975, 147–67.

7 See e.g. R. Hayburn, 'The Voluntary Occupational Centre Movement, 1932–39', *Journal of Contemporary History*, 6, 3, 1971, 156–71; G. Finlayson, 'A Moving Frontier: Voluntarism and the state in British social welfare, 1911–1939', *Twentieth Century British History*, 1, 2, 183–206.

8 Hoyland, *Digging*, 126, 190.

9 *Service civil volontaire de secours en faveur des inondés du midi de la France*, 8/8/30, Hull History Centre (HHC), IVSP 45/J/25.

10 Kitty Lewis, *An Adventure at Rhosllanerchrugog*, reprinted from *The Welsh Outlook*, September 1932, HHC IVSP 39/G/15.

11 *The International Voluntary Service Movement: A history*, Edgar Dunston & Co., London, n.d. [1933?], HHC IVSP 39/G/15.

12 *An International Voluntary Service Camp in South Wales* n.d. [1931], HHC IVSP 45/J/25.
13 IVS, *Annual Report 1934*.
14 IVS 1932. Brynmawr, Rhosllanerchrugog, HHC IVSP 39/G/15; IVS circular, October 1934; HHC IVSP 45/J/23
15 John A. Barnes, *Humping My Drum: A memoir*, Lulu, Raleigh NC, 2008, 43.
16 M. Sims-Williams, *Camps for Men*, Heffer, Cambridge, 1933, 6–7.
17 Universities Council for Unemployed Camps (UCUC), *Annual Report for 1934*, Cambridge University Archives Min.IX.69/24.
18 UCUC Minute Book, 23 May 1939, CUA Min.IX.69/6.
19 UCUC Minute Book, 29 February 1940, CUA Min.IX.69/6.
20 UCUC, Report of Sub-committee on camp expenditure 1936, CUA Min.IX.69/20.
21 UCUC, *Annual Report for 1934*, CUA Min.IX.69/24.
22 *The Times*, 25 August 1934, 29 August 1935, 5 April 1937; *CN*, 11 January 1936.
23 K. K. Patel, *Soldiers of Labor: Labor service in Nazi Germany and New Deal America, 1933–1945*, Cambridge University Press, New York, 2005, 302.
24 *The Times*, 19 July 1934; UCUC, *Annual Report for 1934*, CUA Min. IX.69/24; Ronald Lunt, 'Noah's Flood at Pinkhill Lock', *Eynsham Record*, 11, 1994.
25 UCUC, *Annual Report for 1935*, CUA Min.IX.69/25.
26 Camp Chief's Report, Harome, n.d. [1936], CUA Min.IX.69/43.
27 *Bredon Bunkum*, July 1937, CUA Min.IX.69/54.
28 UCUC, *Annual Report for 1934*, CUA Min.IX.69/24; Bredon Hill Camp photographs, CUA Min. IX.69/61.
29 Oswald Allan to C N Ryan, 29 December 1934, NA LAB/23/3.
30 UCUC, Cambridge Committee Agenda, 18 November 1935, CUA Min.IX.69/1.
31 UCUC, *Annual Report for 1934*, CUA Min.IX.69/24.
32 *Sheffield Telegraph*, 25 May 1937.
33 Recommendations made by Camp Chiefs, 1936, CUA Min.IX.69/5.
34 UCUC, *Annual Report for 1937*, CUA Min.IX.69/27.
35 Sims-Williams, *Camps for Men*, 24–5.
36 Ibid., 4.
37 Ibid., 32.
38 Hoyland, *Digging*, 156–7.
39 *The Times*, 30 August 1930.
40 UCUC, *Annual Report for 1934*, CUA Min.IX.69/24.
41 *CN*, 6 December 1936.
42 Barnes, *Humping*, 65.
43 Personal communication, 26 September 2009.

44 Longland to Duff, 1 March 1937, Girton College Archives (GCA), GCPP Duke 4/3.
45 Duff to Mr Longland, Durham CSC, 15 February 1937, GCA, GCPP Duke 4/3.
46 CSC Durham County circular, 29 May 1937, GCA, GCPP Duke 4/3.
47 A. P. C. Gray, 'The Durham Camp, *Girton Review*, Michaelmas Term 1937, 13
48 CSC for Durham County, Report on Women's Camps, 1938, GCA, GCPP Duke 4/3.
49 CSC Durham Report on Women's Camps held at Marsden Bay, 1937, GCA, GCPP Duke 4/3.
50 *Marsden Camp Magazine*, August 1937, GCA, GBR/0127/GCPP Nevell.
51 CSC Durham Report on Women's Camps held at Marsden Bay, August 3–10, August 12–19, 1937, GCA, GCPP Duke 4/3; CSC for Durham County, Report on Women's Camps, Marsden Bay, 1938, GCA, GCPP Duke 4/3.
52 Duff to Blanche Griffith, 14 July 1937, GCA, GCPP Duke 4/3.
53 Report of Girton College Camp at Marsden Bay, [1938], GCA, GCPP Duke 4/3 .
54 *Marsden Camp Magazine*, August 1939, GCA, GBR/0127/GCPP Nevell.
55 Gray, 'Durham Camp', 14.
56 Zweiniger-Bargielowska, *Managing the Body,* 254.
57 Sheila Nevell, personal communication, 26 September 2009.
58 *Marsden Camp Magazine*, August 1939, GCA, GBR/0127/GCPP Nevell.
59 Gray, 'Durham Camp', 14; Pathé News, *New Dances for Everybody*, 1938, at www.britishpathe.com/video/new-dances-for-everybody (accessed on 21 April 2012).
60 *Marsden Camp Magazine*, August 1937, GCA, GBR/0127/GCPP Nevell.
61 *Marsden Camp Magazine*, August 1938, *Marsden Camp Magazine*, August 1938, GCA, GBR/0127/GCPP Nevell.
62 Camp at Marsden Bay 12–19 August [1938], GCA, GCPP Duke 4/3.
63 CSC Durham Report on Women's Camps held at Marsden Bay, 1937, GCA, GCPP Duke 4/3.
64 Gray, 'Durham Camp', 12.
65 Ibid., 13.
66 Blanche Griffith, Durham CSC, to Duff, 12 July 1937, GCA, GCPP Duke 4/3.
67 C. Dyhouse, *No Distinction of Sex? Women in British universities, 1870–1939*, UCL Press, London, 1995, 17–25.
68 Personal communication, 26 September 2009.

69 J. Field, 'Service Learning in Britain between the Wars: University students and unemployed camps', *History of Education*, 41, 2, 2012, 195–212.

70 D. Hardy, *Alternative Communities*, 220–3; R. Overy, *The Morbid Age: Britain and the crisis of civilization, 1919–1939*, Penguin, London, 2010, 270–5.

71 *North Sea and Baltic (NSB)*, Spring 1935.

72 M. Jefferies, 'Rolf Gardiner and German Naturism', in M. Jefferies and M. Tyldesley (eds), *Rolf Gardiner: Folk, nature and culture in interwar Britain*, Ashgate, Farnham, 2011, 57.

73 *NSB*, Midwinter 1937.

74 ICGC, Summer Vacation Camp, September 1930. Instructions & Regulations, at www.icgcarchive.co.uk/1930s/documents/1930_instructions_summer_camp.pdf (accessed on 21 April 2010).

75 ICGC, Diary of the Annual Camp, September 1931, at www.icgcarchive.co.uk/1930s/documents/1931_summer_camp_report.pdf (accessed on 21 April 2010).

76 ICGC, Summer Vacation Camp: September 1930, at www.icgcarchive.co.uk/1930s/documents/1930_summer_camp_report.pdf (accessed on 21 April 2010).

77 *MoL. Reports of Investigations into the Industrial Conditions in Certain Depressed Areas*, HMSO, London, 1934, 97.

78 Rolf Gardiner to Jim and Ruth Pennyman, 5 December 1929, TA U/PEN/11/28.

79 *First Cleveland Work Camp 1932*, TA U/PEN/11/28.

80 *NSB*, Spring 1936.

81 *Fourth Cleveland Work Camp 1933*, TA U/PEN/11/28; *Northern Echo*, 19 November 2009.

82 *Northern Echo*, 17 February 1933.

83 *North-Eastern Daily Gazette*, 4 August 1933.

84 *NSB*, Spring 1935.

85 Ibid., Spring 1936.

86 Bene to Auslandsorganisation of the NSDAP, 30 August 1934, NA KV2/2245.

87 R. Gardiner, 'Die deutsche Revolution von England gesehen', in R. Gardiner, A. Broderson and K. Wyser, *Naationalsozialismus von Ausland gesehen: an die Gebildeten unter seiner Gegnern*, Verlag die Runde, Berlin, 1933, 15–18.

88 *NSB*, Spring 1935,

89 Ibid.

90 *Springhead Ring: News Sheet 28*, September 1939.

91 *NSB*, Autumn 1932.

92 R. Gardiner, 'The Triple Function of Work Camps and Work Service in Europe', *NSB*, Harvest 1937.

93 Ibid., 28.
94 Memorandum on the development of a Residential Centre for Social Education at Springhead, no date [?1934?], Pennyman Papers, TA U/PEN/11/30.
95 *NSB*, Harvest 1937; Students' Work Camps in North Yorkshire, 1934, Pennyman Papers, TA U/PEN/11/32.
96 Secret – Instruction to the Postmaster General, 30 August 1939.
97 Gardiner, 'Triple Function', 18.
98 *NSB*, September 1933.
99 *NSB*, Autumn 1939.
100 B.7, 6 March 1940, NA KV2/2245.
101 Cited in D. Edgell, *Order of Woodcraft Chivalry 1916–1949 as a New Age Alternative to the Boy Scouts*, Edwin Mellen Press, Lewiston NY, 1992, Vol. 2, 457.
102 Ibid., 463–4.
103 E. Westlake, 'History of the Order of Woodcraft Chivalry', in Westlake (ed.), *An Outline History of the Order of Woodcraft Chivalry 1916–1976*, OWC, London, 1979, 21–3.
104 *CN*, 20 August 1932; Edgell, *Order of Woodcraft Chivalry*, 471.
105 *Daily Express*, 5 September 1932.
106 S. P. B. Mais, *SOS Talks on Unemployment*, Putnam, London, 1933, 245; Edgell, *Order of Woodcraft Chivalry*, 471.
107 D. Bradshaw (ed.), *The Hidden Huxley*, Faber & Faber, London, 1995, 237.
108 *Daily Express*, 9 September 1932.
109 Mais, *SOS Talks,* 245.
110 *Daily Express*, 1 July 1932.
111 Ibid., 5 September 1932.
112 Ibid.
113 Ibid.
114 *Daily Express*, 29 June 1932.
115 A Technique for the Expansion of Rural Life. Memorandum from Grith Fyrd Camps to HM Treasury, August 1933, NA LAB23/19.
116 Ibid.
117 Editorial, *Library World*, xxxii, June 1930, 1; K. C. Harrison, 'Library Association', 465–70, in R. Wedgeworth (ed.), *World Encyclopaedia of Library and Information Sciences,* 3rd edn, American Library Association, 1993, 467.
118 Edgell, *Order of Woodcraft Chivalry*, 475.
119 *Eugenics Review*, 25, 4, 1934, 265.
120 For example, see *BMJ*, 27 May 1933.
121 *The Times*, 11 August 1934.
122 J. A. R. Pimlott (1935), *Toynbee Hall: Fifty years of social progress, 1884–1934*, London: J. M. Dent, 226.

123 WEA, *Annual report 1933*, 14, 51; *Annual report 1934*, 62.
124 *Daily Express*, 29 June 1932.
125 T. H. to Ryan, 1 March 1935, NA LAB23/19.
126 *DM*, 28 September 1935.
127 *DM*, 19 April 1934; Norman Glaister to E. H. E. Havelock, Development Commission, 15 March 1937, NA D/4/372.
128 Memorandum, Havelock, 31 May 1937, NA D/4/372.
129 Edgell, *Order of Woodcraft Chivalry*, 515, 535–6.
130 Ibid., 584.
131 R. Yates, 'A Brief Moment of Glory: The impact of the therapeutic community movement on the drug treatment systems in the UK', *International Journal of Social Welfare*, 12, 3, 2003, 240–1.
132 *Habonim 20 Years* (souvenir brochure), Kettering, 1949, 6.
133 J. Schneer, *The Balfour Declaration: The origins of the Arab-Israeli conflict*, Random House, New York, 2010, 333–46.
134 H. Near, *The Kibbutz Movement: A history*, Vol. 1, Oxford University Press, Oxford, 1992, 101–8.
135 M. Thomson, '"The Solution to his own Enigma": Connecting the life of Montague David Eder, socialist, psychoanalyst, Zionist and modern saint', *Medical History*, 55, 2011, 61–84.
136 A. Sakula, 'Samson Wright (1899–1956): Physiologist extraordinary', *Journal of the Royal Society of Medicine*, 92, 1999, 484–6.
137 *Jewish Chronicle* (*JC*), 8 May 1936.
138 *JC*, 20 November 1936.
139 Interview by Allen Bordoley, 12 July 2011.
140 *JC*, 8 May 1936.
141 *JC*, 20 November 1936.
142 Interview, 12 July 2011.
143 *The Times*, 23 June 1939.
144 Ibid.
145 *JC*, 8 May 1936.
146 *JC*, 20 November 1936.
147 Y. Morris, *Pioneers from the West: A history of colonization in Israel*, World Zionist Organization, Jerusalem, 1953, 29; A. Bordoley, 'Seven Olives for an Egg: Shalom Bordoley – Hechalutz to Kfar Blum, 1933–2003', privately published.
148 *The Times*, 8 May 1939, 23 June 1939.
149 Interview, 12 July 2011.
150 Gillett, 'Jack Hoyland's Work-Camps', 45–6.
151 *Bredon Bunkum*, July 1936, CUA Min.IX.69/52.
152 Peter Hewett and Diana Hewett, *Paradise Regained*, 2008, www.trimleymill.co.uk/paradise-regained (accessed 19/9/2009).
153 *An International Voluntary Service Camp in South Wales*, n.d. [1931], HHC IVSP 45/J/25.

154 Sims-Williams, *Camps for Men*, 8, 40.
155 *The International Voluntary Service Movement: a history*, n.d. [1933?], HHC IVSP 39/G/15.
156 *Daily Express*, 5 September 1932.
157 CSC Durham Report on Women's Camps held at Marsden Bay, 1937, GCA, GCPP Duke 4/3.

10

'Down with the concentration camps!'

Opposition and protest

If they thought at all about work camps, the comfortably paid and regularly employed probably saw them as a rather jolly time under canvas, jollier perhaps than the unemployed deserved. One young woman student from Edinburgh University told Jack Hoyland that unemployed 'lads' thought of work as 'a holiday', offering 'friendship, freedom, health and discipline'.[1] Others took a very different view; this chapter considers those inside the camps who organised and participated in protests of different kinds, as well as those outside who campaigned either for improved conditions or for their abolition.

Of all those who fought against work camp movements, the most consistent were Britain's handful of communists. Normally thought of as small and peripheral, the Communist Party of Great Britain (CPGB) could be formidable when allied with others on the left, or on the rare occasions when it led a popular movement, as it did through the National Unemployed Workers' Movement (NUWM), described by Richard Croucher as 'a highpoint of unemployed organisation in British history'.[2] Much of its success was due to its devoted and efficient organiser, Wal Hannington, who managed to preserve the movement from the worst idiocies of Stalinism, though sometimes at the cost of his own position.[3] Yet even Hannington had to accept party discipline in the end, and the NUWM's fortunes were undoubtedly affected as a result.

Inside the camps, the NUWM had few members if any. It held occasional recruitment drives, but appears to have concluded that its main priorities lay elsewhere, and not with those who had chosen – if under pressure – to enter a 'slave camp'. It did campaign against the camps, though, and its publications are an important source on conditions inside them. As for men who had entered the camps, neither their decision nor their distance from Communist politics can be understood as a signal that they passively accepted their fate. On the contrary, and belying the Communists' claims that the camps were ruled with military discipline, there were protests, strikes and demonstrations in both the labour colonies and Instructional Centres (ICs). These were triggered by a variety of causes, the most common being complaints over food; there is no sign of any wider political rejection of the camp system from within. In the case of the women's home training centres, I am unable to report any trace of rebellion or organised complaint, whether because dissent went unrecorded or because the women were relatively young, largely ignored by the NUWM, and peripheral to the wider labour movement.

Denunciation from outside

Socialist groups had been involved in a number of labour colony movements, but these were largely exercises in land settlement, and their most enthusiastic supporters were quick to distinguish between their ventures into socialist living and those labour colonies that they saw as little more than workhouse farms. Lansbury, as we have seen, protested against what he saw as the betrayal of Hollesley Bay's founding principles, while Thomas Smith, Fels's manager at Mayland, who had helped lay out the estate for Hollesley Bay, described it in 1907 as no more than 'a large relief yard'.[4] The Minority Report triggered more open opposition from the veteran London Marxist Harry Quelch, who mocked the Webbs and their allies as 'practical' people who proposed 'practical' palliatives such as labour exchanges and training schemes, rather than working for socialist revolution, reserving their 'Detention Colony' for the poor while ignoring the 'wealthy workshy'.[5]

In the immediate post-war years, unemployment spread to the industrial areas, proving particularly intractable in the homes of the staple industries. As in earlier decades, there was still lingering support on the left for labour colonies. In Glasgow, the Communist and nationalist John MacLean joined other unemployed leaders in demanding that the town council provide 'work on farm colonies at trade union rates of pay, with representation on all committees employing the unemployed', equipped with municipal restaurants to feed the workers and municipal housing to shelter their families.

They also satirised emigrant training schemes by demanding to emigrate to Soviet Russia.[6]

Such enthusiasm did not last. In 1922, paupers at Hollesley Bay went on strike. The Peckham branch of the electrical trades union expressed its sympathy, as well as its 'disgust' at the policy of sending single men to Belmont and Hollesley Bay, which it claimed was 'a blot upon the reputation of all British People, who have always been credited with giving a square deal to all parties'.[7] E. Harmer of the newly-constituted National Unemployed Workers' Committee Movement (NUWCM) attacked the London Guardians for 'inaugurating into ENGLAND, SLAVERY of a more BRUTAL CHARACTER than even that of CHATTEL SLAVERY or SERFDOM'.[8] While the NUWCM paid little attention to Belmont and Hollesley Bay, concentrating for the rest of the year on organising the first – and by all accounts rather successful – hunger march, it (and subsequently the NUWM) took a sporadic interest in the London labour colonies, and occasionally represented members who refused to enter them.[9]

For much of its history, the precise focus of the NUWM's campaigning depended on the state of Communist Party policy, which in turn followed the broad direction of Soviet policy. As Croucher emphasises, while the NUWM was by no means a puppet that danced obediently to every Party tune, its Communist leaders maintained a firm and growing hold over its organisation and policies.[10] One clear example of this is the way that the NUWM attacked the poor law labour colonies after 1930, when it was particularly interested in undermining democratic socialist parties, above all Labour, and then shifted its attention to the ICs in 1934–35 as it started to build alliances with other left-wing forces. In 1928, the Comintern declared that the capitalist system had entered its third and decisive global crisis since 1917. As a result, it instructed its national sections – the CPGB included – to seize the leadership of the labour movement and break the stranglehold of social democracy. By 1929, the Comintern was attacking other left-wing parties as 'social fascists', who by leading the workers astray were more insidious and dangerous than any actual fascists.[11]

The London labour colonies provided an ideal opportunity for exposing social fascism. In 1930, the *Daily Worker* urged readers to send in stories about local public assistance committees (PACs), 'especially those with Labour majorities'.[12] It had already interviewed men from Belmont, described in the headline as a 'Slave Colony for

London's Unemployed'.[13] This 'exposure' of Belmont was followed by street meetings in the East End, with speeches from men who had been in Belmont, and sometimes their wives.[14] The CPGB attacked the 'cowards who call themselves Labour members' on Stepney PAC for calling police to a demonstration against Belmont, and accused Lansbury of praising the Salvation Army 'slave farm' at Hadleigh.[15] Len Wilson, a Party member and NUWM activist, criticised Walter Greenwood during the 1931 LCC election campaign for his stance as Labour's Minister of Health towards 'London's slave colonies'.[16] The campaign continued through the summer, and in July the movement called for Laindon, Belmont and Hollesley Bay to be closed.[17] Outside London, a number of PAC meetings were disrupted during debates over labour colonies.[18] On one occasion, the Communists even denounced adult education programmes for the unemployed as tantamount to plans for 'slave camps'.[19]

Belmont was a particular focus. It was close to London, where many Party members were concentrated, and was managed by the LCC, whose strong Labour representation made it a particularly attractive target. In 1933, Kath Duncan tried to present a petition calling on the LCC to abolish test work and close its labour colonies, supported by demonstrators who shouted slogans including 'LCC starves the unemployed' and 'Down with slave colonies'. Three unemployed men were arrested after invading the council chamber.[20] A *Daily Worker* report on Dunton Farm was scathing about the porridge and tinned corned beef given to the 140 men in 'this slave institution of the PAC'.[21] Communists also attacked Wallingford as evidence that even the 'Christian Church have Sweat Camps'.[22]

Communist logic allowed the Party, of course, to attack 'slave colonies' in Britain while denying their existence in the Soviet Union. One British communist, while attacking Belmont, explained that reports of slave camps in the USSR were a wicked myth, as in the workers' state 'there are no unemployed'.[23] Social fascism, meanwhile, was everywhere. Harry Pollitt, Communist candidate in the 1933 Clay Cross by-election, denounced Roosevelt's New Deal, with its plans for 'labour conscription'.[24] Another communist denounced Canada as 'a land of capitalist terror and forced labour camps'.[25] New Zealand's 'slave camps' also came in for attack, partly because they confirmed that 'in all capitalist countries, the workers have not only the forces of the State to fight, but also the reactionary Labour leaders of the Labour Party'.[26]

While the NUWM was not immune from the Party's sectarianism, it sought to root its campaigns in what it understood as the realities of working-class life. First, it denounced labour colonies and ICs for harming families.[27] In 1931, Belmont's worst feature was said to be 'separation of the husband from his family for an indefinite period, the wife being left to scrape along on a mere subsistence scale of relief'.[28] Second, the movement complained that working men were mixed with social undesirables. In 1930, one Communist objected to living with the 'mentally deficient, bordering on being insane',[29] while others complained of mixing with 'aged institutional men'.[30] The *Daily Worker* similarly criticised the Durham Diocesan Rescue Association for taking three young unemployed women, who expected to be trained as servants, to a home in Darlington which also cared for former prostitutes and criminals.[31]

Initially, the Communist Party and NUWM showed surprisingly little interest in the TICs. An article attacking 'Maggie's training centres' appeared in the *Daily Worker* in May 1930, proposing a boycott of the home training centres for women.[32] In early 1931, NUWM branch members campaigned outside labour exchanges against 'the action of Maggie Bondfield, the Slavey Queen, in driving the women and girls of this country into "domestic service"'.[33] Bondfield was precisely the type of trade union and Labour figure who exemplified social fascism; moreover, as the minister responsible for the unemployment insurance system, she refused to meet NUWM deputations, and once had Hannington and his colleagues thrown out of the Ministry building.[34] In February, the NUWM planned a day of action around the slogan 'Down with compulsory domestic slavery'.[35] Communists demonstrated against the 'Social-Fascists' Jimmy Thomas and Margaret Bondfield when they spoke at a Labour Party rally in Sheffield, and attacked Dr Marion Phillips and other 'Social-Fascists' for 'glorifying' domestic service at the International Socialist Women's Conference.[36] The TICs, meanwhile, were barely mentioned.

This changed slightly in 1931. Labour-controlled Abertillery PAC came in for criticism when it refused benefit to two young men who had refused to enter TICs.[37] In May, the *Daily Worker* reported on discontent in the 'hellhole' that was the 'notorious' Brandon centre; again, food appears to have been the main issue at stake.[38] Another writer contrasted a lavish 'freak party' at the Kit Kat restaurant with the experiences of a Brandon trainee:

I have now been in the training camp one month, and can tell you without hesitation that the majority of the boys don't think much of it, as the food is rather poor, but plenty of it. The lavatories are buckets which have to be emptied by the trainees every day, a job that is very distasteful to them. We have to wash our own clothes.[39]

Yet otherwise the NUWM paid little attention to the TICs, despite Communist hatred of Bondfield, who had introduced compulsory attendance as a condition of benefit.

Communist and NUWM indifference to the TIC programme is baffling.[40] The TICs did, however, attract attention from some on the Labour left. George Buchanan, ILP MP for Glasgow Gorbals, described TICs as 'places of detention' and 'labour colonies', while Campbell Stephen, ILP MP for Glasgow Camlachie, contrasted 'imprisonment' in Carstairs with the 'walking and golfing' enjoyed by the wealthy when they felt 'run down'.[41] While these were by no means isolated voices, they certainly had little if any influence on Labour policy. And by this time, the Communists had started to pay more attention to the camps, prompted partly by the deliberations of the Royal Commission on Unemployment Insurance.

Established by Bondfield and MacDonald as a delaying mechanism, the Commission was asked to address the funding gap between the costs of benefits paid to unemployed claimants, and the income from insured workers. Wal Hannington and others in the NUWM were suspicious from the outset, suspecting – rightly – that it would lead to benefit reductions. Witnesses like James Maurice Loughran, Public Assistance Officer at Port Glasgow, helped reinforce this interpretation: his evidence to the Commission include a call for 'workshies' to be sent to compulsory labour colonies.[42] In summer 1931, Brennan Ward wrote a pamphlet called *The Real Scandal of the 'Dole'* (the 'real scandal' being the idle rich), claiming that 'Youths are to be driven into slave compounds – so-called "training centres" – under well-nigh incredible living conditions, or into the Army'.[43] Others feared that the government was planning an army of strikebreakers, who would be used to undermine apprenticeship training and weaken trade unions.[44] Hannington, normally a rather scrupulous researcher, claimed in 1936 that the 1932 report of the Royal Commission on Unemployment Insurance 'had referred to a similar labour camp scheme in operation in Germany, and we therefore claimed that this meant the application of Fascist methods in Britain'.[45] The report, of course, was published well before the Nazi seizure of power, at a time when the voluntary *Arbeitsdienst* was managed by a variety of bodies including churches, sports clubs, and youth groups, with little Nazi involvement.[46]

With its huge majority, Ramsay MacDonald's National Government believed it had a mandate to pursue the Royal Commission's recommendations. In 1932, the government began work on the Unemployment Assistance Bill, which would retain the means test and expand the grounds for disqualification, while creating a new body – the Unemployment Assistance Board (UAB) – to administer 'transitional' benefits to those who had exhausted or did not qualify for unemployment insurance benefits. The Bill also brought to an end the long-established practice of parish relief, which since 1929 had been administered by local government, through local PACs. In a particularly controversial development, it combined government's existing power to compel applicants to undertake training with the old poor law power of requiring applicants to undertake test work.

Neil Evans has calculated that the Unemployment Assistance Bill was the single most discussed piece of domestic legislation in inter-war Britain.[47] It triggered immediate protests within Parliament and in the wider community, and while much attention was inevitably focused on likely reductions in benefits and tightening of eligibility requirements, particularly in districts where local PAC members had considerable sympathy for the unemployed, opponents were also anxious – and often angry – about the proposals for training and testing applicants. The government's large majority within the House of Commons meant that the legislation was approved, and new regulations came into force in early 1935.

In the summer of 1933, the NUWM stood at what Croucher calls its 'organisational highpoint'. Popular unrest over the means test had led to violent street battles in a number of cities, including Birkenhead, Castleford and Belfast, followed by police attacks on hunger marchers as they headed for London; meanwhile, the everyday work of legal representation and local lobbying continued. By February 1933, the NUWM claimed a membership of 100,000, organised in 349 branches.[48] Hannington claimed that the National Government's legislation had confirmed all his predictions, warning against 'the biggest attempt at slave labour and the introduction of slave colonies yet made'.[49] By 1934, the NUWM was sending delegations to lobby PACs and others over the Bill, almost invariably including objections to 'slave camps'. At its annual conference, the movement denounced the act as a 'fascist measure', establishing 'a dictatorship' over the unemployed. The conference urged all branches to

> develop an intensive and spirited propaganda against the Labour Camp Schemes. We must organise the unemployed, with the support of the employed workers, to carry out mass refusals to enter these Labour Camps. The spirit of boycott against the Camps must be developed. We must conduct picketing at the Labour Exchanges and collect the names of unemployed workers who have been approached by the Labour Exchange officials to go to the Camps. Meetings of these unemployed workers must be called to discuss resistance to entering the Camps. Where the experimental camps are already in operation, steps must be taken to make contact with the men inside the Camps and to organise strike action against their conditions, on the demand that their work shall be paid for at full trade union rates.

The conference also called on PACs not to participate in sending men to 'the concentration camps', promising 'exposure' of all who failed to comply.[50]

In South Wales, the campaign against the new system mobilised almost the entire community.[51] Here, the NUWM and Communist Party were joined by the South Wales Miners' Federation, many of whose members were themselves unemployed, as well as by many leaders in the churches, the Labour Party (particularly its eloquent parliamentary spokesman Aneurin Bevan) and the social service movement. In early 1935, radical members of the miners' union blocked a bus attempting to take 50 young men to an IC.[52] By March, Llanelli United Front Committee set its mind on closing Brechfa, finding some support from the trainees.[53] Yet if it was particularly strong in South Wales, the campaign won support across Britain. NUWM members in Falkirk lobbied their National Unionist MP against plans 'to develop slave and blackleg labour'.[54] A flute and drum band and 600 demonstrators accompanied the NUWM delegation in Kirkcaldy, where a speaker demanded that the PAC should restore cuts in benefits, and pay benefits to young men who refused to enter the 'slave camps'.[55] In Durham, 54 delegates representing thirteen miners' union lodges decided to lobby the local PAC, and appointed a delegation to visit 'Hamsterley slave camp'.[56] Shortly afterwards, Jarrow branch of the boilermakers' union urged Durham PAC to discuss closing Hamsterley.[57]

By now, the Communists were willing to cooperate with supporters on the Labour left. In early 1935, the Communists issued a joint appeal with the Independent Labour Party, calling for 'mass opposition to the slave camps and solidarity with those who refuse to enter'.[58] Local branches of the Women's Co-operative Guild and the Labour League of Youth also supported the campaign.[59] Even in 1935, though, the Communists continued to denounce Labour for enforcing 'the principle of slavery' at the LCC labour colonies.[60] In April 1935, a 'squad of young worker-cyclists' raided Belmont, putting up posters and holding a meeting in Sutton High Street.[61] By 1936, the Communists were using Belmont to attack Herbert Morrison, Labour leader of the LCC and grandfather of Peter Mandelson.[62]

For its part, mainstream Labour viewed the entire campaign with suspicion. When East Ham Trades Council called for the Trades Union Congress (TUC) to investigate conditions at Belmont, and campaign for its closure, Walter Citrine passed the problem over to Congress's Social Insurance Department, who advised that local government matters were none of the TUC's business.[63] When Frank Day of Brighton Trades Council complained that IC trainees had to parade daily before the Union Flag, and were marched four abreast through local town centres on Saturdays, the TUC replied politely that they had 'no knowledge of these points' and would be grateful for evidence.[64] This was also how the TUC dealt with complaints about a speech by Sir John Gilmour, in which the Home Secretary apparently praised concentration camps.[65]

From the TUC's perspective, ICs and labour colonies fell below the radar. Most trade unions had members who were unemployed, but the work camps mostly recruited unskilled men, particularly those who were in the most precarious areas of a slack labour market, while the unions largely represented men in skilled or semi-skilled trades. The only significant expressions of concern came from the miners' unions in Durham and South Wales, some of whose unemployed members were being encouraged to enter ICs. Some of the building trades unions briefly feared that their members might be displaced by men who had been trained by the Ministry of Labour, and the National Federation of Building Trades Operatives decided to raise its concerns with the TUC. One Glasgow official visited Carstairs in 1930, reporting reassuringly that the men were training 'in ideal surroundings and under ideal conditions' for farm work in Canada, though he added that the joiners' workshop was 'a farce'.[66] In 1934 the TUC described the Unemployment Assistance Act as 'the Slave and Blackleg Act', because of its approach to test and training centres, but this was not followed by any action against the camps.[67] While trade unions took little interest in the camps, Labour leaders usually portrayed critics as proto-Communists. In early 1935, for example, the Labour group on Durham Council expelled Councillor Steve Lawther for openly supporting the NUWM campaign.[68]

After the Act was introduced, the campaign continued, but inevitably it lost momentum. Apart from anything else, the new UAB decided – probably sensibly – not to open centres for work testing and training; rather, it opted to use the Ministry of Labour schemes, treating them as both a de facto work test and a training programme. It also chose – equally wisely – not to apply its powers of compulsion. Though the NUWM retained the language of slavery in its publicity materials, and continued to agitate over the camps, from 1936 it was unable to rouse mass opposition. It continued its legal work, representing men denied benefit by the UAB after refusing to attend 'Slave Camps'.[69] It also represented a number of men who had been refused compensation for injuries incurred in the ICs, challenging the Ministry's argument that the men were trainees rather than employees, and were therefore not covered by the relevant legislation.[70] It organised small-scale protests of a symbolic character, as in March 1939 when NUWM members lay down in the lobby of the House of Commons, holding placards proclaiming 'Work at TU rates – not slave camps'.[71] As for Labour, the first time the ICs were discussed at the Party's conference was in 1939, when Sam Watson, the Durham miners' leader, condemned the 'slave camps', claiming that a trainee ended up 'a much worse citizen than before he went to the training camp'. The conference unanimously demanded 'cessation of training camps for the unemployed'.[72]

How should we make sense of the Communist opposition to the camps? From the vantage point of the present, much of the language seems hyperbolic, even apocalyptic. Even in 1933, Communist writers were still comparing the TICs with Mussolini's Italy.[73] In August, the *Daily Worker* denounced the ICs as a British attempt to produce a 'slave class' of the kind planned 'by the murderous Fascist leader of Germany, Hitler'.[74] Tom Wintringham, a Communist and later prime mover behind the Home Guard, described Belmont as 'a workhouse concentration camp'.[75] As late as 1938, Wal Hannington was warning of the 'pro-fascist gang' within the National Government, which was promoting a 'drive for compulsory labour camps for the British unemployed', in an attempt to prepare them for war.[76]

Changing Communist policies alone cannot explain this, as Guy Aldred's anarchist group similarly attacked the ICs as 'concentration camps', designed to drive the working class 'from wage-slavery to chattel-slavery'.[77] British Trotskyites also held that the ICs proved that the British 'boss-class' was preparing for 'universal totalitarianism' and 'forced labour'.[78] Intriguingly, Britain's Fascists complained about the government work camps, if not frequently. In 1935, for instance, the *Blackshirt* reported the case of a Mr G, aged 32 and unemployed off and on for a decade, who was sent to 'notorious Belmont, the residential occupational training centre', separating him from his family.[79] Two years later, the paper took issue with a Ministry of Labour leaflet, advertising for men to enter an IC, stressing that while the British Union of Fascists (BUF) had no quarrel with the idea of training, 'THE TROUBLE IS THAT THERE AREN'T ANY JOBS.'[80] This was no consistent campaign; Britain's fascists treated the camps mainly as an opportunity to attack 'democracy' and its failings. In Scotland, the nationalist movement had a more specific grievance. A National Party delegation led by the Duke of Montrose told Sir Arthur Rose, Commissioner for Special Areas in Scotland, that the government's transference policy was depriving Scotland of 'the flower of the race'. The delegation favoured camps, so long as they were in Scotland and trained young Scots to remain in Scotland.[81]

Outside the camps, then, only the Communists repeatedly raised questions about the conditions and lives of the men, as well as challenging their wider purpose. Neither the mainstream parties nor such fringe groups as the Scottish nationalists and Fascists had much to say about the ICs. Of course, Communist interest peaked when the Party thought of the unemployed as the most revolutionary regiment in the proletarian army, and waned when the Party focused on building its base and influence in the trade union movement. Even the NUWM was inconsistent in its attention to the camps, partly because the trainees were never likely to bring much to its campaigning, and partly because the NUWM too was subject to the discipline and priorities of the Party. At local level, it defended the right of unemployed men to refuse training, and from time to time it promoted campaigns over conditions inside the camps, as well as attacking the camps' supposedly malign purpose. Fritz Funk, a German pacifist and anti-Nazi who joined the IVS camp in Gateshead, was astonished to arrive at work one morning to find that someone had painted on the wall: 'Down with this Fascist Work Camp'.[82]

Concerns over the camps were pervasive on the left, thanks largely to the NUWM, and while this atmosphere of mistrust may not have undermined the camps' existence, it certainly caused the authorities to tread carefully. In Northern Ireland, the chairman of the local UAB thought that the NUWM's campaigns had made it impossible even to use the word 'centre' and 'camp'.[83] Even without the benefit of hindsight, neither the ICs nor the student camps of the UCUC and the IVS justified the term 'slave camps', let alone stand serious comparison with Nazi concentration camps. But the NUWM was a political organisation, and in many ways a very effective one. Much of its public language was hyperbole, but at the same time its local casework was often highly conscientious and deeply humane. And as a result of the NUWM campaigns, UCUC organisers, UAB officials and Ministry of Labour administrators all had cause to remind their colleagues that their actions needed to be justified before a wider, potentially hostile public.

Protest and resistance

Inside the camps, such debates must have seemed remote. By historical standards, as Croucher suggests, the level of organised protest among Britain's unemployed during the interwar years was rather remarkable.[84] In general, unemployed people tend not to engage in sustained and organised political action.[85] Some sociologists suggest that most successful social movements tend to depend on their members who are able to mobilise resources, including money, contacts with powerful groups, and positive media coverage.[86] Unemployed people who already possess these resources are likely to be the first to move back into jobs, while the long-term unemployed are the least likely to be able to command the resources that will produce durable and influential movements. Within the camps, though, durable and large-scale action was impossible, partly because most of the camps were miles from the main centres of population, and the trainees were isolated. This did not prevent them from participating in periodic outbreaks of dissatisfaction and complaint, usually over practical grievances of an immediate kind.

In the labour colonies, there is simply insufficient evidence of protest to be confident about generalisations. Bolton Smart, superintendent at Hollesley Bay, admitted to the Royal Commission on the Poor Laws that there had been 'one trouble' on his watch, which he dismissed as 'a very foolish thing, there was nothing behind it' (this did not prevent him from having the ringleaders dismissed).[87] The Reverend Brooks claimed that Lingfield had seen a number of 'isolated cases where discipline was needed', but never 'open subordination'.[88] Nevertheless, there is scattered evidence of organised protest. Men from Laindon joined unemployed demonstrations in London in 1905.[89] There were reports of a 'riot' in Belmont in December 1910, reportedly provoked by a mixture of complaints over the diet and frustration caused by the lack of work in bad weather, and the magistrates imprisoned 80 men for refusing to work.[90]

Rather more organisation went into the 1922 strike at Hollesley Bay. Between 85 and 98 men walked out of the colony in protest at the working conditions.[91] Twenty-one of the strikers, including three 'ringleaders', came from Camberwell, where they apparently persuaded local union members to lend their support.[92] A subsequent enquiry by Poplar Board of Guardians heard that Albert Sutherland wanted a set of false teeth and a suit for 'walking out', while Robert Christie complained that the men had cold dinners on Sunday, though he retracted after hearing that this was so the kitchen staff – themselves unemployed – could have the day off. The Poplar Guardians concluded that, on the whole, the men were 'fairly treated'.[93]

Protests within the labour colonies rose in number and scale from the late 1920s. In 1929, the Hollesley Bay inmates protested once more, prompting a delegation from the Stepney Guardians to investigate complaints from the 70 men they had sent to the colony. Once more, the Guardians decided that conditions were satisfactory, dismissing the complaints as 'an organised grouse'.[94] In 1930, a group of inmates walked out of Belmont, complaining of the food, the resemblance of the clothing issued to convict uniforms, and the presence of men who were 'mentally deficient, bordering on the insane' among their ranks.[95] In 1933, 200 men struck at Hollesley

Bay; their grievances centred on food, with the strikers complaining that they were underfed, and had been given milk from a cow infected with tuberculosis. The superintendent called the police, and six men subsequently appeared, in handcuffs, at Woodbridge Police Court. On this occasion, the Bench attempted to intervene, asking the colony to take the men back while their grievances were investigated, but the superintendent refused to take them 'under any consideration'. The men were sentenced to a week each in prison, after which they were taken straight to the nearest railway station with a one-way ticket to London, where the NUWM decided to fight their cause.[96]

Food was the single most frequently quoted cause of protest in the labour colonies. However, this can be slightly misleading. Depending on their reception, initial complaints over food could easily lead to wider grievances. In late autumn 1931, for example, men at Belmont complained to the Master after they were served meat pies that, they alleged, had gone bad. The Master arranged for the kitchen to provide cold meat, pickles, bread and tea, but by this time the 'shop stewards' had progressed to demands for an extra day's Christmas holiday. When the Master rejected this demand, they demonstrated outside a meeting of the PAC's visiting committee, and were again turned down. They therefore held an organised march back to London, where they tried to see the PAC. By this time, the superintendent had decided to discharge 41 ringleaders, which itself became the subject of a new grievance.[97]

Only in one case can I find evidence of a purely economic grievance in a labour colony. Sixty men working at Palacerigg struck in 1930 because they were paid less than men on other relief work projects run by Glasgow Corporation; the Corporation compromised, paying £2 weekly to men it deemed satisfactory for three months.[98] But there may have been other, unreported disputes. When one civil servant was exploring possible work centre sites in Scotland, the Director of Public Assistance for Glasgow warned against residential camps, as 'unless a lot of recreational provision is made the men are apt to get in a bad state and burn the huts down'.[99] Was this based on experience or anxiety?

In the ICs, protests were more frequent and more organised; the protesters were also more likely to have connections with the NUWM. One Lanarkshire man claimed that when he had been in Glenfinart, spontaneous walk-outs were a familiar occurrence:

'During the first eight weeks there were five strikes, due to the men having to sit all day in the wet weather sheds, corrugated iron sheets wrapped to a half moon, with a rain-sodden earth flooring.'[100] Food was also an issue. At the non-residential IC in Slough, the 'Leigh boys' organised a petition in 1929 over the quality of the food. Again, though, there was more to the complaint. As well as disliking the lunches, the Lancastrians complained of 'not receiving civility from servants employed by the caterers', then took umbrage when the camp manager ignored them. A further petition in May 1930 claimed that on some days the men were unable to eat the lunch at all, leaving them without sustenance between breakfast and tea.[101] Bondfield had the Ministry investigate the allegations; an official tasted the meals, confirming that the meat was overcooked and poor quality, the tea weak. He thought the kitchen equipment poor, and the canteen cold, while 'the service, I should say, was not very appetising'.[102] In July, 60 men left Carstairs after one was discharged for complaining over the food.[103]

Camp hygiene could also provoke action. According to the camp manager at Fermyn Woods, 63 men walked out in 1930 after being asked to submit to a medical examination, then were joined by a smaller group who were angry about the Sunderland head-lice cases.[104] Fermyn Woods had form, for in 1929 Robert Beddall from Sheffield had died from influenza in the camp.[105] The Ministry agreed that the strikers could return to complete their courses 'if they so desire'.[106] In the following year, the *Daily Worker* claimed that discontent at nearby Bourne was so great that trainees smashed the windows in the recreation hut, workshops and staff room. This protest appears to have had a political dimension, for in the evening trainees gathered in the village where they sang the Red Flag, then chalked hammers and sickles and Communist slogans on huts. The police had apparently been unable to disperse the men, but one Communist sympathiser was subsequently fined 10s. 10d. for malicious damage and expelled from the camp.[107] The cause is unknown. So is the trigger for a 1933 strike at Carstairs, after which 91 trainees walked out or were discharged.[108] In summer 1933, a strike at Carshalton IC over food and bullying lasted all of half an hour, but still got a mention in the *Daily Worker*.[109]

In 1935, the protests acquired a more political tone as the NUWM sought to involve trainees in the campaign against the Unemployment Assistance Act. In February, twenty-one men from

Brechfa IC joined a rally in Llanelli against the Act, complaining of the food and heavy quarry work, and wearing – according to the *Daily Worker* – 'heavy corduroy trousers, with heavy boots and a rubber cape'.[110] Fifty men from Brechfa attended a similar rally a month later, where one of the speakers read a letter complaining about the food, bedding and lack of recreation in the camp.[111] Two weeks later, Brechfa trainees marched at the head of another rally in Llanelli, attracting attention in their corduroy trousers and brown jackets, and meeting Hannington to discuss their grievances.[112] Enoch Collins, representing the steelworkers' union on Llanelli United Front Committee, reported that three strikes had taken place in the IC, and the men were forming an NUWM committee to represent their interests.[113] This campaign fizzled out, but was the one occasion on which the NUWM was able to mobilise effectively a group of camp trainees.

Further protests took place shortly before the camp programme came to an end. In March 1938, 150 men walked out at Glentress in a dispute over discipline. Once more, this was more complex than it first seemed. The walk-out had its origins in an argument about working in wet weather, which led to eight men being dismissed. Subsequently, other trainees walked out after one of their number was discharged for allegedly causing a disturbance in the canteen; when the deputy manager refused to reinstate the sacked man, others struck work and were sent home. Thirty men who had taken no part in the protest remained in the camp, meeting the Ministry of Labour official investigating the dispute.[114] Finally, in what seems to have been the last recorded protest before the camps closed, 150 men struck over grievances about the food in Hamsterley in March 1939.[115]

Overall, a simple analysis suggests that food was the men's main grievance, followed at some distance by wet weather working. How did the authorities view the protests? Croucher, for example, supports claims that strikes and other demonstrations made relief works unattractive to the authorities.[116] Logically, then, one might expect the authorities to suppress disruption, and hush it up when it took place. The absence of reports from the Ministry of Labour's training branch inspectors is likely to fuel cynicism: when one Cumberland MP asked in 1936 about the experiences of unemployed constituents in a Lincolnshire IC, the government replied that the Centre – possibly Bourne – had received six visits by officers of the training branch inspectorate within the last six months.[117] Perhaps, but I could find none of their reports among the Ministry's records.

On several occasions, the camp manager expelled protesters, on grounds of discipline. In these circumstances, the men lost their eligibility to unemployment benefit, and had to turn to the PAC – later the UAB – for support. This was not deterrent enough for at least one civil servant, who hoped that any man expelled for misconduct would find himself treated 'as a case of special difficulty', and sent 'if incorrigible, into a penal settlement'.[118] In practice, though, many grievances were settled quietly, with minimal fuss. When Christie Tait visited Kershopefoot, he learned of a grievance about the heating in the huts; after a delegation to the manager, the problem was resolved.[119]

One file sheds some light on the Ministry's perception of discipline.[120] In 1933, R. W. Connelly applied to the Leeds labour exchange for a place on an IC course. The local exchange dealt with his application, but after he passed both the interview and the medical examination an official learned that Connelly belonged to 'a group of local communists, who are extremely hostile to the recruitment of men to the Centres, which they describe as "Slave and Concentration Camps"'. The Leeds exchange consulted the Controller for the North-east Division, who was minded to reject Connelly's application but decided to sound out his superiors. Whitehall officials took rather a more relaxed view than their Yorkshire colleagues. 'This is an interesting case', reported a mid-ranking officer to Beryl Power, for if Connelly were rejected, the outcome could be 'awkward questions on political persecution', while if accepted, 'the anticipated adverse influence on other applicants may be troublesome'. His advice was to accept Connelly and 'minimise the trouble with the help of the Centre Manager'.[121] Power in turn sought advice from her superiors, who ruled that Connelly should be offered a place at Fermyn Woods, where Mr Kettley, the manager, was said to have 'an excellent influence over troublesome trainees'.[122] After serving as an employment clerk at Leamington Spa exchange, Kettley managed Shobdon testing centre then spent a period in charge of Carshalton TIC before taking on the role at Fermyn Woods IC in October 1932.[123] He was an experienced camp manager, but in the meantime Connelly had found work; no more was heard of the troublesome Communist.[124] At this point the file ends.

The Connelly episode is revealing, confirming that while the

Ministry was confident enough to leave a known Communist militant to the discretion of an experienced local manager, it was nonetheless sensitive to Communist criticism. Senior civil servants would have been keenly aware of allegations that NUWM agitation had affected recruitment. Sir Arthur Rose was particularly indignant that 'organisations whose intentions are entirely subversive of the present order of society' were claiming 'that the schemes perform essential work under "slave" conditions'.[125] Fear of NUWM protest also influenced the debate on compulsion, with one civil servant justifying his reluctance to compel young men to enter ICs as due to 'fear lest the Board be criticised for "starving young men into slave camps"'.[126] The Ministry may or may not have resorted to more underhand methods, but we do know that it used publicity and openness against its critics. Camps were thrown open to the public from time to time, while trainees and managers gave broadcasts on the BBC, in a concerted drive to prove that the Ministry had nothing to hide. One journalist, invited by the Ministry to visit Weeting Hall, dutifully complained of the 'unscrupulous and completely false epithet of "slave camps"'.[127] Openness was, on the whole, a successful strategy.

Conclusions

In 1940, Walter Hannington looked back at what he called 'ten lean years'. By this time, like many of Britain's jobless, the veteran campaigner had found work, in his case as an organiser for the Amalgamated Engineering Union. The Party to which he had devoted so much of his life, and which had disciplined and tried to rein him in, was now telling its members to tone down their criticisms of the Nazis, and campaign against the war.[128] In his final angry and detailed denunciation of the National Government's treatment of the unemployed, Hannington offered a surprisingly balanced account of the ICs. He avoided such terms as 'concentration camp' or 'slave camp', and acknowledged that while some camp managers were authoritarians, he had also met men 'with an intelligent outlook upon their job', who were 'anxious to create pleasant conditions in the Camp'.[129] After September, of course, Hannington and his Party were opposing the war, and were anxious to stress any sign of similarities between Britain and Germany. In this context, Hannington knew that he could afford to tone down his criticism of an institution that Britain had abolished, but which was integral to the Nazi labour market.

In some respects, though, Hannington shared at least some of the core assumptions that underpinned the work camp movements. He completely endorsed the idea that work was a human necessity, though he thought it an outrage that the men were not paid at union rates; he agreed that the unemployed were 'unfit', but blamed the government and capitalist system for leaving them idle and under-nourished. Otherwise, his main grievance was that the camps cut the men off from the rest of the working class, giving them an 'undignified feeling' of inferiority and creating an underclass of potential strikebreakers.[130] More broadly, while the Communist movement ridiculed 'slave camps' and 'slave colonists', they ran their own summer camps with 'a just distribution of the toil and of the play' (together with a 'fine lecture' denouncing Trotskyists), while the *Daily Worker* regularly carried photographs of powerfully sculpted Soviet workers' bodies, as well as equally finely proportioned Soviet women athletes.[131] In short, the cult of the body and the comrade-ship of the camp were as palatable to the radical left as they were to the political mainstream.

Notes

1 J. Hoyland, *Digging for a new England: The co-operative farm for unemployed men*, Jonathan Cape, London, 1936, 126–7.

2 R. Croucher, *We Refuse to Starve in Silence: A history of the National Unemployed Workers' Movement*, Lawrence & Wishart, London, 1987, 11.

3 A. Campbell and J. McIlroy, 'The National Unemployed Workers' Movement and the Communist Party of Great Britain Revisited', *Labour History Review*, 73, 1, 2008, 64–82.

4 *RCPL*, Appendix, Vol. VIII, *Minutes of Evidence*, HMSO, London, 1910, 136.

5 H. Quelch, 'The Prevention of Destitution', *Social Democrat*, 14, 8, 1910, 337–46.

6 *Vanguard*, November, 1920.

7 C. Holbourn, Secretary, Peckham Branch ETU, 24 June 1922, NA MH63/8.

8 E. Harmer, Southwark, 31 August 1922, NA MH63/8.

9 Croucher, *We Refuse*, 164–5.

10 Ibid., 202–3.

11 For a sympathetic view see M. Worley, 'To the Left and Back Again: The

Communist Party of Great Britain in the Third Period', in M. Worley (ed.), *In Search of Revolution: International Communist Parties in the Third Period*, I. B. Tauris, London, 2004, 67–74.

12 *Daily Worker (DW)*, 21 May 1930.

13 *DW*, 16 May 1930.

14 *DW*, 20 May 1936.

15 *DW*, 22 May, 4 June 1930.

16 *DW*, 28 February 1930.

17 *DW*, 2 June, 15 July, 18 July 1930.

18 As in Dumbarton: *DW*, 24 February 1931.

19 *DW*, 17 May 1932.

20 *DW*, 18 May 1933.

21 *DW*, 29 June 1933.

22 *DW*, 9 November 1931.

23 *DW*, 28 February 1931.

24 *DW*, 24 August 1933.

25 *DW*, 5 September 1933.

26 *DW*, 13 September 1932.

27 Harry McShane repeated this complaint in his autobiography: H. McShane and J. Smith, *Harry McShane: No mean fighter*, Pluto Press, London, 1978, 228.

28 *DW*, 21 October 1931.

29 *DW*, 16 May 1930.

30 *DW*, 21 October 1931.

31 *DW*, 8 May 1933.

32 *DW*, 24 May 1930

33 *DW*, 23 January 1931.

34 P. Kingsford, *The Hunger Marchers in Britain, 1920–1940*, Lawrence & Wishart, London, 1982, 114.

35 *DW*, 31 January 1931.

36 *DW*, 27 May 1930, 1 August 1931.

37 *DW*, 19 August 1931.

38 *DW*, 8 May 1931.

39 *DW*, 27 June 1931.

40 Croucher, *We Refuse*, 100–101.

41 *RCUI: First Report, Appendices, Part I*, HMSO, London, 918–19.

42 *DW*, 17 April 1931.

43 *DW*, 18 July 1931.

44 *DW*, 2 February 1932, 4 August 1932.

45 W. Hannington, *Unemployed Struggles, 1919–36*, Lawrence & Wishart, London, 1978, 301; see also Hannington's *The Problem of the Distressed Areas*, Gollancz, London, 1937, 99.

46 K. K. Patel, *Soldiers of Labor: Labor service in Nazi Germany and New Deal America, 1933-1945*, Cambridge University Press, New York,

2005, 46–7.

47 Neil Evans, 'South Wales has been Roused as Never Before': Marching against the Means Test, 1934–1936, in D. W. Howell and K. O. Morgan (eds), *Crime, Protest and Police in Modern British Society*, University of Wales Press, Cardiff, 1999, 183.

48 Croucher, *We Refuse*, 148.

49 *DW*, 21 July 1933.

50 National Unemployed Workers Movement, *The Fight Against Unemployment and Poverty: Our plan for action*, NUWM, London, 1934, 5–6; see also W. Hannington, *Work for Wages not Slave Camps*, NUWM, London, 1934.

51 Evans, 'South Wales', 178.

52 *DW*, 1 February 1935.

53 *DW*, 28 March 1935.

54 *Stirling Journal and Advertiser*, 17 January 1935.

55 *Scotsman*, 12 February 1935.

56 *DW*, 13 March 1935.

57 *DW*, 23 April 1935.

58 *DW*, 3 January 1935.

59 *DW*, 2 February 1935, 3 April 1935, 8 May 1935.

60 *DW*, 8 January 1935, 11 May 1935, 18 May 1935.

61 *DW*, 30 April 1935.

62 *DW*, 30 May 1936.

63 Social Insurance Committee, 13 December 1934, TUC Mss, MRC 292/131/3/3.

64 J. L. Smyth, TUC, to Frank Day, Brighton Trades Council, 14 March 1934, TUC Mss, MRC 292/131/3/3; for another view, see Hamilton Fyfe, *Press Parade: Behind the scenes of the newspaper racket and the millionaires' attempt at dictatorship*, Watts & Co., London, 1936, 161.

65 J. L. Smyth, TUC, to E. Allan Robson, Cardiff Trades Council, 20 March 1934, MRC 292/131/3/3.

66 National Federation of Building Trades Operatives, Government Training Centres: Report submitted to General Council of the TUC, February 1930, TUC Mss, MRC 292/131/3/3.

67 S. Shaw, 'The Attitude of the TUC Towards Unemployment in the Interwar Period', PhD, University of Kent at Canterbury, 1979, 376.

68 *DW*, 21 March 1935.

69 *DW*, 3 July 1937.

70 *DW*, 22 July 1937.

71 *The Times*, 3 March 1939.

72 Labour Party, *Annual Report, 1939*, 267.

73 *DW*, 29 June 1933, 15 July 1933.

74 *DW*, 10 August 1933.

75 T. Wintringham, 'Who is for Liberty?', *Left Review*, 1, 12, 1936, 483.

76 W. Hannington, *Beware!! Slave camps and conscription*, NUWM,

London, no date [?1938], 5, 10.

77 'Concentration camps for the workless!!!', at http://gdl.cdlr.strath. ac.uk/redclyde/redcly138.htm (accessed on 15 May 2006).

78 *Workers' International News*, July 1939.

79 *Blackshirt*, 8 March 1935.

80 *Blackshirt*, 6 February 1937. Upper case in the original.

81 *Scotsman*, 25 April 1935.

82 *Le service civil*, 1 November 1936.

83 UABNI. Memorandum by the Chairman on Training, 1 January 1935, PRONI LAB/5/2.

84 R. Croucher, 'The History of Unemployed Movements', *Labour History Review*, 73, 1, 2008, 2.

85 F. F. Piven and R. A. Cloward, *Poor People's Movements: Why they succeed how they fail*, Random House, New York, 1979.

86 J. McCarthy and M. Zald, 'Resource Mobilization and Social Movements: A Partial Theory', *American Journal of Sociology*, 82, 6, 1977, 1212–41.

87 *RCPL*, Appendix, Vol. VIII, *Minutes of Evidence*, HMSO, London, 1910, 321.

88 *Minutes of Evidence taken by the Departmental Committee on Vagrancy*, HMSO, London, 1906, 181.

89 *The Times*, 3 July 1906.

90 S. Webb and B. Webb, *English Poor Law History, Part II: The last hundred years*, Longmans, London, 1929, 751.

91 *Parliamentary Debates*, 17 May 1922, 31 May 1922.

92 Handwritten note on letter from C. Holbourn, Peckham ETU, 24 June 1922, NA MH63/8.

93 Poplar Board of Guardians. Report of committee appointed to visit Hollesley Bay, 4 October 1922, NA MH63/8.

94 *City and East London Observer*, 20 July 1929; Central (Unemployed) Body for London, Minutes, 6 December 1929, NA MH63/6.

95 *DW*, 16 May 1930.

96 *Daily Express*, 23 September 1933; *Daily Mirror*, 23 September 1933; *DW*, 23 September 1933.

97 *DW*, 26 November, 2 December 1931.

98 *Scotsman*, 16 December 1930.

99 C. N. Ryan, UAB, Notes of a discussion with Mr Reynard, 11 October 1934, NA AST10/3.

100 *DW*, 3 November 1937.

101 J. Leather, 61 Gloucester Ave, Slough, 2 December 1929; Petition to Manager, GIC, 11 May 1930 [in Leather's handwriting], NA LAB2/1266/TFM332/19.

102 Dowling to Passmore, 14 May 1930, NA LAB2/1266/TFM332/19.

103 *Scotsman*, 10 July 1930.

104 Manager, Fermyn Woods, to G. Wade, Leeds Divisional Office, 1

October 1930, NA LAB2/1275/ET5990.

105 B. Simon, 'Robert Beddall at Brigstock Camp', *Bygone Brigstock*, 12, 2011, 13.

106 Circular to Managers of TICs, 12 November 1930, Manager Cranwich Heath TIC to Director of Training, MoL, 6 November 1930, NA LAB2/1275/ET5990.

107 *DW*, 7 July 1931.

108 Allen to Passmore, 17 August 1933, NA LAB2/2040/ET6119.

109 *DW*, 22 July 1933.

110 *DW*, 27 February 1935.

111 *DW*, 28 March 1935.

112 *DW*, 8 April 1935; Hannington, *The Problem*, 96.

113 *DW*, 22 April 1935.

114 *Scotsman*, 2 March, 3 March 1938.

115 *Parliamentary Debates*, 23 March 1939

116 Croucher, 'History of Unemployed Movements', 1–17.

117 *Parliamentary Debates*, 11 June 1936.

118 O. Allen to Passmore, 15 January 1934, NA LAB2/1286/ET6097.

119 D. Christie Tait, 'Unemployment of Young People in Great Britain', *International Labour Review*, 31, 2, 1935, 185–6.

120 Discussion on admittance to instructional centre of an active member of a local communist group, NA LAB2/1286/ET6097.

121 Divisional Controller, NE Division, Leeds, to Headquarters, 9 December 1933, NA LAB2/1286/ET6097; Leggett to B M Power, 11/12/33, NA LAB2/1286/ET6097.

122 O. Allen to Passmore, 15 January 1934, W. C. Osmond to Allen, 16 January 1934, NA LAB2/1286/ET6097.

123 Selection of Officers for Posts of Managers of Testing Camps, 20/12/28, NA LAB2/1778/CEB202; W. Wilson, MoL to H. Biggs, Treasury, 31 October 1932, NA LAB2/1775/SE774.

124 Notes from Divisional Controller, NE Division Leeds, 25 January and 9 March 1934, NA LAB2/1286/ET6097.

125 *ML. Reports of Investigations into the Industrial Conditions*, 228–9.

126 Bowen to Eady, 11 January 1935, NA AST10/4.

127 *The Times*, 19 July 1935.

128 Campbell and McIlroy, 'The National Unemployed Workers' Movement', 64–82; K. Morgan, *Harry Pollitt*, Manchester University Press, 1993, 108–16.

129 W. Hannington, *Ten Lean Years: An examination of the record of the National Government in the field of unemployment*, Victor Gollancz, London, 1940, 192–204.

130 Hannington, *The Problem*, 111–13.

131 *DW*, 5 August 1937.

Conclusion –
Understanding work camps
Memory and context

For some sixty years, work camp movements flourished in Britain. But Britain's work camps were far from unique. We have already seen the international nature of the labour colony movement, but there were similar debates and exchanges, on an even larger scale, between the wards. In 1935 the International Labour Organisation's officers detailed camp systems in Austria, Canada, Czechoslovakia, Finland, Germany, Poland and South Africa; in the following year, they added Estonia, France, Japan and Switzerland to the list.[1] This catalogue was still incomplete, as there were also work camps in Bulgaria, Denmark, Finland, New Zealand, Netherlands, Norway and Sweden, not to mention the Civilian Conservation Corps (CCC) in the USA, or the Construction Corps in Ireland.[2] By the end of the decade, the Nazis had introduced an interlocking network of labour camps, ranging from those attended by all young German males for a period of compulsory labour service to forced labour by prisoners in the growing system of concentration camps.[3] The vast Soviet forced labour system, meanwhile, was really a case on its own, although it was mirrored on a small scale in the punitive labour camps developed by both sides during the Spanish Civil War.[4]

If we set aside the punitive work camps of Nazi Germany and the Soviet Union, we are still left with a wide variety of work camp systems, each with its own distinctive features and origins. Many claims were made at the time about the similarities and differences between systems, but these were either largely descriptive or inspired more by contemporary political preoccupations than by any interest in the phenomenon itself. How did these schemes differ, and how did they compare with the British schemes – and how do they help us to understand the British schemes?

International experiences

The most obvious starting point is the eruption of work camp systems between the wars. While the British debate over the merits of labour colonies was certainly fuelled by international comparisons, there was nothing in the 1880s and 1890s to compare with the back and forth of policy makers, journalists, film-makers, holiday-makers and interested members of the public during the interwar years. Some work camp systems, particularly the IVS, were determinedly internationalist in character, drawing members from many countries to promote pacifism and unity. Rolf Gardiner was also an internationalist, though of course his interests were primarily limited to the Nordic and Germanic cultures that nurtured the youth movements he so admired. Girth Fyrd (GF) also had wider links, some of them through its ties with Gardiner. National Socialists visited Sandy Balls and GF men met Nazis at Gardiner's Springhead camps.[5] Another of Gardiner's GF connections was Glynn Faithfull, who represented the movement at the Second International Work Camp Conference in 1937, where he was introduced to the audience as 'Mr Ficefull'.[6] Faithfull was certainly no Nazi, and the conference itself – though addressed by Nazi officials – was dominated by Service Civil International, the parent group of the IVS.

These overlapping networks and memberships should not obscure the enormous ideological differences between systems. We can start by distinguishing between states with public benefits schemes and those which did not provide benefits. A number of countries fall clearly into the latter category, including the United States, Australia, Canada and Ireland. In these countries, governments created work camps as a means of providing relief. British Columbia's provincial government opened 200 lumber and construction 'sustenance camp's in 1931, ensuring that Vancouver's unemployed worked in exchange for relief payments.[7] State governments in California, Washington and New York similarly collaborated with the federal Forest Service to open work camps.[8] Nationwide schemes followed in Canada in 1932 and in the United States in 1933, administered in both cases by the department for defence.

For most contemporaries, the most prominent relief camp scheme was the CCC, which rapidly became a showpiece for Roosevelt's New Deal. Once a decision was made, the Americans moved quickly: the first detailed plans went out in April 1933, and within less than three months some 275,000 young men were placed in 1,300 camps, mostly in forests and National Parks, where they took on large-scale public works such as dam building. Like the *Reichsarbeitsdienst* (RAD) after 1933, the men wore uniforms and were under military command, and they were also participants in a project of 'national education'.[9] In contrast to the RAD, however, the CCC did not require men to engage in drill or other preparations for war, and attendance was voluntary, while the men were free to quit if they wished. Like the Canadian system, the CCC removed potentially troublesome youths from the cities, and provided relief in exchange for heavy labour. The CCC still had 160,000 enrolees in 900 camps when the Japanese decided to attack Pearl Harbor. But while the Canadian sustenance camps became centres of protest and complaint, resulting in their closure in 1936, the CCC was so popular that politicians lobbied and competed to have camps located in their own electoral districts.[10]

Germany, of course, presents a different, and misleadingly familiar, case. Unlike the USA, Britain and Germany shared a broadly similar approach to insurance-based benefits.[11] However, early work camps in Germany emerged as an offshoot of the youth movements rather than as a response to unemployment. The best known German camps were those of the *Schlesische Jungmannschaft* in 1928, theoretically underpinned by ideas of Eugen Rosenstock-Huessy, law professor and historian at the University of Breslau, and Adolf Reichwein, leader of the adult education centre in Jena.[12] Patel describes this initiative, which emerged from the adult education movement, as primarily 'socio-pedagogical' in its approach, focusing mainly on citizenship development and community-building through shared living and labour.[13] But the Breslau group were not alone. Catholic youth groups had been creating work camps since the mid-1920s, usually based in residential adult education colleges, while the *Alt-Wandervogel* ran their first work camp in 1925.[14] These groups usually saw work camps as a means of community-building, while also debating the future of German society.[15] Their role in combating unemployment was still secondary.

Work relief schemes, often conducted locally by voluntary bodies and local government, played a much larger role in Weimar Germany than Britain. In June 1931, the Brüning government introduced a national system of voluntary labour service, or *Freiwilliger Arbeitsdienst* (FAD), which combined public works with camp life. Patel views the FAD, at least in many of its manifestations, as a 'socio-pedagogical' initiative, whose primary purpose was to combine a broad training in work discipline with welfare payments of up to two Reichmarks daily, for a period of up to twenty weeks. Work projects were organised by a variety of *Dienstträger* (providers), mostly from the churches, youth movements, sporting associations, local government and, on a much smaller scale, some of political groups, including parts of the labour movement and the right-wing paramilitaries of the *Stahlhelm*. The movement grew quickly, peaking at 285,000 – mostly male – in November 1932, before falling back to 177,000 by the end of the winter.[16] Most of the work was on land reclamation and other public works projects, while each provider also aimed at promoting the values and beliefs of its parent organisation. Peter Dudek argues that by early 1933, however, such wider perspectives – often radical and sometimes utopian – had been overwhelmed by the scale of the crisis, with most FAD camps concentrating on meeting the immediate needs of their parent organisation's unemployed members.[17]

With the Nazi seizure of power, social democratic and Catholic work camps came under attack by the Brownshirts and, some-times, the *Stahlhelm*. Their leaders often found themselves gaoled, and the Nazis imposed their own authority over the camp, so that many unemployed socialists and Catholics now found themselves supervised by their political enemies.[18] From the early summer of 1933, the Nazis – who had previously shown little interest in FAD – started to remould it, initially on a voluntary basis (mainly as a result of international suspicions of their intentions), and renaming it the *Reichsarbeitsdienst* (RAD). From 1935, it became compulsory for all 18–25 year-old men to serve for six months in the RAD, with a much smaller parallel voluntary initiative for women.

The RAD camps were strongly militaristic. Sentry boxes guarded the main entrances, and the men wore a uniform which bore a number of similarities to the brown shirts of the *Sturmabteilung*. As well as carrying out the usual heavy labour, they were given political instruction, and undertook a fairly intense physical training, with a strong emphasis on exercises of military value, as well as parading in formation through the local area. Because labour service was universal, the RAD had the mission of binding young Germans together, creating what Konstantin Hierl, the Reich labour leader, called a 'new National Socialist man', a concept of manhood that the Nazis reinforced through a proliferation of publicity materials showing healthy, spade-wielding, bare-chested young men.[19]

In particular, we must be careful, when comparing the German work camp systems with their British counterparts, to distinguish between the voluntary movement before 1933 and the increasingly authoritarian RAD. But we also need to be very clear about the fundamental differences between the RAD, which was fundamentally concerned with creating 'new National Socialist man', and the punitive camp systems into which the Nazis threw their enemies. The *Arbeitslager*, or work camps, were primarily concerned with pedagogic goals, of training proud and obedient German citizens, not as individual workers but as a national whole. As one Nazi journalist wrote after the Party Day of Labour in 1937, 'Work is the moving and shaping element of the true community.'[20] The RAD's slogan, duly etched into commemorative plaques and dagger blades, was *Arbeit adelt* (work ennobles). Unlike the famous sign outside Auschwitz, this message was intended without irony.

After the injustices of Versailles, one did not need to be a Nazi to view Germany with sympathy, or take an interest in its youth work camps. The independent-minded journalist Gareth Jones visited five voluntary camps in Dresden, and was much impressed by what he saw. On his return, he calculated that

> If Wales had done as much as Germany for the unemployed there would now be 300 camps here, and about 10,000 young Welshmen between 18 and 25 years of age would be engaged at useful work, repairing boots, singing, doing physical exercise, playing football or cricket, and discussing everything under the sun.[21]

Jones made it clear that he was thinking not only of what government had done, and might do, but also of the voluntary contribution, above all from the churches. A group from a Workers' Educational Association (WEA) summer school visited a camp in summer 1933 where unemployed university graduates were growing crops; the earnest adult education students from Yorkshire were particularly impressed by the 'democratic way of living' in the camp, where all wore the same field-grey uniform and dined together.[22]

WEA members were not so enthusiastic after the Nazi seizure of power – though one, visiting Germany in 1935, pointed out that if life in RAD camps was strict, there was not much freedom in being unemployed.[23] As the RAD became more overtly militaristic, so foreign observers tended to view it as part of the Nazi's wider rearmament programme. One British artillery officer reported from visiting an RAD camp that 'the work is hard and the life is healthy', concluding that it was mainly designed to produce a 'physically hard and well-developed conscript'. He ended by asking pointedly for what exactly this 'great nation' was preparing.[24]

Generally speaking, the tendency to conflate the RAD with more punitive camps was confined to the Left, at least until 1939. In 1940, under wartime conditions, the Adult School Union (ASU) hoped to encourage its members to discuss the merits of public works and 'Labour Camps', providing they had an 'English character' – in other words, that they were voluntary and civilian in character. The ASU also noted the existing ICs, which it described as places of 'training and recuperation'.[25] What is clear is that while we can compare the RAD with British work camps, the differences are more striking than the similarities. This was pretty obvious for most of the social service camps, as well as the Ministry of Labour ICs, but even Rolf Gardiner's Nordic-themed harvest camps were mild entertainments by comparison with the average RAD camp. Otto Bene, leader of the Nazi Auslandsorganisation in Britain and Ireland, acknowledged this when he reported to Berlin on one of Gardiner's camps that 'of course one mustn't judge this sort of camp by German standards', even if he judged it 'well above the average English one'.[26]

By way of a contrast, national strategy of a different kind influenced the Irish government, which in 1940 created the Construction Corps (*An Cor Déantais*) in response to the economic disruption caused by wartime disruption elsewhere. The Corps' main aim was to retain young men in neutral Ireland, by providing an alternative to emigration to nearby Britain.[27] Recruitment was compulsory, in so far as refusal of employment in the Corps constituted grounds for discontinuing benefit payments.[28] Set to work for up to a year digging bogs and building roads, the men wore Army uniform, lived in military barracks, and formed part of the Irish Army's command structure; they even paraded in formation through the streets of Dublin.[29] The move was welcomed by the *Catholic Herald* as promising 'hope for a better manhood when the trial is over'.[30] While there may have been elements of militarism, and nationalism, the Construction Corps seems a temporary and pragmatic response to what De Valera's government termed 'The Emergency', and lacked entirely the deep ideological roots that characterised the labour service movement in Germany, or the passionate radical nationalism of Roosevelt's New Deal.

Understanding Britain's work camps

What light does this brief survey of work camp systems internationally shed upon the 'average' British experience? The first and simplest point to make is that British work camp systems were part of a broader international movement, and compared by the standards of other systems, Britain's endeavours seem relatively modest. Even the IC system, which was the largest and most coherent work camp programme in Britain, dealt with tiny proportions of the male unemployed when set against its counterparts in Germany and the United States. Contemporary observers such as the American researcher Kenneth Holland recognised this all too well: in his comparative study of European work camps, completed when the Ministry of Labour's programme was at its peak, Holland described enrolment in the ICs as 'still small'.[31] We can easily understand this relatively minimalist approach as the result of the British focus on reconditioning, which was pursued more or less to the exclusion of other purposes. While the early labour colonies often had therapeutic and health-related objectives, these were achieved primarily through a regime of bodily strengthening based on daily doses of heavy labour, and this remained the main concern of the ICs during the 1930s. Their existence was not required in order to legitimate relief payments, and nation-building only featured in the schemes for emigration. If we also take the ICs' appalling placement record into account, it is clear that the Ministry of Labour did well to maintain the programme at all.

Yet if the British system was relatively small and narrowly focused, it nonetheless shared a number of features with schemes elsewhere. In Erving Goffman's phrase, these were total institutions. As he described it, a total institution was a place where a large number of individuals, with a shared status, lived and worked together for an extended period, were more or less isolated from the wider society, and were controlled by common, formal structures of behaviour.[32] These features can be seen in all of the British work camp systems, as well as their international counterparts, and Goffman saw them as serving to strip away established identities, by removing the usual set of foundations upon which an individual's self-concept relies. He was, though, keen to emphasise that this 'democratic' and equalising process could be a source of support as well as deprivation, helping inmates to build new concepts of themselves in the world.[33] In this sense, all total institutions serve a pedagogic function, which can be more or less explicit in the institution's espoused aims. But, of course, they do not all adopt the same methods, and what was distinctive about work camps was the central role of labour.

Within Britain's work camps, labour almost invariably involved heavy manual toil. Unlike the workhouses and penal labour camps, the work camps provided 'meaningful' and purposive labour, rather than work for its own sake, as punishment, or simply as test of willingness to work. In more punitive institutions, work was often without intrinsic purpose. Paupers and prisoners might be set on a treadmill or picking oakum, or they might hoe gardens and wash laundry; as long as their labour did not compete with the outside world, all that mattered was the fact that they were put to work. Labour camp inmates, by contrast, were told – and presumably believed – that they were doing something useful. They built sea defences, drained marshes, grew their own food, kept bees, dug ditches and cleared scrubland. Engagement in such socially useful tasks endowed the work with an intrinsic meaning.

Work camps were almost always divided along gender lines. Where they were concerned with the unemployed, their primary focus was largely with men. Most of the poor law colonies dealt solely with men, as did all the major work camp systems of the interwar years. Women's colonies existed, mainly for inebriates, and on one occasion for prostitutes. In these cases, the women usually lived in some sort of cottage system, or in converted middle-class suburban homes, while the men usually lived under canvas or in dormitories. Rather than heavy labour, women trainees usually engaged in lighter work of some kind. At Duxhurst and Cope Hall, women inebriates worked in the greenhouses or gardens and kept bees; they were also encouraged to undertake handicrafts and other 'artistic' occupations that, the managers believed, might serve a therapeutic purpose. In the HTCs, unemployed young women learned the skills and demeanour appropriate to domestic service. Rough and heavy labour was emphatically off the agenda; on the contrary, the aim was to produce bodies that looked suitably biddable.

Marked gender distinctions were found in all types of labour service. Women played no part in the CCC, other than in background support roles such as administration. I am not aware of any discussion in Ireland over women's role in the Construction Corps, which was entirely male. In Germany, women played a minimal and marginal role in the voluntary labour service movement. Middle-class feminists had considered the possibility of a women's labour service (non-residential) before 1914, but this came to nothing.[34] In general, women's unemployment was largely discounted in Weimar Germany, as elsewhere; where it was discussed, largely by feminists, the 'work home' rather than the camp was seen as the most appropriate form of labour service for women. By summer 1933, Dudek estimates that some 10,000 young women were involved in the FAD, in what remained a largely marginal role.[35] This remained the case under the Nazis; although in principle labour service became compulsory for both genders, in practice it was only mandatory for men. The women's service remained small until 1937, when Frau Scholz-Klink managed to expand it to some 25,000 trainees.[36] Most lived in relatively small groups of 30–40 in country homes, combining land work with singing, dancing and education, including political instruction. While distinctly *völkisch* in character, and certainly designed to ensure subordination to the national will, it lacked the militarism that was so characteristic of the dominant male labour service.[37]

Male labour, and male living, took place in a largely distinctive world. Dudek notes that along with geographical isolation went celebration of the primitive, in both the living conditions and the work.[38] He connects this valuing of the primitive with the spiritual crisis of the Weimar Republic, but it can also be found in some British discussions. We have seen that Rolf Gardiner, the IVS and Grith Fyrd all took great pride in the austere pioneer conditions of their own camps, and the demands they made on their inmates' courage and determination. Sir Henry Betterton, Minister of Labour in MacDonald's National Government, boasted that the tented ICs 'reproduce the conditions of a pioneer camp', where 'the men must improvise for themselves their amenities and recreations'.[39] While there was an element of moral critique in such views, it was always clear that their target was men. It was male bodies that were being 'reconditioned', male minds that were recovering their questing spirit of adventure through pioneering conditions, male guilt and aggression that were being sublimated and redeemed through 'pick and shovel'. In short, the camps can be understood as sites where the values and practices of masculinity were produced and enforced.

Manliness was also evoked and enacted through sports. British men's camps tended to produce team sports, such as football and cricket, or athletics contests in the form of a camp sports day, with races and a tug-of-war. Swimming was also practised, usually in the sea or a river, though some of the hutted ICs had their own pool. In so far as sports featured in the women's camps, it was usually in a semi-humorous and non-serious manner, as in the sports days at the Marsden Bay camps (though here too swimming was serious, if non-competitive). Sport at the men's camps was almost always competitive, often fuelled by rivalries between men from different towns or regions. Harry Rée was mightily impressed by an inter-tent seven-a-side football league at Harome which, although never reaching a conclusion, generated 'the most bloodthirsty arguments' among the men.[40] Unlike the German camps, sports in British camps usually had no obvious military value. Westlake's dream of teaching young men to shoot was never realised in Grith Fyrd; only Gardiner included anything remotely resembling the German traditions of *Wehrsport* and *Kampfspiele*, organising for some of the Springhead events to conclude with a night-time 'flag-raiding contest' between Scots and English participants.[41]

There has been much debate in recent years over the idea of 'hege-monic masculinity', a concept which is associated with the Austra-lian sociologist R. W. Connell.[42] We often forget that our values and behaviour are played out in specific conditions, and involve people as agents on all sides. In the case of the work camps, what we see is the repeated rehearsal and enactment of the belief that performing work, and particularly heavy manual labour, is a central part of what it means to be a man. But by bringing men together in isolated conditions, the camp organisers were also creating the risk of resis-tance and transgression. Camp life was an integrating mechanism, and the organisers often spoke of it as producing a sense of bounded community, though they often used terms such as 'fellowship' to explain its importance. More broadly, camp life together with work were often spoken of as binding men into the wider society, or in the words of contemporary discourse, as making them into full citizens. But these common bonds also occasionally forged a community of camp inmates who organised against and resisted the conditions under which they had been brought together in the first place.

British work camp systems were fundamentally civilian in character. Of course, they certainly had indirect implications for the armed forces: some at least in Britain's military were concerned about the physical standards of the male population, particularly after the Boer War, but also in the late nineteenth century and again during the interwar decades. But we should not exaggerate this; during the 1930s, the officer class in Britain, which was responsible for a relatively small standing army, did not show much concern over the physique of the civilian population, and there was certainly no attempt by the War Office to take over the labour colonies or the ICs.

The German situation was quite different. Particularly after 1930, the German military authorities took an active interest in the FAD, while for their part some of the right-wing organisations increasingly treated their labour service camps as part of the process of *Wehrhaftmachung*.[43] British diplomatic reports, particularly after 1935, frequently referred to the RAD, which the British government now viewed as a paramilitary training force.[44] But there was also a marked military dimension in democratic countries such as Canada and the United States, where the military ran the camps, while in Ireland the Construction Corps was formally and in practice a unit of the army.

There is also another comparison to be made, though it can be dealt with briefly. In their study of Scottish ICs, Walsh and Kenefick are so keen to overthrow what they see as the conventional account of work camps as places of despair that they invite us instead to view them as 'relatively relaxed' places that in some respects can even be compared with holiday camps. They do not help their case by presenting a detailed menu for Glenbranter without making it clear that their source for a 'typical day's meals' was an unsuccessful tender from a North Lanarkshire catering firm.[45] Nevertheless, we should certainly understand the interwar work camp movements in the wider context of camping as a leisure activity.

Camping thrived in the 1930s: by 1939, an estimated 1.5 million holiday-makers spent their summer break in a hutted camp or under canvas. For most, the experience was a highly organised one; if the routines were not actually military in nature, they were followed daily; and the camps themselves were often held under austere conditions.[46] They ranged from the highly standardised mass camps associated with commercial entrepreneurs like Butlins to the small communities of huts and tents that sprouted up on unwanted edges of land.[47] And if some camps were thought to be irregular to the point of anarchy, there were plenty who were willing to step in and sort them out. The Reverend John White, convener of the Church of Scotland's Home Board, opened a summer mission hut at Port Seton with 150 seats, to ensure that the working-class Clydesiders who camped there would be 'well organised and well disciplined'.[48]

Like the ICs, and the labour colonies before them, holiday camp organisers firmly believed in the benefits of exposure to rural life and fresh air, and in some cases in the value of strenuous exercise. Even the Communists embraced this belief, organising annual camps by the seaside for socialist youth, with sports days alongside the speeches. Even the revolution was bound to benefit, as one correspondent wrote to the *Daily Worker*: 'Apart from the pleasure derived from camping, I do not know of any sport which is so dependent upon discipline, order and a spirit of co-operation.'[49] But of course these camps were not confined to the unemployed, the mentally deficient, or epileptics; and neither did they have work at their core. The only work camp participants who saw heavy labour as a holiday were, it seems, the middle-class student volunteers.

What became of the camps and their archives?

There is a persistent belief that the story of Britain's work camps has somehow been 'hidden from history'. The suggestion is not only that most historians have other interests, but that this story has actively been suppressed. The BBC included material on the ICs in its six-part series on 'Forbidden Britain', and a chapter covering 'slave camps and skivvy schools' was included in the accompanying book, whose authors complained that their investigation of our 'secret past' had been hampered by 'Government censorship of information and ideas considered to be damaging or dangerous'.[50] One Internet source, based at a leading Scottish university, alleges that in August 1939, 'the Ministry of Labour issued instructions that the managerial records of its own concentration camps should be weeded out, and much of the documentation was destroyed'.[51] What truth is there in these claims?

While researching this study, I have found no shortage of information and ideas, but I have certainly faced gaps and omissions. Archives generally hold written records, and therefore privilege the accounts compiled by the highly literate and articulate. Written accounts of work camp life as experienced and authored by trainees are incredibly rare, and are mostly confined to those who went to the interwar camps of various kinds. And in my experience, the longest-lived are those who helped organise the student camps. The documentary records, then, are dominated by the voices of administrators, managers, funders and leaders, or at best by those who organised protests or reported for the press.

We are, as a result, faced with significant silences. Most of the interesting but unanswerable questions concern the experiences and lives of the people who went to the camps, and developed ways of living within, despite and around the official regime. We have some insider accounts from people who ran and lived in camps during the 1930s, and we can interview the dwindling number of survivors from that period. We have barely any insider accounts of earlier movements, and hardly any that describe everyday life from the perspective on an inmate. One risk – which I hope I have largely managed to avoid – is that of understating the agency of the inmates, and overestimating the authority of those who ran the camps. Beyond that, even where we have insider narratives, significant gaps remain. We know next to nothing of sex life within the camps, a topic on which almost all the surviving accounts say nothing. Here I have to admit to a character flaw: I found myself utterly unable to ask the seniors whom I interviewed about attitudes and practices that I expected to be deeply embarrassing for men and women of their generation. We know that there was cross-dressing during some ritual occasions, such as when Sheila Nevell acted the part of Hitler. We also know that there was a general propensity to publish photographs of muscular young men with bare torsos, wielding pick and shovel. Perhaps this is a muted form of the more overtly homoerotic sensibility that Colin Johnson discerns in the literature and practices of the CCC?[52] Unfortunately, this is speculation.

As for the Ministry of Labour, it is true that local records were destroyed. This was under its policy on records management, which long predated 1939. A 1921 circular to exchanges and local offices noted that all files should be sent to Whitehall, where personal files, receipts, vouchers and other low-level and routine documents were to be destroyed seven years after they had last been used.[53] The Ministry revised its procedures in 1938, requiring local managers of exchanges and other bodies to destroy some categories of records, usually after seven years, including most of the records of individual centres and their trainees.[54] Weeks before the outbreak of war, the Ministry told centre managers to prepare for immediate closure. Trainees' personal files, staff personnel files and the medical record book would be kept at Weeting Farm for seven years from termination, and correspondence files would be kept for three years; meanwhile, centre managers should burn their monthly reports, staff forms, goods receipt records.[55] While I cannot read anything sinister into the destruction of material that at the time had no obvious value, plainly a rich archival resource went up in flames.[56]

The legacy

In September 1939, virtually overnight, the ICs were closed, and the premises turned over to other purposes. After the war, most were quietly forgotten. Hardly any of the old work camps survived intact. Lingfield is a rare exception, evolving from epileptic colony into a national specialist centre for young people with epilepsy. Its history was not entirely uninterrupted, for in 1944, two V1 rockets hit the colony, damaging buildings and injuring a number of girls; shortly afterwards the colony was evacuated to Mansfield, where they lived in a former miners' camp until the war was over.[57] The German Industrial and Farm Colony also survived two world wars, and Libury Hall continued as a residential care home. Osea Island returned to its role with inebriates, and later achieved an unusual degree of fame as a clinic, treating such celebrities as Amy Winehouse. But most of the former work camps and labour colonies quietly vanished from history, their sites built over and their purposes forgotten.

Their stories have also been neglected, partly because they never had the scale and impact of much more memorable institutions, such as the workhouse, and partly because their role in late nineteenth- and early twentieth-century welfare did not survive the Second World War. They are, though, worth remembering, not least as a component in what became the welfare state. Paths not taken are as important in understanding later institutions and practices as are the trails that lead more directly to recognisably contemporary ways of delivering services.

The camps also left a pedagogic legacy. Lingfield, Wallingford and Hadleigh were particularly important as centres for training social workers, while the epileptic and tuberculosis colonies served as training grounds, centres for research and as agencies for the professionalisation of specialist nurses, doctors and other health professionals. GF and the social service camps certainly had an influence on the therapeutic community movement. But it was not only the young utopian community builders who helped to create therapeutic communities. David Wills, camp chief at Hawkspur from its inception in 1936, had entered Wallingford as a Brother in 1923, later becoming a House Father. A Quaker, Wills studied social work at Birmingham and New York, before serving as warden of the Oxford House Settlement at Risca, in South Wales, between 1931 and 1935.[58] Hawkspur was intended to help disturbed young men come to terms with themselves, while socialising them into the wider community. In turn, it has been one of the many influences on the various outdoor and outward bound residential communities that were later targeted at young offenders, the long-term unemployed, and other stigmatised young people.

There was far less continuity in the treatment of the unemployed. Vocational training often seems like a practice without a past, destined to repeat its mistakes in each generation. In 1931, Noel Barlow, Principal Assistant Secretary at the Ministry of Labour, claimed that the post-war programmes for ex-servicemen had 'no direct connection with the training schemes for men which are now in existence'. Even so, Barlow accepted that the earlier experience had been 'valuable in indicating the possibilities and limitations of adult vocational training'.[59] Between the wars, the brief flirtation with compulsion produced a recognition that adults must be motivated to learn, and simply cause problems for trainers when they are coerced. These were lessons long in the learning: British policy makers still seem to learn them afresh every few years in our own times.

Sometimes, consequences were unintended. The students and others who worked in voluntary service camps soon found that if they were to lead unemployed men and women effectively, they had both to earn their respect and to involve them in decisions. There were, as we have seen, some obvious limits to this democratic approach to leadership. Moreover, this sense of leadership as a relational practice, rather than simply a command structure, had many parallels in the human relations approach to management, as well as in wider cultural reactions against Taylorist systems of hierarchy and control.[60] In this, then, those who organised social service camps were moving in a similar direction to many others, but I found it very noticeable that a number – including Harry Rée, Glynn Faithfull and Sheila Nevell – played highly effective leadership roles later in their lives, and also became distinguished public servants.

Finally, Britain's work camps had a much more tangible influence. The men who were sent to labour colonies, TICs and ICs helped to create our landscape: many modern forests, for example, were scrubland and marginal pasture before they were taken over by the Ministry of Labour, whose trainees prepared the land for use by the Forestry Commission. Labour colonies and farm camps also helped to produce modern Canada and Australia, through the children of the young men who learned rudimentary agricultural skills in labour colonies and training camps in Britain.

A balanced assessment must view the British work camps as creatures of their times. Yet, even judged by their own criteria, the British systems were invariably too small (and often too inefficient) to have made more than a marginal difference to overall levels of unemployment. Undergoing a period of training in a government work camp was a stigmatising experience, which left some of the trainees embittered, and resulted in no great increase in employability. Yet other trainees remembered the experience with affection, and there is also evidence that the camps did indeed help improve the physical well-being of some very undernourished and dispirited young men. The camp regimes, while certainly hierarchical and spartan, were far from being authoritarian, illiberal or inhumane.

At the same time, without following Foucault too far down the path of auto-repression, the camps existed in order to regulate and re-educate human beings. This was not simply a socialisation function nor simple physical reconditioning. The camp regimes taught their stigmatised inmates that through work, they were rejoining – because they were contributing to – the wider community. This was often articulated through the language of citizenship and belonging. As Violet Markham put it when speaking of her role in the UAB, 'The big job before them was to give the unemployed a sense of usefulness and the feeling that they were once again living units in the life of the community.'[61] Work remains, in our own century, a route to community and citizenship, and thus to welfare.

Notes

1 *The ILO Yearbook, 1934–35*, ILO, Geneva, 1935, 317–22; *The ILO Yearbook, 1935–36*, ILO, Geneva, 1936, 340–2.
2 See K. Holland, *Youth in European Labor Camps*, American Council on Education, Washington DC, 1939.
3 J. Caplan and N. Wachsman (eds), *Concentration Camps in Nazi Germany: The new histories*, Routledge, Abingdon, 2010.
4 J. Ruiz, 'Work and don't lose Hope: Republican forced labour camps during the Spanish Civil War', *Contemporary European History*, 18, 4, 2009, 419–41.
5 Hans Pollmann, Königsberg, to Mrs and Major Pennyman, 25 May 1933, Teesside Archives U/PEN/11/28; *NSB*, Spring 1936.
6 *NSB*, Harvest 1937.
7 *Labour Gazette* (Ottawa), March, June 1932.
8 J. A. Salmond, *The Civilian Conservation Corps, 1932–1942: a New Deal case study*, Duke University Press, Durham NC, 1967, 5.
9 Patel, *Soldiers*, 209–11, 261–4.
10 *Labour Gazette* (Ottawa), June, October 1933; R. Liversedge, *Recollections of the On to Ottawa Trek*, McClelland and Stewart, Toronto, 1973, 129–45; Patel, *Soldiers*, 157–8.
11 G. A. Ritter, *Sozialversicherung in Deutschland und England: Entstehung und Grundzüge im Vergleich*, Beck, Munich, 1983.
12 J. Olbrich, *Geschichte der Erwachsenenbildung in Deutschland*, Leske and Budrich, Opladen, 2001, 163, 205.
13 Patel, *Soldiers*, 31.
14 M. Göbel, *Katholische Jugendverbände und Freiwilliger Arbeitsdienst 1931–1933*, Ferdinand Schöningh, Paderborn, 2005, 44–9.
15 P. Dudek, *Erziehung durch Arbeit: Arbeitslagerbewegung und Freiwilliger Arbeitsdienst, 1920–1935*, Westdeutscher Verlag, Opladen, 1988, 234.
16 Patel, *Soldiers*, 42–4; Göbel, *Katholische Jugendverbände*, 160–79.
17 Dudek, *Erziehung*, 252.
18 Göbel, *Katholische Jugendverbände*, 268–9.
19 Patel, *Soldiers*, 194–231.
20 *Parteitag der Arbeit*, Zeitgeschichte Verlag, Berlin, 1937, 1.
21 *Western Mail & South Wales News*, 27 April 1933.
22 *Outlook*, 1 October 1933.
23 *Highway*, January 1935.

24 G. F. Cooke, 'The Young German: His organization and training', *Journal of the Royal United Services Institution*, 81, 1936, 788–9.

25 *Today and Tomorrow: The Adult School Lesson Handbook, 1940*, National Adult School Union, London, 1939, 42.

26 Bene to Auslandsorganisation of the NSDAP, 30 August 1934, NA KV2/2245.

27 B. Evans, 'The Construction Corps, 1940–1948', *Saothar*, 32, 2007, 19–31.

28 *Parliamentary Debates* (Dáil Éireann), 19 March 1941.

29 *Irish Press*, 9 December 1940.

30 *Catholic Herald*, 11 October 1940.

31 Holland, *Youth in European Labor Camps*, 156.

32 E. Goffman, *Asylums: Essays on the Social Situation of Mental Patients and Other Inmates,* Penguin, Harmondsworth, 1968, 4–10.

33 Ibid., 112.

34 Dudek, *Erziehung*, 54.

35 Ibid., 211.

36 Patel, *Soldiers*, 106.

37 J. Stephenson, 'Women's Labor Service in Nazi Germany', *Central European History*, 15, 3, 1982, 241–65.

38 Dudek, *Erziehung*, 234–5.

39 Training and Occupation for the Unemployed Next Winter. Memorandum by the Minister of Labour, 21 July 1933, NA CAB24/242.

40 Camp Chief's Report, Harome, n.d. [1936], CUA Min.IX.69/43.

41 *NSB*, Spring 1936.

42 R. W. Connell, *Masculinities*, Polity Press, Cambridge, 1995; see also Connell and J. Messerschmidt, 'Hegemonic masculinity: rethinking the concept', *Gender & Society*, 19, 6, 2005, 829–59.

43 Dudek, *Erziehung*, 185–6.

44 Samuel Hoare, Cabinet Memorandum, German Rearmament, 25 November 1935, NA CAB24/257; Anthony Eden, Cabinet Memorandum, The German Danger, 17 January 1936, NA CAB24/259.

45 L. Walsh and W. Kenefick, 'Bread, Water and Hard Labour? New perspectives on 1930s labour camps', *Scottish Labour History*, 34, 1999, 14–33. The menu is from William Austin, Ltd, Bellshill, 21 January 1933, NA LAB18/31.

46 J. Walvin, *Beside the Seaside: A social history of the popular seaside holiday*, Allen Lane, Harmondsworth, 1978, 115–16.

47 A. Durie, 'No Holiday this Year? The depression of the 1930s and tourism in Scotland', *Journal of Tourism History*, 2, 2, 2010, 74–5.

48 *Glasgow Herald*, 5 July 1939.

49 *DW*, 27 June 1930.

50 S. Humphries and P. Gordon, *Forbidden Britain: Our secret past 1900–1960*, BBC Books, London, 1994, 7.

51 http://gdl.cdlr.strath.ac.uk/redclyde/redcly138.htm (accessed 12 July 2012).

52 C. R. Johnson, 'Camp Life: The queer history of "manhood" in the Civilian Conservation Corps, 1933–1937', *American Studies*, 48, 2, 2007, 26–33.

53 Staff Circular, Preservation and destruction of documents, 21 June 1921, NA LAB2/1809/ S+ER129/Part I.

54 Circular, Preservation and destruction of documents, 17 February 1938, NA LAB2/1809/S+ER129/Part II.

55 Letter to managers of ICs, 14 August 1939, NA LAB25/31.

56 I have tried unsuccessfully to verify Dave Colledge's claim that a file about a riot at High Lodge was deliberately destroyed: *Labour Camps*, 24–5.

57 'Forest Town Miners' Hostel, 1944–59', at www.ourmansfieldandarea. org.uk/page_id__22_path__0p20p.aspx (accessed 2 June 2010).

58 'Therapeutic Living with Other People's Children: an oral history project', at www.charterhousegroup.org.uk/otherpeopleschildren.ppt (accessed 2 June 2010).

59 *RCUI: First Report, Appendices*, 409.

60 D. A. Wren, *The Evolution of Management Thought*, Wiley, New York, 1979, 347–68.

61 *Scotsman*, 4 September 1934.

Select bibliography

Archival holdings

British Library of Political and Economic Science
Beveridge Papers.
Lansbury Papers.
Markham Papers.

Cambridge University Archives
Min.IX.69 Universities Council for Unemployed Camps, Cambridge
    Committee.

Devon Record Office
M 118/1/6/11/3–17 Royal Western Counties Institution, Colony corre-
    spondence.

Girton College Archives
GCPP Duke – Papers of Alison Duke.
GCPP Nevell – Papers of Sheila Nevell.

Hull History Centre, Records of International Voluntary Service for Peace
IVSP 2/ A/17 Annual general meetings, correspondence.
IVSP 21/E/114 Second International work camp conference.
IVSP 39/G/15 Booklets and leaflets.
IVSP 42/J/5 Reminiscences.
IVSP 45/J/23 Blaenavon and Oakengates camps.
IVSP 45/J/25 Hugh Horsfield collection.

London Metropolitan Archives
Charity Organisation Society, A/FWA/C/D/254/001.
Hollesley Bay Labour Colony, CUB/93.
London County Council, Farm Colonies LCC/CL/WEL.
Popular Board of Guardians, Admission and Discharge Books for the
    Labour Colony at Sumpner's Farm, PO/BG/180.

Poplar Branch Workhouse, Dunton – Chaplain's Report Book, 1909–1916, PO/BG/187.
Poplar Farm Colony Workhouse Punishment Book, 1907–1914, PO/BG 188.

Lothian Health Board Archives, University of Edinburgh Library
Minute Book, of the Sub-Committee appointed in connection with the Working Colony, LHB41/3/1.

Modern Records Centre
Women's Colony MSS 16C/3.
Trades Union Congress, training centres and relief schemes MSS.292.

National Archives
Unemployment Assistance Board, work centres AST10.
Cabinet Minutes CAB23.
Cabinet Papers CAB24.
Cabinet Sub-committee on Oversea Settlement CAB32.
Development Commission correspondence D4.
Dominions Office, Oversea Settlement DO57.
Forestry Commission Inspections F43.
Security Service file on Rolf Gardiner KV2/2245.
Ministry of Labour Training Department LAB2.
Ministry of Labour correspondence LAB23.
Ministry of Labour Records policy LAB25.
Hollesley Bay MH63.
Belmont Institution MH68.
Treasury Correspondence T161.
Unemployment Assistance Board, Training and Work Centres AST10.

National Archives of Scotland
Emigration AF51.
Disposal of Palacerigg DD10/195.
Purchase of Midlocharwood E824/607.
Scottish Labour Colony Association HH1/1351.
Inebriate Reformatories HH57/70.

National Film Archive, British Film Institute
E. Anstey, 'On the Way to Work', Ministry of Labour, 1936.

Public Records Office of Northern Ireland
Unemployment Relief Schemes CAB9C/13.
Unemployment CAB9C/20.
Adult training LAB5/2.

Teesside Archives
Pennyman Papers, Boosbeck Industries and Springhead Ring U.PEN/11.

Official publications
(unless otherwise stated, all published by HMSO, London)

Report from the Select Committee of the House of Lords on Poor Law Relief, 1888.

Board of Trade Labour Department, *Report on Agencies and Methods for Dealing with the Unemployed*, 1893.

Report of the Interdepartmental Committee on Physical Deterioration, 1904.

London Unemployed Fund, *Preliminary Statement*, 1905.

Minutes of Evidence taken before the Departmental Committee appointed to consider Mr Rider Haggard's Report on Agricultural Settlements in British Colonies, 2 vols, 1906.

Minutes of Evidence taken by the Departmental Committee on Vagrancy, 1906.

Royal Commission on the Poor Laws, Report and Appendices, 1909–1910.

Report of the Committee appointed to consider settling within the empire ex-servicemen who may desire to emigrate after the war, 1917.

Conference of Prime Ministers and Representatives of the United Kingdom, the Dominions and India, 1921, 1921.

Industrial Transference Board Report, 1928.

Ministry of Labour, *Reports of investigations into the industrial conditions in certain depressed areas*, 1934.

Secondary texts

Alden, P., *Democratic England*, Macmillan, New York, 1912.

Armytage, W. H. G., *Heavens Below: Utopian experiments in England, 1560–1960*, Routledge & Kegan Paul, London, 1961.

Berry, R. L. and R. G. Gordon, *The Mental Defective: a problem in social inefficiency* McGraw-Hill, New York, 1931.

Beveridge, W., *Unemployment: A problem of industry*, 2nd edn, Longmans, London, 1910.

Booth, W., *In Darkest England and the Way Out*, Salvation Army, London, 1890.

Bush, J., 'The Right Sort of Woman: Female emigrators and emigration to the British Empire, 1890–1910', *Women's History Review*, 3, 3, 1994, 385–409.

Chase, M., '"Wholesome Object Lessons": The Chartist Land Plan in retrospect', *English Historical Review*, 118, 2003, 59–85.

Cole, G. D. H., *The Next Ten Years in British Social and Economic Policy*, Macmillan, London, 1929.

Cole, M. (ed.), *Beatrice Webb's Diaries 1924–1932*, Longmans, Green & Co., London, 1956.

Colledge, D., *Labour Camps: The British Experience*, Sheffield Popular Publishing, Sheffield, 1989.

Colledge, D. and J. Field, 'To Recondition Human Material: An account of a British labour camp in the 1930s', *History Workshop Journal*, 15, 1, 1983, 152–66.

Constantine, S. (ed.), *Emigrants and Empire: British settlement in the Dominions between the wars*, Manchester University Press, 1990.

Croucher, R., *We Refuse to Starve in Silence: A history of the National Unemployed Workers' Movement*, Lawrence & Wishart, London, 1987.

Crowther, M. A., *The Workhouse System, 1834–1929: The history of an English social institution*, Routledge, London, 1983.

Davison, R. C., *British Unemployment Policy: The modern phase since 1930*, Longmans, London, 1938.

Dudek, P., *Erziehung durch Arbeit: Arbeitslagerbewegung und Freiwilliger Arbeitsdienst, 1920–1935*, Westdeutscher Verlag, Opladen, 1988.

Edgell, D., *Order of Woodcraft Chivalry 1916–1949 as a New Age Alternative to the Boy Scouts*, Edwin Mellen Press, Lewiston NY, 1992.

Fels, M., *Joseph Fels: His life-work*, Huebsch, New York, 1916.

Foss, W. and J. West, *The Social Worker and Modern Charity*, Adam & Charles Black, London, 1914.

Foucault, M., *Discipline and Punish: The birth of the prison*, Vintage Books, New York, 1979.

Göbel, M., *Katholische Jugendverbände und Freiwilliger Arbeitsdienst 1931–1933*, Ferdinand Schöningh, Paderborn, 2005.

Goffman, E., *Stigma: Notes on the management of spoiled identity*, Prentice Hall, Englewood Cliffs, NJ.

Hamilton, P. and B. W. Higman, 'Servants of Empire: The British training of domestics for Australia, 1926–31', *Social History*, 28, 1, 2003, 67–82.

Hannington, W., *The Problem of the Distressed Areas*, Victor Gollancz, London, 1937.

Hannington, W., *Ten Lean Years: An examination of the record of the National Government in the field of unemployment*, Victor Gollancz, London, 1940.

Hannington, W., *Unemployed Struggles, 1919–36*, Lawrence & Wishart, London, 1978.

Hardy, D., *Alternative Communities in Nineteenth Century England*, Longman, London, 1979.

Hardy, D., *Utopian England: Community experiments, 1900–1945*, Routledge, London, 2000.

Harper, M., *Emigration from North-East Scotland, Vol. 2*, Aberdeen University Press, Aberdeen, 1988.

Harper, M., *Emigration from Scotland Between the Wars: opportunity or exile?*, Manchester University Press, Manchester, 1998.

Harris, J., *Unemployment and Politics: A study in English social policy, 1886–1914*, Clarendon, Oxford, 1972.

Hazell, R.C., *Walter Hazell, 1843–1919*, Hazell, Watson & Viney, London, 1919.

Hill, A. C. C. and I. Lubin, *The British Attack on Unemployment*, Brookings Institution, Washington DC, 1934.

Hobson, J. A. (ed.), *Co-operative Labour upon the Land*, Swan Sonnenschein & Co., London, 1895.

Hobson, J. A., *The Problem of the Unemployed: An enquiry and economic policy*, Methuen, London, 1904.

Horn, P., *The Rise and Fall of the Victorian Servant*, Gill and Macmillan, Dublin, 1975.

Horn, P., 'Ministry of Labour female training programmes between the wars: 1919–1939', *History of Education*, 31, 1, 2002, 71–82.

Hoyland, J., *Digging for a new England: The co-operative farm for unemployed men*, Jonathan Cape, London, 1936.

Humphries, S. and P. Gordon, *Forbidden Britain: Our secret past 1900–1960*, BBC Books, London, 1994.

Jefferies, M. and M. Tyldesley (eds), *Rolf Gardiner: Folk, nature and culture in interwar Britain*, Ashgate, Farnham, 2011.

Kelynack, T. (ed.), *Human Derelicts: Medico-sociological studies for teachers of religion and social workers*, Charles H. Kelly, London, 1914.

King, D., *In the Name of Liberalism: Illiberal social policy in the USA and Britain*, Oxford University Press, Oxford, 1999.

Kropotkin, P., *Fields, Factories and Workshops*, Nelson, London, 1912.

Langan, M., 'Reorganising the Labour Market: Unemployment, the state and the labour movement, 1880–1914', in M. Langan and B. Schwarz (eds), *Crises in the British State*, Hutchinson, 1985.

Langfield, M., 'Voluntarism, Salvation and Rescue: British juvenile migration to Australia and Canada, 1890–1939', *Journal of Imperial and Commonwealth History*, 32, 2, 2004.

Laybourn, K., '"Waking Up to the Fact that there are any Unemployed": Women, unemployment and the domestic solution in Britain, 1918–1939', *History*, 88, 292, 606–23.

Lees Smith, H. B., 'The Unemployed Workmen Bill', *Economic Journal*, 15, 58, 1905, 248–54.

Lowe, R., *Adjusting to Democracy: The role of the Ministry of Labour in British politics, 1916–1939*, Clarendon Press, Oxford, 1986.

Mais, S. P. B., *SOS Talks on Unemployment*, Putnam, London, 1933.

McKibbin, R., 'The Economic Policy of The second Labour Government,

1929–1931', *Past & Present*, 68, 1975, 95–123.

Mills, H. V., *Poverty and the state, or work for the unemployed: an inquiry into the causes and extent of enforced idleness*, Kegan Paul & Tench, London, 1886.

Moore, N. V. *Problems of Brotherhood. By a Brother*, Wallingford Farm Training Colony, Turners Court, Oxfordshire, 1913.

Patel, K. K., *Soldiers of Labor: Labor service in Nazi Germany and New Deal America, 1933–1945*, Cambridge University Press, New York, 2005.

Plant, G. F., *Oversea Settlement: Migration from the United Kingdom to the Dominions*, Oxford University Press, London, 1951.

Rider Haggard, H., *The Poor and the Land, being a Report on the Salvation Army Colonies in the United States and at Hadleigh, England, with a scheme of national land settlement*, Longman's, Green & Co., London, 1905.

Rowbotham, S., *Edward Carpenter: A life of liberty and love*, Verso, London, 2008.

Rowbotham, S., *Dreamers of a New Day: Women who invented the twentieth century*, Verso, London, 2010.

Salmond, J. A., *The Civilian Conservation Corps, 1932–1942: a New Deal case study*, Duke University Press, Durham NC, 1967.

Searle, G. R., *The Quest for National Efficiency: A study in British politics and political thought, 1899–1914*, Ashfield Press, London, 1990.

Shaw, S., 'The Attitude of the TUC towards Unemployment in the Interwar Period', PhD, University of Kent at Canterbury, 1979.

Shepherd, J., *George Lansbury: At the heart of old Labour*, Oxford University Press, Oxford, 2004.

Sims-Williams, M., *Camps for Men*, Heffer, Cambridge, 1933.

Stedman Jones, G., *Outcast London: A study in the relationship between classes in Victorian society*, Penguin, London, 1970.

Sutter, J., *A Colony of Mercy; Or, social Christianity at work*, Hodder & Stoughton, London, 1893.

Sutter, J., *Britain's Hope*, James Clarke & Co., London, 1907.

Thane, P., *The Foundations of the Welfare State*, Longman, London, 1982.

Thane, P., 'The Working Class and State "Welfare" in Britain, 1880–1914', *Historical Journal*, 27, 4, 1984, 877–900.

Thomas, M., 'Paths to Utopia: Anarchist counter-cultures in late Victorian and Edwardian Britain, 1800–1914', PhD thesis, University of Warwick, 1998.

Thompson, M., *The Problem of Mental Deficiency: Eugenics, democracy and social policy in Britain, c.1870–1959*, Oxford University Press, Oxford, 1998.

Todd, N., *Roses and Revolutionists: The story of the Clousden Hill Free Communist and Co-operative Colony, 1894–1902*, People's Publications, London, 1986.

Walsh, L. and W. Kenefick, 'Bread, Water and Hard Labour? New perspectives on 1930s labour camps', *Scottish Labour History*, 34, 1999, 14–33.

Webb, S. and B., *The Prevention of Destitution*, Longmans, Green & Co., London, 1911.

Webb, S. and B., *English Poor Law History, Part II: The last hundred years*, Longmans, London, 1929.

Welshman, J., 'The Concept of the Unemployable', *Economic History Review*, 59, 3, 2006, 578–606.

Zweiniger-Bargielowska, I., *Managing the Body: Beauty, health and fitness in Britain, 1880–1939*, Oxford University Press, Oxford, 2010.

Index